I0895380

Lyric Powers

Lyric Powers

ROBERT VON HALLBERG

The University of Chicago Press ✻ *Chicago and London*

ROBERT VON HALLBERG is Helen A. Regenstein Professor of English and Comparative Literature at the University of Chicago.

The University of Chicago Press, Chicago 60637
The University of Chicago Press, Ltd., London
© 2008 by The University of Chicago
All rights reserved. Published 2008
Printed in the United States of America
17 16 15 14 13 12 11 10 09 08 1 2 3 4 5
ISBN-13: 978-0-226-86500-3 (cloth)
ISBN-10: 0-226-86500-2 (cloth)

Library of Congress Cataloging-in-Publication Data
Von Hallberg, Robert, 1946–
Lyric powers / Robert von Hallberg.
p. cm.
Includes bibliographical references and index.
ISBN-13: 978-0-226-86500-3 (cloth : alk. paper)
ISBN-10: 0-226-86500-2 (cloth : alk. paper)
1. Lyric poetry—History and criticism. I. Title.
PN1356.V66 2008
809.1'4—dc22

2007044619

∞ The paper used in this publication meets the minimum requirements of the American National Standard for Information Sciences—Permanence of Paper for Printed Library Materials, ANSI Z39.48–1992.

For Danielle Allen

Contents

Contents

Acknowledgments

I have discussed with friends the general issues of this book—even long before I wrote a word of it. Now I recognize the benefit I have drawn from these people, and I wish to name them. My thanks to Danielle Allen, Kelly Austin, Cal Bedient, Charles Bernstein, Frank Bidart, John Bishop, Graham Burnett, Jim Conant, Bradin Cormack, Maria Damon, the late Donald Davie, Jeff Dolven, Chris Faraone, Ken Fields, Barbara and Al Gelpi, John Gery, Raymond Geuss, Reg Gibbons, Rudy Gintel, Allen Grossman, Robert Hass, Lyn Hejinian, Beth Helsinger, Oren Izenberg, Travis Jackson, Alison James, Ralph Johnson, David Langston, Nate Mackey, Maureen McLane, Jerry McGann, Diane Middlebrook, Steve Monte, Michael Murrin, Tenney Nathanson, Liesl Olson, Mark Payne, Marjorie Perloff, Robert Pinsky, Jim Powell, Chicu Reddy, Gareth Reeves, Joshua Scodel, Alan Shapiro, Laura Slatkin, Ellen Stauder, Susan Stewart, Mark Strand, Richard Strier, David Wray, and John Wright. With this list of distinguished interlocutors, this book should be better, I know.

The Division of the Humanities at the University of Chicago generously supports the Poetics Program that regularly provides me occasions for conversation and enlightenment. The students who edit the *Chicago Review* ensure that the intellectual atmosphere at Chicago is literary as well; their efforts have sustained my work. My thanks as well to the master's students who have discussed poetics with me every fall for the last five years or so. Justin Evans, Marat Grinberg, and Marta Napiorkowska assisted me with research.

Versions of chapters 1, 3, 4, and 5 were presented variously as talks for an ALA conference in San Diego, for an *Arizona Quarterly* conference in Tucson, for a conference on knowledge and poetry at Princeton, for the Comparative Literature Department at USC, and for the English Department at Berkeley. I received useful, challenging questions from those audiences, for which I am grateful. Essays drawn from chapters 4 and 6 appeared in *TriQuarterly* 120 and *Michigan Quarterly Review;* my thanks to editors Susan Hahn and Laurence Goldstein for their interest in my work.

Introduction

Poetry, not prose: the distinction proposes a limit on what prose can be expected to do. The currency and institutionalization of legal, journalistic, and academic discourses make secular, rational explanation, conventional syntax, and sequential narrative seem comprehensive—the orders of truth itself. But the differential concept of poetry identifies a range of language beyond the orders of most institutionalized communication. Exactly what lies within the scope of poetry is indefinite; successive generations reconsider inherited definitions. Moreover redefinitions are constructed along two tracks: in essays by poets, but more reliably in poems. The essays are conjectural; they propose a range of extravagant language as belonging to poetry. Whether these proposals have been or will be effectively realized depends on the powers of individual poets. Because of the indefiniteness of the term "poetry," there is always a utopian element to prose definitions of this art's powers. Poems that redefine the operations of poetry do so by instantiation, not conjecture; they are rather evidence of what truly can be done outside the conventions of prose.

My objective is to clarify issues that arise when one prefers one kind of poem over another. Various concepts of poetry circulate now in U.S. literary culture, and among them are some family resemblances. The following chapters are oriented on two rival families: one the orphic, and the other the rhetorical approach to the art. Chapters 1 and 2 elaborate an orphic, chapters 3 and 4 a rhetorical poetics. Chapters 5 and 6, on music and universality, examine resources available to both for constructing lyric power. Particular poets tend to write more closely to one mode than to the other, but a few move back and forth from poem to poem. Neither poetics excludes the other. The categories presented here are merely heuristic; they identify entrances to poems, not features of the One True Poetry. I opportunistically use whatever distinctions serve understanding and appreciation of particular poems. This book is intended to lead readers who want guidance—students, or poets, or general readers—in understanding the pleasures and ambitions of poetry, especially in our time.

Poetry is retentive: it preserves the beliefs but also the wishes, misgivings, and doubts of poets and their cultures. My eclecticism rests on faith in the preservative capacity of poetry, and the longevity of even theories of poetry. Theories, constructed at a remove from actual poems, have an uncertain, hypothetical existence. Just where they exist, and whether they ever cease to exist, are open questions. Even very old theories are not entirely superannuated; they survive as vestigial and, like modern theories too, approximate accounts of the art, resources for acquisitive workers in a deeply traditional art. Spenser and the Bhagavad Gita were fully alive for an American poet in a Swiss sanitarium in 1921; modernist poets felt unconstrained by any sort of historical continuity, and later poets obviously retain that example. "Poetry is the sum of its attributes," according to Stevens.[1] It is an art of ideals, and they persist well in time. The theory with which I begin descends from Orpheus, who had the power to charm leaves off trees, to make rocks weep, and to bring the dead nearly all the way back to life. There followed a tradition of poetry and prophecy that was central to ancient Greek, Roman, Hebrew, and Koranic Arabic poetry.[2] The Aristotelian account of poet-makers and rhetoricians is the main countervailing line of poetics. Individual poets choose their predecessors and model their art accordingly.

›››‹‹‹

Literary interpretation has not been oriented, for decades, on what Wordsworth called "the grand elementary principle of pleasure" that attracts and sustains readers.[3] A discouraging gulf yawns between the experience of a poem and professional explanations of the importance of this art. Intellectuals have reason to avoid straightforward appreciation, because that alone doesn't advance understanding. Nonetheless one wants to understand which pleasures a particular poem provides, and more generally which are the pleasures most worth seeking. When, for instance, is the amusement of a pun worthy of the claims made for the art of poetry? What is the significance of the pleasure of sonority? A criticism that analyzes first the pleasures and then the meanings of poems, or always the pleasures *with* the meanings, might gradually help to offset the dominant interpretive model. Classroom teachers need to explain why one returns to poems, or memorizes them. A skeptical interpretive model that analyzes only other people's pleasures will not account for the interests of some students right there in the room; nor will it allure others. One wants criticism to account for the ardor of expression and appreciation.

Are the observations of great critics—of Pound, Eliot, Arnold, Coleridge, Johnson—sufficient to warrant the conviction that criticism can account for the pleasures of poetry? They are, but one recognizes the persistent and widely held judgment that poems are never adequately represented by prose statements of their significance. Walter Benn Michaels notes that the distinction between a sensual experience and a cognitive understanding of a text requires a prior understanding of the particular features of a text that are significant.[4] Certain features of a poem's sensuality—the shape of letters, the leading between lines—usually seem trivial, but others, not so: sounds—vowels, consonants, beats—but also the shapeliness of phrases, clauses, and sentences. All these features affect one's experience of a poem, but some sources of formal pleasure are less sensual than others. What Michaels calls the experience (or sensuality) of a text is surely central to poetry. Does one have what one needs when one identifies the cognitive features of a poem? What is missing from a plausible paraphrase, or even from a cogent account of a poem's historical context? Only what makes a poem: access to the remainder of language use that lies outside expository prose. Stevens believed that a poem requires two elements in struggle, intelligence and sense: "Poetry must resist the intelligence almost successfully."[5] Neither element alone will serve. Most criticism aims at the triumph of understanding, but poetry, often at the nearly complete frustration of understanding. John Crowe Ransom, who mistrusted rational analysis, says that "the art of poetry depends . . . on . . . the faculty of presenting images so whole and clean that they resist the catalysis of thought."[6] Poetry's appeal to the mind's eyes and the body's ears is meant to arrest analysis. The illusion of sensual presence effectively intimidates the impulse to dismantle experience. Orphic poets do not ask a reader to continue interpretation endlessly; they expect instead what Coleridge called "poetic faith" that their statements require no supplementation, at least for the duration of a reading.[7] Professional intellectual culture knows no such duration. Although poetry is an intellectual discourse, great poems are often not directed toward secular enlightenment.

Some critical procedures reveal the pleasures of poetry better than others, but all reasoned judgment, according to Montaigne, fails the poem—less because rationality is faulty than because poetry expresses power more than truth. According to him, "the good, supreme, divine poetry is above . . . rules and reason. Whoever discerns its beauty with a firm, sedate gaze does not see it, any more than he sees the splendor of a lightning flash. It does not persuade our judgment, it ravishes and overwhelms it."[8] His specific words repay scrutiny: some poetry is "divine" and it "ravishes" readers. He is recalling the Longinian observation that "sublimity flashing forth at the right moment scatters everything before it like a thunderbolt."[9] Accounts of the sublime draw on the idioms of eros and religion—sudden surrender. The Horatian notion that art improves one is remote from Montaigne's understanding. On the contrary, poetry is disabling. Some people struck by lightning are lastingly altered by the bolt, but they are all stopped, at least for a while, right in their tracks. The fitting response to a poem of this order is to read no further. Poems are at odds with language in that, when they succeed, the process of absorbing textually coded information comes to a halt, and one is left alone with one's thoughts. This is one of many signs that poems are not meant to extend ordinary discourse; a poem's triumph rather silences discourse. The mission of criticism pulls against poetry itself.

There is good reason, then, why definitions of poetry are so often antithetically formulated. Negative formulations open an indeterminate conceptual space, as though all that is not ordinary discourse might be poetry. Theorists rightly leave indeterminate just what poetry is, in positive terms, so that the art may respond to the utopian desire for new language. On this view, poetry is writing that has not yet come entirely into being; it remains an idea. This line of thinking underlies both avant-garde advocacy, like Marinetti's, on behalf of an art that is not yet there, and all literary theory that nobly presses for a fuller sense of what poetry might be. Gerald Bruns has recently adduced the logical basis of this view: "What we take poetry to be cannot be exhausted by examples; because examples are always in excess of our experience and understanding."[10] His point is that the actualization of ideas of poetry sets no constraint on concepts of poetry because every actual poem thought to be great exceeds interpretive accounts. But he claims further that poetry is a philosophical problem:

> What I want to argue is that poetry is philosophically interesting when it is innovative not just in its practices but, before everything else, in its poetics (that is, in its concepts or theories of itself). Poetry is as much a conceptual art as it is an art of language. . . . What is intellectually challenging is the possibility that anything, under certain conditions, may be made to count as a poem: The conceptual task is to spell out these enabling conditions.[11]

I prize the utopian element of poetry but resist the appeals that Bruns articulates, partly because the subtlest theorizations of poetry are expressed more often in poetry than in prose, partly too because I presume, as he does not, that the theorizations that count are the ones that engage realized poems that provide significant pleasure. Theorizations that do not engage exceptional poems seem to me merely academic. I attend closely to actual poems as a corrective to speculative poetic theory.

Bruns's point about the excessive significance of particular poems is important: the analyses that are congenial to abstract poetic theory tend to move poems through a set of coordinated categories at the risk of simplifying poems. I focus on poems that seem to give immediate, but significant pleasure to readers, in the hope that they also refine distinctions made by the prose theorists I cite. To just the extent that, as Bruns says, "anything . . . may be made to count as a poem," anything may be relevant to an explanation of poetry. My intent is not to make a case that readers *should* be interested in some poem or other on theoretical grounds. I presume that they seek pleasure, and that they wish to understand less what they should feel than what they do feel; but the temptation to regulate taste is nonetheless difficult to resist. Those who read only the inset verse quotations here may adequately estimate whether this book has anything to say to them. The case I make is no stronger than the poems my claims support. Other critics make compelling arguments for quite different views of the art of poetry. If the poems that support their arguments are superior to the ones that support mine, I concede defeat. Even a clever argument supported by routine art should hold no authority among literary critics. However, if I have the better poems, I probably have the better arguments too.

Lyric poetry has stood for the power of art in a way that other literary genres have not.[12] A successful lyric, as Montaigne said, is stunning, forceful, compelling: a language of power conventionally supports the advocacy of lyrics. It makes easy sense to speak of the authority of lyric poetry, as I will show in the next chapter, and that authority is allegorical of the capacity of all the arts. "The poem," Heidegger notes, "has a privileged position in the domain of the arts."[13] Yet he spoke from the cultural hierarchies of the early twentieth century: intellectual critiques of the last half century have produced strenuous suspicion concerning the special status of poetry, literature, and art generally. As Steven Knapp observes, the last few decades have seen "a growing agreement, among literary critics and theorists, that literature's uniqueness is an illusion."[14] Inevitably, the prestige of lyric poetry has been eroded, even though poets themselves continue to write as though, as Williams said, everyday people die from want of what is found in poetry.[15] Throughout literary history, the authority of poetry has fluctuated widely: skeptical, agnostic periods have been followed by reassertions of the highest claims for this art, as in England between 1590 and 1660. Doubt about poetry's special status . . . this too will pass. My argument, put simply, is that the authority of lyric has three sources: first, traditions of religious affirmation; second, the social status of those who speak the idioms from which particular poems are made; third, extraordinary cognition produced by the formal, and in particular musical, resources of some poems. Lyric authority is inextricable from its sister art, music: Euterpe, the muse of lyric poetry, needs a flute; Terpsichore, the muse of choral poetry, a lyre. Diverse forms of musicality are attractive to poets, but no poet can afford to tap only lightly the musical resources of language. Moreover there will always be a limit in the analysis of poetry, as there is too in the analysis of music. Critics know that in the end they cannot account adequately for the power of either poetry or music. But this side of complete enlightenment, there remains much to learn.

1

Authority

Poetry is quoted in public, even from memory, and read aloud among friends, as often by working people as by intellectuals.[1] And of course it is taught everywhere in schools. It circulates because its words seem to count, but what is the source of its authority, and is that source secure? Intellectuals often speak of the "poetics" of all explanatory discourses, but even some professional critics of poetry doubt that poetry itself has distinctive authority: on this view, it is just one more variety of rhetoric; anyway, its devoted readers are too few and disempowered (it has recently lost curricular centrality in the academy). Canonical narratives (epics, novels, romances) "provide criteria, implicit or explicit," as Steven Knapp observes, "by which contemporary models of action can be shaped or corrected"; lyrics preserve only locutions.[2] Poetry's authority—however great or slight—derives from linguistic forms, not approved patterns of behavior. This chapter identifies several sources of poetic authority—some sonic, some syntactic, and others semantic. The deepest well of authority is religious, though no one source works entirely on its own, and the chapters that follow examine various facets of poetic authority. Behind this deepest authority, I will explicate in this and the next chapter an orphic poetics, and then set some of its limits in chapters 3 and 4. My argument is that the most distinctive authority of lyric rests still on its affirmative function, whereas the intellectual disciplines derive from doubt. Insofar as the achievements of the art are measured by the criteria of skeptical intellectual disciplines, lyric inevitably seems slight.

The term *authority*, as Hannah Arendt observes, comes from the root of "augment": with what does poetry augment ordinary language? If there is one answer, it is: music. Musicality authenticates poetry, a crucial function in a discourse that strains against social conventions. Poetry enjoys distinctive credibility: a reader is often asked to credit less *what* a poet says than the earnestness or genuineness of the effort. Poets do not expect simply to be believed where a prose writer would be doubted; they do not even expect to be fully understood. They need instead to pursue significance at the edges of conventions, where no significance is assured. Readers stay with poems, moving into uncertainty and even obscurity, because the history of this art demonstrates utter seriousness, and because shapely sounds draw them on. The worst that can be said of a poem is not that it is obscure, or without paraphrasable sense, but that it is frivolous or fake. A "high seriousness," according to Arnold, is the defining feature of great poetry. A figure of authority does not exercise power, as Arendt notes, but rather approves or disapproves of a power or policy: a priest or judge, not a king, is an authority. "The most conspicuous characteristic of those in authority is that they do not have power."[3] A sense of displacement is built into the concept of authority. The indirectness of poetic expression corresponds directly to its authority. Poets are far removed from power, and that *strengthens* their authority. What they wield is not power but approval.

Autonomy is poetry's special aspiration: an independence from politics, philosophy, history, or theology, so that poetic value does not depend upon political conformity, logical argumentation, historical accuracy, or religious faith. If poetry has distinctive value, it must have special features that other discourses either lack or cannot exploit fully. Poems, in Fanny Howe's phrase, engage directly with what is bewildering. Intellectual disciplines reduce bewilderment, but poetry cultivates it. Poets write in forms that resist rational criteria. Many poems leave syntactic and prosodic structures open and unresolved. Even conventionally structured poems ring with traditional but bewildering echoes. The musical structure of symmetrical formal poems often pulls signification toward uncertainty. The separable syntactic and prosodic structures of a poem vie with one another for the focused attention of readers. Only the first leads directly to semantic sense. Critics reassuringly show how sound echoes sense, but it does so only occasionally; sonics are often bewildering, even in poems as shapely as Shakespeare's sonnets.

What is called lyric is more effort than thing, a variety of language use differentiating itself from other discourses. Lyrics are conventionally distinguished from speech or prose by diction, syntax, prosody, and typography. Poetry's conventional markers facilitate memory, but provide no guaranty of poetic value; light verse and doggerel display the same markers. Roman Jakobson said that "form exists for us only as long as it is difficult to perceive, as long as we sense the resistance of the material, as long as we waver as to whether what we read is prose or poetry."[4] The marking of poetry as distinct, as he saw, initiates a contest of uncertain outcome. Although some poets continue to write gnomic lines, more often poetic craft serves ways of thinking and formulating that rarely settle into judgments, or even generality, and often dissolve altogether. Poetry explores language usage beyond conventional prose or speech; it competes with other discourses for authority or credibility, but is hobbled in that competition by an indefinite account of its own distinctiveness. The most ancient contest is between poetry and philosophy, which Goethe addressed in his autobiography: "In poetry a certain faith in the impossible, . . . as in religion a like faith in the inscrutable, must have a place[;] the philosophers appeared to me to be in a very false position who would demonstrate and explain both of them from their own field of vision."[5] Poetry solicits the faith of adherents. But faith in what? Not in doctrine or dialectic. Poems try to move past the points where rationality rests to recover a remainder of the impossible, inscrutable, overlooked, negligible, or even erroneous. Poets are thinkers, but they are believers too in the value of what eludes rationality.

English-language intellectual culture has been preponderantly secular for over a century, though the religious roots of poetry have remained, however buried, vigorous. The Polish poet Adam Zagajewski acknowledges the inevitable limit on the knowledge that poetry offers: "Poetry is condemned to live with mystery, alongside mystery, in endless, energizing uncertainty."[6] Even the rationalizing methods of New Criticism relied on a sense of mystery. John Crowe Ransom's understanding of the contest of discourses—poetry, theology, philosophy, political theory, economics, sociology, history—was mundane: he measured their relative command of power, economic and political, and social prestige. Poetry is weak in these ways, though it has a distinctive strength because it is less abstract than philosophy, political theory, and economics. The unexplained specificity of life is honored in the language of poetry, according to Ransom, whereas other discourses try to explain everything. Poetry needs the unexplained, even the inexplicable. At its core is approval of the fullness of experience made evident by the unwillingness of poets to subordinate difficulties to explanatory principles: this distinguishes it from other discourses. A lyric conveys exaltation, but also a sense of limits—those of agency as well as rationality. Poetry and religion both lead toward submission. Schiller argued that the most developed poetry produces a "serene clarity," a moment when there is nothing to be done.[7] Adorno follows him much later in saying that the lyric strives "to remain unaffected by bustle and commotion."[8] From this point of view, a didactic or provocative poem is a contradiction in terms. A journalist hews closely to what is said to be known and delineable. In poetry, prayer, and song what is not known is affirmed; these uses of language acknowledge, as others more rarely do, that the wavering boundary between understanding and misapprehension is a threshold of value. Ignorance and incomprehension are necessary horizons of the art.

Poetry is an art of ideals shadowed by failure. The "language of the actual," as Ransom says, is plainly prose, which dominates "the marketplace, the senate, the camp, the executive offices, the laboratories, the learned professions, and nearly all the public occasions." Idealistic prose is projected toward a future: space travel, artificial intelligence, triumphalist histories, and so on. But the idealism of poetry is retrospective: "it handles the past, and in particular those clearly marked alternative paths which we came to in the past but did not take."[9] Poetic diction consists of faux archaisms. Poetry, archival and utopian, resurrects forms of expression and conception that might be more regularly accessible if history's losers had been winners. Yes, if the South had won the war, in Ransom's case. An appalling thought: slavery and agriculture. But Ransom had a pertinent point in that poems, after Virgil, sing of lost causes, and figure the costs of historical choices. What one hears is a minority report. "Over every poem which looks like a poem," Ransom wrote, "is a sign which reads: This road does not go through to action; fictitious."[10] Past choices, made differently, might have enabled some fictions to be facts, and vice versa. The categories of academic literary interpretation are aligned against this poetic project. Daniel Tiffany, for instance, has argued that Pound's "crypt aesthetic," his pursuit of the cherished dead, is a version of fascist kitsch. Pound's retrospective orientation seems to many scholars now void of allegorical significance, rich only in "the rhapsodic sensibility of kitsch." The most musical passages of the *Cantos* are the worst violations of the academic taste for paraphrasable sense.[11] Orpheus wore jackboots, on this view.

Dark, lost causes. Lyric poets have no reason to expect their art to transform the future, to right wrongs, or redeem loss. An expectation of failure, not triumph, is built into poems. "There is no poetry," according to Bonnefoy, "but that which is impossible."[12] Lyric begins in a sense of implacable limits, against which it is appropriate to strain; tough odds justify strenuous language. Music's power to charm is validated by the apparent impossibility of overcoming these limits. So "strain" in both senses: a hard push and a song too. The impossibility of poetry is not a historical development; journalism about the death of poetry, or its regrettable adversity, is off point. Poets are drawn less to questions that can be answered, than to those that cannot, to irresolvable problems, and inevitably obscure issues. "Poetry is a search for the inexplicable," Stevens says.[13] Not a confrontation with the inexplicable, but a search for it. Poets look for trouble, taking only the long shots. And they plan to lose. Whitman's young poet, in "Out of the Cradle Endlessly Rocking," grows "ecstatic" in response to a birdsong of loss and misery. Pleasure in the bird's adversity sets the poet apart from others, from the natural order of things, and from the boy he was before his vocation. The prospect of a thousand songs yet "more sorrowful" than the bird's excites him. The peace the boy knew before he felt his inspiration is gone forever; in its place: "the sweet hell within, / The unknown want."[14] He will now live in paradox and yearning for a lost satisfaction; that is perversely thrilling to the poet. "The word of the sweetest song and all songs" is "death." His destiny is to hear in the sea that dark song, "some drowned secret hissing." The exact nature of the secret, as the phrase suggests, is beside the point: it might be one secret or another. What counts is that it is drowned, irrecoverable, mysterious. That is the birth of song.

Ovid tells the story of Orpheus as a first poet. Book 10 of the *Metamorphoses* begins with the wedding of Orpheus and Eurydice; their union is impossible from the start. Hymen waves his torch in a celebratory fashion, but it gutters and smokes, bringing tears to everyone's eyes. This couple had only one night together; on the morning after the wedding, she dies suddenly of snakebite. Orpheus sings his laments the world over, and all the species weep at his music. He takes his laments to the underworld and charms even the Furies to tears. He is allowed to revive his dead bride and lead her back to her mortal life, on condition that he not look back at her as they ascend the path out of Hades. As they are about to emerge from the underworld, he turns in doubt, and she recedes into the gloom, whispering goodbye.[15] He is driven by devotion to his lost beloved Eurydice, but their union was impossible from their wedding day. His song is extraordinarily persuasive; it falters, though, on a doubt. Orpheus turned away from women then. As Seamus Heaney translates the last lines of book 10:

> Many women loved him and, denied
> Or not, adored. But now the only bride
> For Orpheus was going to be a boy
> And Thracians learned from him, who still enjoy
> Picking those spring flowers bright and early.[16]

Book 11 narrates the death of Orpheus. Wild women, hearing his song and resentful of his disdain of women, launch an attack. His song charms even the sticks and stones thrown at him. He is beaten, though, because they make a rival music: his sweet songs cannot be heard over their wild sounds, and the stones begin to reach their mark:

> The furies were unleashed. And his magic note
> That should have stalled their weapons was drowned out
> By blaring horns and drums, beatings and yells
> And the pandemonium of those bacchanals
> So that at last his red blood wet the rocks.[17]

Orpheus dies horribly, torn limb from limb, in a sonic combat; noise, bad music drives out the good. The women misuse tools as weapons and brutally slaughter farm animals. Charles Martin's translation connects the struggle to religious authority:

> having torn apart the oxen
> whose horns had threatened them, they hastened back
> to finish off the seer, who, with raised hands,
> spoke words unheeded for the first time ever,
> his voice not moving them the slightest bit;
> the sacrilegious women struck him down. . . .[18]

The death of the poet ends an era of faith: his song thereafter fails to charm. His singing head washes up on the shore at Lesbos, where Sappho's song begins. What we know as lyric has the musical and religious crisis (he succumbed to doubt) of Orpheus behind it. The musicality of poetry is not going to be entirely extricated from issues of faith. Music solicits a hearing, as a speech does too, but a belief as well in the indefinite power of words.

Fanny Howe, as I noted, refers to "a Muslim prayer that says, 'Lord, increase my bewilderment,' and this prayer belongs both to me and to the strange Whoever who goes under the name of 'I' in my poems . . . where error, errancy, and bewilderment are the main forces."[19] This wonderful notion of seeking confusion is related to Stevens's point, but not quite the same. When she puts error and errancy together, she evokes a sense of movement, wandering without direction. The objective of expunging or correcting error is irrelevant. There is no criterion of rightness, in this way of thinking, only a technology of error. She especially feels a need for movement, or change, to develop a project without any profound truth to support its authority. Just one line after another, wayward, bewildered. Errant poets do not resolve issues—in this they are close to Stevens—but they are especially determined to find paths of continuing surprises, and that is not exactly Stevens's point. "The serial poem," she writes, demonstrates an attention to what is "cyclical, returning, but empty at its axis. To me, the serial poem is a spiral poem. In this poetry circling can take form as sublimations, inversions, echolalia, digressions, glossolalia, and rhymes."[20] The formal language of poetry echoes, approximates, or digresses from, something else; the poem itself is not the thing. A poetics of the achieved artifact misses the authority of the art. A spiral is hollow.

›››‹‹‹

The attraction to impossible subjects is ancient. Pindar celebrates the efforts of mortals to excel and invokes the blessings of the gods for his athletes and their benefactors. He tells stories about the gods and the achievements of his athletes, but he refuses to explain fully all that he celebrates. In Nemean 5 he says, "And often silence is man's best art."[21] W. R. Johnson credits him with inventing the vatic personality.[22] This ancient Greek poet,

Johnson shows, "resolutely avoids analysis" of legends; silence expresses his piety and understanding of the limits of choral lyric. Very near the start of Western lyric, then, poetry derived authority from religion; but more important the limits on lyric's explanatory power were explicitly made to express the piety of both poet and audience. Prolixity remains suspect in poetry: poets who explain fully are accused of being outside the art altogether. Arnold referred to Pope as a prose writer. The taciturnity of poets derives less from character than from faith in what cannot be adequately explained.

Lyric poems can seem intellectually modest, and not only because they are cut short. Poets behold and approve the value of the women, men, and landscapes that move them, but they don't *explain* that value. The identification of value is itself intellectually ambitious in a context dominated by skepticism and irony. Ancient Greek choral lyrics designate someone worthy of praise, as a champion is designated. Praise poems name particular people, but the naming of athletes and even of benefactors is carefully restrained. Gods and places are specified just as prominently; less is made of particular athletes than one might expect. The point is more to connect athletes (and auditors) with the eternal forces of the gods than to name mortals. Praise poems articulate general categories; the challenge for ancient Greek poets was to set standards by which particular leaders and communities might be well measured. A poet's intellectual work was not definition or explanation of values, but rather the naming of such values and the articulation of linkage between them and particular leaders or scenes: poets join general and particular.

Orpheus as founder has not determined the history of criticism. The dominant line of poetics since Aristotle is rhetorical: the craft of achieving particular poetic effects. For nearly a century poets have written inventively about technique: Yeats's masks, Eliot's objective correlative, Pound's ideogram, Ransom's irony, and so on; the *Cantos* and the *Waste Land* are far darker, though, and stranger than these prose accounts of technique. Any Aristotelian shot necessarily falls short of the mark. The now subordinate, orphic line of poetics claims instead that a true poet does not know just what to say. Asked whether he begins with a definite idea of what a poem will say, Robert Creeley responded, "Not at all. If I knew that I wouldn't bother to write it. What's the point of doing what one already knows?"[23] "Old men ought to be explorers," according to Eliot (and then Roethke), and Stevens thought similarly about all intellectual pursuit.[24]

> That the unknown as the source of knowledge, as the object of thought, is part of the dynamics of the known does not permit of denial. It is the unknown that excites the ardor of scholars, who, in the known alone, would shrivel up with boredom. We accept the unknown even when we are most skeptical. We may resent the consideration of it by any except the most lucid minds; but when so considered, it has seductions more powerful and more profound than those of the known.[25]

The grandest poetic aspiration—despite all analysis of style—is not to produce resplendent forms, but to reach into darkness. "Poetry, despite its great design," Bonnefoy says,

> has always preserved within its closed dwelling the sense of an unknown existence, an alternative way of salvation, a different hope—in any case, of a strange and inadmissible pleasure. . . . The truth is that there is something ambiguous about all great works. And this makes them more deeply akin, among all edifices, among all mansions whose eternity is assured, to a temple, to the dwelling of a god.[26]

The pursuit of the unknown by experimental scientists progresses through collaboration, but poets who turn away from rhetorical poetics come very quickly to the overlap of poetry and religion. Orphic poets are not invariably priestly; however, this dimension of Western poetics feeds intellectual and spiritual drives that are poorly served by the agnostic enlightenment disciplines of academic organization. Where intellectual aspiration ends and religious belief begins is unclear. Criticism has no difficulty with poetry as lament, or critique. But before Orpheus lamented the loss of Eurydice he presumably sang songs of praise. Laments require a prior state of blessedness or amplitude. Without spring songs and hymns, no elegies, though the converse is not true.

A will to get beyond what is already known drives poetry to distinguish itself from discourses that render their subjects transparent, known. Traditionally, among poets, obscurity is a sign of profundity; the dark modernists would be recognizable to Spenser and Milton. Boccaccio observed that "some things are naturally so profound that not without difficulty can the most exceptional keenness in intellect sound their depths."[27] Obscure poems seem to come from a hidden source, not from the beliefs of their audience. Oracles, for instance: when a god speaks, men are not expected to follow easily.[28] "Alienation of an audience," Michael Murrin observes, "is actually a sign of divine inspiration."[29] The obscure poets have marked their language as nonconformist, as exceptional. Poetic diction and syntax are like robes: "The poet is the priest," Stevens says, "of the invisible."[30] Conspicuous devices of the art all signify "Not of This World." Yet the aesthetics (and politics) of representation have led modern readers and critics alike to treasure realistic art. "The highest problem of any art," Goethe says, "is to produce by semblance the illusion of some higher reality. But it is a false endeavour to realize the appearance until at last only something commonly real remains."[31] He sees plainly the hollowness where art's core is thought to be. Artists trade in illusions, conjuring an uncommon sense of "some higher reality." Goethe accepts the hocus-pocus, as Yeats, Robert Duncan, and James Merrill later did too. "Malachi Stilt-Jack am I." The nadir of poetic credibility, where art's authority rests on trickery. "Any taste remains barbaric," according to Kant, "if its liking requires that *charms* and *emotions* be mingled in, let alone if it makes these the standard of its approval."[32] Academic literary theory rests just here, suspicious of all claims that literary writing has a distinctive character, let alone authority.

Yet distinguished poets, particularly in cultures that seem to need poetry, retain the tradition of poetic authority. Even in the United States at least the separateness of poetic discourse, though contested, is a settled fact. In 1945 Pound was incarcerated for treasonous speech; the U.S. government did not recognize a poet's authority to contravene that of the state. Many literary critics and poets, however, claimed in 1948 that his poetic authority entitled him to override state authority. He was given the Bollingen award for poetry in 1949, though he was not released by the government until 1958. In 2001 Baraka, then poet laureate of the State of New Jersey, published a poem asserting that the Israeli government knew in advance of the attacks on the World Trade Center and advised Jewish employees to stay home from work on September 11. The State of New Jersey could not even end his term as laureate. He was ridiculed but not disciplined for his provocative allegations. The conventional protection of poets is ancient; Pound and Baraka are not anomalies. Plutarch tells the story of Solon disguising himself as a fool to advocate in verse an Athenian military expedition to recover the island of Salamis—despite a new law specifically against just such advocacy. His cause was thoroughly unpopular; the Athenians were then tired of fighting the Megarians for Salamis. But Solon was not stoned for his advocacy, partly because he set his speech to verse, partly because he played the fool. And his poem persuaded the Athenians. He was appointed to lead an expedition to recover control of Salamis, and the expedition was successful.[33] Solon was right. The possibility is acknowledged by the sufferance of the majority that a poet-fool may get something important right. Some causes a reasonable orator cannot advocate with impunity, but poets can do much more because theirs is a separate discourse. The outrageousness of Pound and Baraka has widely discredited poetry, but it has also revealed how firm is the supposition that poetry should not be measured against literal truth or held to civic responsibility.

No surprise, then, that Seamus Heaney wrote that poetry "is credited with an authority of its own." He quotes the Polish poet Anna Swir, who claims that, when writing, "a poet becomes . . . an antenna capturing the voices of the world, a medium expressing his own subconscious and the collective subconscious. For one moment he possesses wealth usually inaccessible to him, and he loses it when that moment is over." On this view, a poet speaks for—that is, represents—others. This is not Pope's notion that a poet articulates "what oft was thought but ne'er so well expressed." Swir's poet rather reveals something surprising that had been if not exactly thought then deeply felt by all others. Her sense of poetic authority is based only partly on a representational model—one voice counting for many. The indispensable feature of poetic authority, for her, derives from something normally hidden and revealed only momentarily. This special authority is unsustainable; it interrupts ordinary discourse, or reading, or silence. One thinks of Arnold quoting only his touchstones to demonstrate the high seriousness of poetry. This authority does not belong to narrative or dramatic poetry; it belongs only to lyric, or lyric moments in longer poems.[34] The oldest evidence for this view, Heaney observes, is the Greek notion that in a lyric, "it is a god that speaks."

Inspiration is a traditional figure for moments when someone else seems to speak through a poet; verbal craft then seems not felicitous but profoundly meaningful.[35] Facility seems to descend on the poet, and art to come effortlessly. Milton says that Urania comes in the night and "inspires / Easy my unpremeditated Verse."[36] The pagan model of inspiration was quite different: a poetic furor, not a Christian calm.[37] The authority of inspired writing, pagan and Christian, was specially related to its musicality. Augustine says that "David was a man skilled in songs, who dearly loved musical harmony, nor with a vulgar delight, but with a believing disposition, and by it served his God, who is the true God, by the mystical representations of a great thing. For the rational and well-ordered concord of diverse sounds in harmonious variety suggests the compact unity of the well-ordered city [of God]."[38] The (mysterious) musicality of the Psalms in particular symbolizes a harmony and order that is to come. Milton's melodious numbers do not ornament; they warrant the profound truth of his poem. The poet William Matthews, writing enviously of music, describes its didactic or rhetorical office as persuading

> without argument. . . . Orpheus could make the stones move and the trees shake. . . . It's by envy of his powers that poets are forced to admit it: Orpheus was a musician. In order for us to be moved by a poem—and this is the interior equivalent of the stones shifting about—an assent is required. We concur, somehow, with the proposition of a poem. Some part of this curious transaction, not the major but crucial part, requires an intellectual assent.[39]

Orphic poetry disdains argumentation, but nonetheless means to convince. Lyric poetry does not lack the power Matthews hears in music; its musicality has exactly this significance still: the orders of sound symbolize another order held in place, beyond argument, by faith. Lyricism implies that a poem's representations, thoughts, claims, beliefs are ordered, reconciled, at least, one to the other, too deeply for explanation. People could not interpret Orpheus's song, but sticks, stones, birds, and the Furies all assented.

Allen Grossman claimed that the figure of inspiration continues to mark the distinctiveness of poetic utterance.

> The very nature of the poetic tradition seems to me to propose . . . a way out: an origin of discourse (the "muse," let us say) outside of the system constituted by family, by secular instruction and social formations, from the point of view of which "outsidedness" it is possible to introduce into the exchange between mortal persons a kind of knowledge which is not vulnerable to the bitter ironies of social construction and vernacular particularity at any given moment in social space and time. . . . The traditional account in the West of poetic vocation, for example, is a story about a social person whose mortal voice is replaced by a transhistorical and, in the language of the West, an "immortal" voice.[40]

The traditional notion of poetic inspiration settled some critical questions at the outset: Why does a poem have distinctive authority? Because, as Socrates tells Ion, "there is a divinity moving you." What makes one poet great and another less so? Again, Socrates: "All good poets, epic as well as lyric, compose their beautiful poems not by art, but because they are inspired and possessed." What is the relation of rationality to poetic discourse? "No man," Socrates continues, "while he retains that faculty [of reason], has the oracular gift of poetry."[41] The Platonic account of poetic authority has not survived at the level of theory; Timothy Clark calls it embarrassing at the outset of his *Theory of Inspiration* (1997). Yet the authority of inspiration did not depend on naiveté; it was always chosen, willed, constructed. No reason to think that any poet effortlessly inherited a functional convention of superdiscursive authority.

Through elaborate artifice, orphic poets mark distinctions from the plainness of instrumental speech and prose, and thereby request special authority from readers. One might expect that orphic poetry would thrive only when literary and religious cultures are tightly bound, but that is not the case. The transition from a religious to a secular model of poetic authority occurred in English well before the Renaissance, the period of greatest distinction in religious poetry. English literary theory of the sixteenth and seventeenth centuries, as William Kerrigan shows, did not earnestly investigate relations between poetry and prophecy.[42] "Why a Christian should think it an ornament to his Poem," Hobbes wrote, "either to prophane the true God, or invoke a false one, I can imagine no cause, but a reasonless imitation of Custom, of a foolish custom; by which a man enabled to speak wisely from the principles of nature, and his own meditation, loves rather to be thought to speak by inspiration, like a bagpipe."[43] Milton's assertion of the divine authority of his poem ran against the temper of his time.[44] He was, as Richard Helgerson says, the most isolated poet in the seventeenth century.[45] The literary culture he inherited was significantly secular; he invented his own milieu. "The claim to divine inspiration," Helgerson says, "could not survive the new astringent realism of the 1590s. Such stilt-walking stuff had become the exclusive prop of fools."[46] In 1667 Milton nonetheless made an uncompromised claim to divine inspiration. By what authority does a poet "justify the ways of God to man"? Spenser and Milton had labored to inherit ancient models of poetic authority from Greek, Latin, and Hebrew poets, as John Guillory shows, and managed successfully to adjust archaic, exotic poetics to the needs of English poetry. Thereafter the question of poetic authority has necessarily entailed their poems. Both poets like Heaney and literary historians like Helgerson, who reveal how poetic authority has been constructed, are right: poetic authority has been audaciously manufactured by certain poets—Spenser, Milton, Jonson, Pope, Wordsworth, but also Eliot, Pound, Lowell, Duncan, Ginsberg, and Rich—and some residual authority, thanks to these constructions, remains for all poets as part of the genre itself.

Poets who tap this resource are motivated more by vocational ambition than by religious piety, and the display of self-regard is not sublime. Petrarch had himself crowned poet laureate in 1341 on the Capitol in Rome. Helgerson shows how great poets (not all orphic: he includes Ben Jonson among his examples, alongside Spenser and Milton) construct personae calculated to command poetic authority. They first seem to ask Cowley's question—

> What shall I do to be forever known,
> And make the age to come my own?[47]

—and then shape their careers accordingly. Spenser, Milton, and Jonson were driven by ambition "to fill the role of the great poet," as Horace, Virgil, and Petrarch had been too.[48] This analysis exposes egotistical men who knew that they wanted to wield authority within a literary culture before they knew what they wanted to write. Such ambition has no particular theological or philosophical source; it begins rather with an appetite for preferment among rivals. This authority derives not from poems, nor even, originally, from literary communities that recognize artistic greatness, but from individuals who contrive in the critical discourse of their time (whatever that may be) to seem special. The ego, not the poem, may be the fundamental unit of literary history: "For a laureate," Helgerson observes, "the poetry could not stand alone."[49] There is no one formula whereby a poet achieves such stature; instead "a laureate's self-presentation will be couched in the language of his own generation." Contemporaneity is the criterion whereby careers are made, even lasting careers. The laureate poets directly contest the terms their contemporaries invoke to justify literary importance, and paradoxically come to preside over the art of their moment.[50] They represent the art of poetry by transcending the representations of contemporary practitioners, and persuade their readers to choose an art at odds with mainstream taste.

I stress poets' choices in order to show that extreme poetic authority does not claim to be inevitable or natural; orphic poetry may produce religious significance, but it is a product of literary ambition, not of religious conviction. Pound was a master of musicality and a vigorous proponent of the orphic authority of lyric; yet behind his orphic aspiration lay also a rhetorical ambition and sense of poetic craft. His sense was that poetry begins in extraordinary emotion, which alone is insufficient to produce poetry, of course, but it is necessary. "An intentness on the quality of the emotion to be conveyed," he said, "makes for poetry."[51] His formulation imagines a rhetorical situation in which emotion is conveyed to a reader, though in fact only representations are conveyed by poems. He wanted the immediacy of emotional experience, but with a distinctive motivation—"intentness." Emotion can be produced accidentally, but intention is itself significant. For all his emphasis on mysterious or intense emotions, he maintained a sense of rhetorical propriety; the language of poetry was instrumental for him. Orphic poetics collaborate with rhetoric. Here is a famous passage in which he constructs the origin of myth.

> The first myths arose when a man walked sheer into "nonsense," that is to say, when some very vivid and undeniable adventure befell him, and he told someone else who called him a liar. Thereupon, after bitter experience, perceiving that no one could understand what he meant when he said that he "turned into a tree" he made a myth—a work of art that is—an impersonal or objective story woven out of his own emotion, as the nearest equation that he was capable of putting into words. That story, perhaps, then gave rise to a weaker copy of his emotion in others, until there arose a cult, a company of people who could understand each other's nonsense about the gods.[52]

Myth, verbal art, and religious cult originate in a narrative failure, or an alleged deception; they reconstitute credibility, or authority, after failure. Conventional expectations determine boundaries for discourse; myth, poetry, and religion suspend such conventions so that extraordinary emotional experience can be communicated. The truth of Pound's story is that poetry is a second discourse, understood in relation to a first in which speakers may lie. As Sidney said, a poet cannot lie, because he nothing affirmeth. Pound wrote this passage in an essay on the union of music and poetry that begins with his own representation of an extraordinary experience of hearing the tones of a recorder: "I have seen the God Pan and it was in this manner: I heard a bewildering and pervasive music moving from precision to precision within itself . . ." He seems to be describing his own experience of the originating moment of allegory—"I have seen the God Pan"—but music, not mimesis, carries the freight of bewilderment. This is the sister art that moves furthest beyond discursive explanation. The profundity of poetry, Pound suggests, may lie not behind a veil of allegory, but in the qualities of sounds. Allegory is a sign of a parallel discourse, but musicality may be just such a sign too, and that has great consequence for the art of poetry. Pound asks: What do poets do after hearing remarkable music? His answer: they cunningly mediate between the music and a skeptical audience.

The concept of inspiration is archaic and was already regarded as anachronistic by Milton's contemporaries, but it lives in ordinary language still, and poets continue to draw on it, though rarely. Ronald Johnson and James Merrill were exceptional among contemporaries.[53] The idea of another power speaking through a poet says something distinctive and permanent about this art; various features of poetic technique refer to a displaced source. The meaning of the traditional "rules and principles of poetic construction" that supplement ordinary language, as Grossman puts it, derives from the notion of inspiration.[54] Even prosody, which is conceived more often as superficial than profound, on this account, signifies an immortal origin or authority. Susan Stewart similarly claims that "inspiration does not always precede *techne*, and *techne* can itself provide a source of inspiration as aspects of the material only come forward within the process of *poiesis* itself."[55] The source of inspiration for her is the body and the mind of a poet; the term *inspiration* seems justified to her when the source lies deep in a poet. "Certain types of music and rhythmic form in one's writing signal the possibility of a recovered somatic meaning. In other words, we might read the symptoms of meter just as the painter, or other maker of visual images, can attend to the obsessional image or the rebus structure of certain scenes. In the accumulation or accrual of returns to certain meters, the poet can come to learn *in time* and in an ongoing practice the deeper structures of his or her own thought and emotion in relation to the world."[56] Grossman holds that the musicality of poetry comes from poetry itself, which is beyond the social and historical existence of the poet; Stewart understands the subjectivity of each poet to underlie the musicality of his or her poems. But for both poet-critics, the music is profound.

›››‹‹‹

I want to examine at length the contemporary formal consequences of the theory of displaced authority. The fact that poetry does not ultimately justify its claims is an obvious handicap in its competition with other discourses for rational assent, but that handicap may be turned to advantage. Because poetic authority is assumed in the end, rather than explained, it may instead be presumed at the outset. Language that has been made to sing may be presumed to have just authority. Old songs, on this view, are the judges of our time. Poets looking back on their predecessors often feel enormous confidence in the resources accessible to them. Milton's monumental blank-verse paragraphs, his Latinate syntax, and his Christian piety might all be reckoned obstacles to his influence on contemporary poetry. However, in 1977 Ronald Johnson published an extraordinary volume, *Radi os*, comprised entirely of words selected judiciously from books 1–4 of *Paradise Lost.* Erasing most of Milton's words, Johnson found this poem in lines 582–634 of book 1:

And all [582]

with all [586]

above the rest [589]

Stood [591]
All [592]

: as when the sun [594]
Looks through the horizontal [595]
Behind the moon, [596]
Eclipse [597]

Archangel : [600]

heaven's fire [612]

From wing to wing, and [617]

Words interwove with [621]
Mortal [622]
Matchless, [623]

change [625]
of mind, [626]
[page-break]
For who can yet believe [631]
To re-ascend, [633]
and re-possess [634]

in close design, [646]
At length from us [648]
Space may produce new Worlds [650]

to pry [655]

Abyss [658]

For who can think [661]

the sudden blaze [665]

There stood a hill [670][57]

This is no précis of Milton; Johnson transforms his source freely. In this passage, toward the end of the procession of fallen angels, Satan first addresses his followers. Johnson erases the specificity of Milton's language: very few proper nouns survive this process. Aspramont, Montalban, Damasco, Marocco, Trebisond, Biserta, Afric, and Charlemain, all enticing words, fall to Johnson's mighty eraser. They become simply "And all / with all." For the effect that Johnson wants, the language must be comprehensive and general—just what Pound mistrusted. His is an idiom of praise, not critique; praise lifts toward a level of ideals. Milton tells of "all our woe," but Johnson prunes back the adversity of his source text. That Satan spoke through tears, an extraordinary passage in Milton, and his "words interwove with sighs" is kept from Johnson's reader, who is not made clear even that Satan's words follow. The last eight lines cited suggest that words might change mind, that heaven might be repossessed. Satan rather asks, "Who can yet believe, though after loss, / That all these puissant Legions . . . shall fail to re-ascend / . . . and re-possess thir native seat?" Johnson's reverence of Milton is enormous, but it allows him nonetheless surprising liberty to revise his source. Milton's "immortal" (622) becomes his "mortal"; phrases of negation, like "shall fail to" (633), are silently dropped, and Milton's local sense reversed. A précis would track closely the thematic sense of the original. Johnson understands that Milton's poem is so fully realized that it requires no such assistance. He can mine it freely and retain the authority of the original, for its great power resides not in its paraphrasable sense, nor even in Milton's exact words; or if in his words, so deeply there, that "mortal" can be extracted from "immortal," and elsewhere the word "cell" from "excell'd" (359) and "star" from "Astarte" (439). Johnson takes the form of inspiration from Milton, but what else must come with this form? Theologically, much of Milton disappears in Johnson's poem, but this too is a Christian poem by almost any standard. Considerable doctrine accompanies the form of inspiration: mortality followed by reascension; redemption of an exemplary new world; heaven; angels. Johnson alters the inspired language of Milton, and that is a controversial thing to do. In ancient Greece special vigilance was exercised concerning the accurate conveyance of inspired utterances. When a messenger was dispatched to consult an oracle, he was explicitly forbidden to alter in any way the utterance of the oracle. The ancient poet Theognis of Megara, as Gregory Nagy observes, is explicit about editorial intrusion: "You will not find any remedy if you add anything, / nor will you escape from veering, in the eyes of the gods, if you take anything away."[58]

Johnson feels his way along Milton's text, alert to buried senses; the history of words—the path recommended by Emerson and later Pound—is not the one he follows ("Astarte" does not derive from "star"). The words used by historical communities of English-speakers are not importantly the source of Johnson's text; the source is just the words that Milton used in his 1667 scripture. Johnson models his poem not on the narratives Milton took from the Bible but on the words and, sometimes, the letters he received from Urania during the night. Johnson's poem is inspired by Milton's, and Milton's by Urania; this lineage is not trivial. Johnson does not claim any religious transport behind his writing, though he represents transport; he works coolly as an editor, paring away the excess of Milton's baroque epic until a celebratory lyric remains, as though the poem on his pages were a figure camouflaged in the ground of Milton's diction.[59] Johnson has no use for Milton's dramaturgy: characters as agents matter not at all; who is speaking in any particular source passage is irrelevant. What characters do in their struggles against antagonists is similarly immaterial; Johnson omits all signs of conflict, even most signs of adversity. The oratory of Hell is dissolved. His poem celebrates the light.

Johnson's solar hymn is a meditative lyric too, exactly because he has constructed a skeleton of implicit syntax. Various readers will doubtless flesh out the skeleton with variations, but here is my reconstruction. The first five lines (from *Paradise Lost* 1.582–89) express in terms of a paradox the sense of sublime unity one derives from the sight of the sun on the horizon: how can all be supplemented by all ("with all") and separate from "the rest"? This language of exaltation leaves parts behind, as it strives toward a great overriding unity. The next seven lines (from *Para-*

dise Lost 1.594–617) liken the sun on the horizon (a figure of sublime union) to an archangel, a higher-order, semidivine creature spreading the light of heaven from wing to wing. The last five lines of this page (from *Paradise Lost* 1.621–26) return to the past tense of "Stood / All." The movement of words in response to this solar vision is said not to provoke but to accompany a change of mind. Johnson applies two distinct modifiers to "change / of mind." The first suggests that such change belongs in particular to the condition of mortality, and the second incorporates that mortal feature into a superlative state fitting this solar eclipse. (There is too a secondary-order pun on "matchless" as without a match, or light, implying that light cannot originate in the mind.) The word "For," which structures the remainder of this poem, with the exception of the last line, initiates a discursive dimension to the hymn. Johnson engages a hypothetical adversary with two rhetorical questions, both implicitly Christian, not secular, amounting to: Who can believe that mortals can recover a blessed state? Who can conceive of the apocalypse that would so transform existence? His answer: "There stood a hill." This conclusion echoes the main clause of the poem's opening: "Stood / All." The hill is Zion.

Johnson's poems are hymns sung in real joy, with little resistance from anyone or anything, and this is hard for a poet to manage. Hopkins's gorgeous "God's Grandeur" is wrenchingly eloquent on the corruptions of natural beauty.

> . . . Why do men then now not reck his rod?
> Generations have trod, have trod, have trod;
>   And all is seared with trade; bleared, smeared with toil;
>   And wears man's smudge and shares man's smell: the soil
> Is bare now, nor can foot feel, being shod. (4–8)[60]

From these weighty lines Hopkins's ecstatic sestet can take flight. Every critic knows that not all is joy. The intellectual disciplines are arrayed against uncritical joy. Johnson sustains elation and music by not staging a character in or against the world. Hymns are impersonal and universal in that there is no speaker or scene, no specificity of the voice. Johnson's poems are like translations: their words issue from another text. He selects the words to bring over not into another language but into another poem. He translates words, not syntax, not narrative, not music. Since he rarely selects the anonymous little words that define syntactic relations, and he does not interpose words between the ones he selects from his source text, he produces texts that are comprised of implicit declarative sentences, when any grammatical structure seems relevant. The declarative sentence may be all that a praise poet really needs. Intellectual disciplines need syntax.

What range of language suits a poetry of praise? Does a praise poet have any range at his or her disposal? Hopkins usually writes syntactically, but the sound structure of his lines seems a generator that might at any point overtake the rules of English grammar. A poet's management of the resources of language—syntactic and sonic—is one reliable source of credibility. The artful elaboration of syntax demonstrates a respectful understanding of conventions of expression and explanation. Rules of syntax govern mutually constituted orders of understanding and explanation. Syntactically artful writing not only presses a claim to authority, as I explain in chapter 4; it alludes to a distinctive way of constructing authority: namely by negotiation between parties within the constraints of recognized rules. Poets like Johnson make very little use of the structures that generate elaborate syntax. His sentences are elementary, when they conform at all to grammatical rules. The authority to which he appeals is not mutually constructed; it derives from a source beyond the linguistic realm of the poem, beyond social relations among autonomous individuals. Some poets—Johnson is one—write within an authoritarian regime, even though practical politics may be remote, as here, from the references of the poem. Much devotional poetry is authoritarian in this specific sense.

Consider Johnson's *Ark* (1996). This book-length poem suggests that syntax—rule-governed elaboration of clauses—is beside the point; *Ark* consists largely of atomized words, many of them chipped out of other texts.[61] The specificity of these words is striking: "chrysoprase," for instance. And their sound contours forcefully generate line after line. Here is *Ark* 89, *Arches* 23, *The Cave*:

up from the bones of the earth,
hew plasma stone
eye lent by granite

middle of a lake
scroll on malachite scroll
topaz city, Samarkand

downdrift X'd celadon,
calcedony zephyr
sapphires surpassing rapture

Perfect in detail,
one opalized reptile skeleton
(found Australia 1909)

One snowball geode
Lined within pyrite phantoms,
in shape of the earth

One bloodstone panorama
whole starred sky,
beasts portrayed in porphyry

luminous and ominous
open cupboard of chrysoprase,
set lapis-lazuli as Seas

Beneath the surface
root hexagonal crystals
upward, many multiples a water

seams aflame in luster
—Mind amid a play of colors
banded impurities

cut readily in all directions
taking high polish,
universal building stone

an Age of Bronze,
ores of peacock copper
tarnished with iridescence

Mercury wrung cinnabar
rooms prism rooms
pillars of basalt, obsidian

quartzlight, mother-of-pearl
cluster bristling embryo
self caught in amber

heavens gem Clay
layered, full play of time
days onyxed with night

Stir moment alabaster!
Pour cup silvery
Step chance by needle ends

memorable pebbles
rolled mountain torrent,
arrested prime amethyst falls

emerald, revealer-of-truth
noinnerfirehid ruby
fit for a King's finger

hands mirror diamond maker
Adam, engoldened
enter into the Grotto[62]

Johnson wants only to name, not to explain; in this sense, he needs little syntax for worship or adoration. "Stir moment alabaster" is a phonically coherent line because of the symmetry of the initial and terminal syllables (Johnson is fond of such constructions). The line is syntactically obscure, though: is it, as it seems, an imperative? What can such an imperative mean? "Alabaster" certainly has a semantic sense in this poem about semiprecious stones—one more admirable stone. The verbs of this stanza—Stir, Pour, Step—seem only vaguely to direct one through a cave of beauties. But the sounds of the lines are very specific, and their symmetries structure what is printed on the page. A paraphrase of lines 46–48 is not possible (however tantalizing line 46 is), but their sonic palpability is certain. Johnson has excised all the coordinating conjunctions that facilitate the reading of prose, leaving readers to imagine syntactic structures, or even sentences, that might underlie his words. There are almost no articles and just enough prepositions to awaken some sense of relationship that might eventuate in a sentence. The words sit one by one on the page, each jewel-like in its uncompromising setting. The words that draw him are specific (a pronoun is nearly unknown in *Ark*). (That said, the closing line of this poem registers with force exactly because its syntax is elementary and its sense is lucid.) One might think that, like Williams and Stein, he was developing that antiseptic strain of modernism that sought to clean words of their histories of accumulated usage, but the contrary is actually the case. He is a profoundly allusive poet, concerned repeatedly to have his words measured against the literary contexts of their former lives. The contemporaneity of his work is likewise insistent: he stages the differences between poetic tradition and current practice on every page.

The syntax is not just telegraphic; it is nearly all modeled on one structure: "behold: . . ." The objective of the syntax is merely to assert existence: "there is" is implicitly ubiquitous. Johnson's job seems done once he has presented what exists. The point is theological; this is all Creation. (How intellectually reduced this is, one has to concede, from Milton's explanatory project.) Words, isolated from syntactic structures that transport attention from one point to another, are effectively opened to alternative modes of scrutiny. An appetite for sense moves one along. By blocking that sort of motion Johnson means to make the words expand: "words sundered swell," he says in *Ark* 51. They swell with resemblances to partner words, and with sonic identity. The logic of this poetic derives from Pound, Zukofsky, and Bunting, certainly. But Johnson constructs a very different relation to the most canonical texts of the West. The Bible and the

Book of Common Prayer are constant sources for his words, and that matters profoundly. One question raised by his work is how deep poetry lies in its traditions. Can his modernist excavations adequately express a wide range of spiritual experience? That he can make poems with shards of Milton is astonishing. Johnson's lines express wonder and reverence, but can he convey the gravity of spiritual awareness? The object of his worship is ambiguous: nature's wonders, or scripture's prophecy? The issue of range is critical. Is there room for doubt or misgiving in his hymns, as there is in the Hebrew Psalms? Johnson writes "luminous and ominous." But what mechanism has he for bringing luminosity and ominousness into relation with each other? Actually all is luminous in *Ark*; the spirit's resistance to splendor can be identified here—ominousness—but not examined.

Johnson was a postwar American experimental poet. He inherited, as all Americans do, the orphic precedents of Whitman, Dickinson, Pound, Eliot, and Crane—that is the main line of U.S. poetry. But his time, and ours still more, is dominated by technological. not religious, wonders. How much freedom does an appropriative poet actually enjoy? Can a poet easily transpose a doctrinally assertive text—*Paradise Lost*, Revelations, or *Mein Kampf*, say—to any contemporary purpose? The model for *Ark* 89 is Revelations 21–22. But John's vision is naturalized here. There are neither "geodes" nor "plasma," nor "ores" in Revelations. Johnson draws on the idioms of the Bible but just as much on the settled terminology of geologists too. This is the central instability of the poem. It is a geological hymn: a mix, that is, of two rival explanations of the "full play of time," as he calls it (41). Charles Lyell's *Principles of Geology* (1830–33) was understood as a direct challenge to biblical authority in that Lyell, working from an analysis of rocks and landforms, argued against catastrophic accounts of the earth's origin, and constructed a timeline far outstripping the six thousand years of biblical history. He argued for a uniformitarian sense of the earth's history: geological changes occur very gradually; the earth is in a more or less steady state of energy. One is commanded to live in the beauty of the earth, to accept one's inevitable home on earth. In Revelations 21–22 an angel displays a New Jerusalem reaching down from heaven. It matters that Johnson's cave poem begins "up from the bones of earth." These bones are made to speak of a life on earth, nowhere near another heaven. Johnson celebrates a New Jerusalem he sees in geology, as John saw it in Revelations 21–22. Johnson, though, goes into a cave in the earth to call up crystals and stones. John is carried aloft by an angel and shown the New Jerusalem from a great high mountain. (Revelations 21:10) The walls of the New Jerusalem are made of precious stones—some of the same stones that Johnson sees (Revelations 21:18–20). Johnson is also thinking of Satan's journey to earth in the third book of *Paradise Lost*: Satan sees the gates of Heaven and admires their jewels, and Milton compares him to John (623). Satan looks at innocent earth in wonder, as Johnson looks too at the crystals of the cave. (Eden as a bejeweled place seems traditional [Ezekiel 28:13].) The stones that interest Johnson are metamorphic; they have changed form due to heat or water. Change is what engages him; the cave is a chamber of natural wonders. But it is also the foundation of a New Jerusalem into which an Adam, a new you, can enter. *Radi os* is solidly Christian, but *Ark* is more ambiguous; it expresses the joy of living on the earth. This is surprising because Johnson's model is in no sense an expression of tolerance or really of joy either. How remote from this poem are Protestant concerns about sin, damnation, atonement, justification, election. This is a Catholic Christianity focused on the transformations of grace. Only a small part of Revelations lives for Johnson: the changes that some rocks go through (from dirt to jewels), a greater promise of a new future for Adam.

›››‹‹‹

The authority of poetry is displaced, as I have said, approximate; its source not on the page. The page stands for something elsewhere; poetic language, far from being full, is only a part of something greater that will not be adequately represented by the poem. That language represents faith itself, line by line, its practice. Even when a poet invokes no religion directly, a familiar structure of belief, if not doctrine itself, underwrites poetic aspiration. What I am calling the authority of lyric derives more from orphic, than from rhetorical, poetics, even when a rhetorical ambition generates orphic achievements, or when rhetorical tools, such as syntax (as in chapter 4), sustain a poet's authority. From Aristotle comes a civic poetics that I discuss in chapter 4; yet the more ambitious account of lyric authority is orphic, and that account is never entirely absent from the reading of lyric poetry. Poems that derive from a secular understanding of the art are nonetheless measured by orphic aspirations. So, yes, orphic poetics is a special case; but its account of authority is strong enough to survive even in other traditions, if only as a reproach. However, alongside the theory of displaced authority has been, since the Renaissance, a suspicion of counterfeit authority; David Quint shows that suspicion of the source or origin of poetry was a central humanist concern. Merrill's intermittent irony about his own inspiration, however coy, keeps this suspicion in plain view.[63] The Ouija board, *sortes Virgilianae*, or Miltonian, or Shakespearean, are all ambivalent: rite and hoax. The question of the counterfeit particularly arises, as in *Radi os*, from formality itself. The arbitrary constraints of avant-garde production of course provoke suspicion, but so too do traditional prosodic structures. Extraordinary prosodic facility is significantly unstable in just these terms: sestinas and villanelles signify a secular, merely technical source of poetry; Milton's "unpremeditated verse," though, elicits wonder at the improbability of a human source. The work of a god, or an engineer?

Johnson's work is especially revealing of the aspirations, but also the limits, of the line of poetic theory I have explicated. He once said, "My myth is Orpheus and Eurydice"; but that can't be the whole story.[64] Orphic poetry is grounded in lament, not praise: the loss of the beloved, not the presence of divinity. How can the first poet of loss authorize songs of celebration? Something crucial is missing from orphic poetics. In the fourth *Geor-*

gic, Virgil presents Proteus as an alternative (or, as I prefer, supplement) to Orpheus; David Quint shows that this revision was developed by Renaissance poets:

> The transformations of Proteus and the song of Orpheus which summons Eurydice back into being are antithetical models of the poetic act. Proteus is the vessel of timeless, originary truth. . . . But Orpheus's song has its "source" in death, that is, within a human history conditioned by mortality. His poetry attempts to recreate and repeat the experience of his love for Eurydice—now part of an irrecoverable past. Wrestled with and bound, Proteus delivers his oracle. But Eurydice speaks only to bid Orpheus farewell and slips out of his vain embrace: by raising her up again, Orpheus merely confirms the fact of her loss.[65]

Proteus is a shape-shifter from whom prophesy must be wrestled: this is no account of inspiration; it figures instead strenuous poetic labor.[66] Proteus sponsors a sense of poetic form as constraint; notions of organic or expressive form are irrelevant to his legend.

> For only by constraint will he give answer:
> He bends to no entreaty; capture him
> With ruthless force and fetters; only these
> Will circumvent and shatter his designs.
> (*Georgics* 4.399–400)[67]

His story reveals some of what an account of poetic authority requires: struggle and labor, unstable and forceful formality, and repetitiveness; but also the merely temporary arrest of truth. Proteus is an oracle, not a figure for rhetorical artifice. One grasps him, holds on, and after his resistance is spent, he yields a truth. A grip on truth and an effort at retention, however temporary: that is what Proteus brings to a religious poetic—a stubborn, willful grasp on an elusive oracle. We speak of orphic fragments, enigmas, but not of forms fulfilled. Proteus supplements orphic poetics by sponsoring perseverance within explicit bonds: the origin of poetry, for him, is metamorphosis.

2

Praise

What does it mean to expect affirmation from poetry? The darkness of so many great poems is a problem, and not only for my argument here. Poetry must tell a truth, and that is often a grim assignment. As Samuel Johnson observed, human life is a condition in which much is to be endured and little to be enjoyed. Poets and critics frequently wonder, though, whether this is a useful truth. Emerson asked how we know that life is mean; his point was that we all *conceive* of a better life, and that is a sound basis for hope.[1] Critics tend to worry about dark poems at the point where poetry is considered in relation not to its deepest authority but to its widest audience. What can poetry do for others? these critics ask. Are many or only very few helped by knowing what Johnson knew? The objective of poetry is encouragement. Even the inveterate avant-gardist Ezra Pound said that poets "incite humanity to continue living."[2] Poets cannot praise constantly, granted, and yet the deepest power of poetry comes from praise, not criticism. When Plato gets to censoring poetry, the dark poems in particular are the ones that lose place in the republic. Socrates tells Adeimantus that representations of the underworld do not encourage a spirit of freedom and resistance among Homer's audience. "Our view is that a good man," Socrates says, "does not regard it as a disaster when death comes to another good man, his friend."

> Yes, that is our view [Adeimantus replies].
>
> . . .
>
> A good man is the most capable of meeting his own needs, and has less need of other people than anyone else has [Socrates continues].
>
> True.
>
> So he least of all will regard it as a misfortune to lose a son, or a brother, or some money, or anything like that.
>
> And he least of all will grieve over the loss. He more than anyone can take it in his stride when an accident of this kind happens to him.
>
> He can indeed.
>
> We shall be right, then, to get rid of the heroes' songs of lamentation, putting them in the mouths of women—and not even the best women, at that—and cowards.[3]

This is an extraordinary, brittle passage. First, Socrates is stunningly callous about the most painful losses one can endure; and indiscriminate too in lumping them together with a financial setback ("anything like that," as if the loss of capital and of a child might be equated). This is one of many points in the text where Plato offers a far from plausible representation of the human heart. Second, Socrates advocates censoring poetry in the sense not of excluding poets from the republic, for which he is notorious, but of actually altering the texts of poems inspired by the gods, if we recall the *Ion*. Plato strains grotesquely to reconcile his civic ambition with the poetry he knew. Is poetry in any way a civic art? he seems to ask.

Part of what he looks past in this passage is the affirmative effect of poetic form; he examines encouragement only in terms of mimesis. He asks whether the poets' representations of loss and suffering might discourage an intelligent warrior class from the struggle to preserve the autonomy of the republic. One may instead ask whether the pleasures of fully realized art do not encourage one to achieve a peace so well crafted that it seems divinely sanctioned. James Merrill imagines himself, near the close of "The Thousand and Second Night," teaching his poem to a class of undergraduates. One student finds his poem vulnerable to Arnold's judgment against passive suffering. The teacher responds that the poem's affirmation is in its formal achievement; "Form's what affirms," he says.[4] That a poem of this order can be made at all—this is encouraging. That poetic language bears a sediment rich in various experience, that words in some combinations seem to sing—also encouraging. Intense praise is surely heard in the dense, tight language of Hopkins and Bunting: their poems express joy taken in sounds in the throat, in the discrete syllables of the English language, one by one, and in the presence of objects in the world.

The orphic notion that poetry begins in loss—of the Beloved, as Allen Grossman says, or the gods, as Heidegger says—is deeply traditional and very powerful. For just that reason, one might ask what it would mean to find a basis for lyric in affirmation, rather than complaint. The expression of joy is but one small and simple part of affirmative poetry. The traditional genre of affirmative lyric is choral praise poetry—in Greek and Hebrew. Post-Enlightenment literary theory has not helped to retain understanding of this poetic function: one needs to return to ancient models to reconstruct what affirmative poetry entails. In particular ancient Greek poetry shows that praise is a medium of exchange whereby general values were allowed to circulate through a culture. The loss of a theoretical basis for this poetry is due to a shift from a religious to a secular intellectual culture. With this shift has come a narrowing of the range of passion: secular, skeptical culture—that of universities—is at a disadvantage in the expression not just of joy but of conviction more generally.

›››‹‹‹

Poetic affirmation begins in the richness and physicality of language. Sounds accompany written signs, but the acoustic features of poetic language often become signs themselves. Think of birdsong: a traditional figure first for musicality in poetry, and then for an imperfectly known worldly order. Shelley makes a skylark's song at twilight signify the grandest aspirations of poetry. His first question is the origin of song.

Hail to thee, blithe Spirit!
  Bird thou never wert,
That from Heaven, or near it,
  Pourest thy full heart
In profuse strains of unpremeditated art.
(1–5)[5]

The bird is plausibly spirit, rather than animal, because it cannot be seen, only heard (20); nor can Shelley say exactly where the bird comes from, possibly from some spiritual demimonde ("Heaven, or near it"). A little Milton of a bird (Milton speaks famously of his own verse as "unpremeditated" exactly when he claims the authority of inspiration).[6] This song in flight seems a sourceless power in the dark; somehow

Like a Poet hidden
  In the light of thought,
Singing hymns unbidden,
  Till the world is wrought
To sympathy with hopes and fears it heeded not.
(36–40)

Invisibility suits song: music and poetry are powers behind visible forms; the world is changed as the light withdraws. Shelley presses hard to make the analogy: a bird disappearing into night is likened to a poet paradoxically hidden in light; this poet must not be a voice from the dark. Rather than confront agents of villainy, this poet, like a bird, makes the world over by extending sympathy. The bird challenges poets to sing unencumbered by mixed motives; if only a poet could, like a bird, leave half-heartedness and exult in joy. Intellectual inquiry into causes and consequences—Shelley's procedure in this poem—dilutes poetry with melancholy.

We look before and after,
  And pine for what is not:
Our sincerest laughter
  With some pain is fraught:
Our sweetest songs are those that tell of saddest thought.
(86–90)

Joy, not intellectuality, is a poet's greatest resource; a poem's authority derives from pleasure. At the end, Shelley explicitly distinguishes the power of "gladness" from prosodic craft: the music he hears is beyond measures (96–97). Milton's apparent resources—prosodic facility and learning—are as nothing to a full heart (96–100).

Celebratory poems seem only to twitter in an intellectual culture, and not only because they are short. They must be short, or repetitive, because they are not skeptical. Doubt has been the engine of intellectuality since Descartes; without a counterforce, joy raises no problems to solve or issues to develop, unless one traces its change into something else. However, joy is emotionally as well as rhetorically unsustainable. Bliss comes to despair, Shelley observes in "Mutability." More subtly, he speaks of pain, languor, annoyance, and satiety, in "To a Skylark." But its fiercest antithesis is temporality, not misery. What joy changes to is less important than the fact that it changes. Keats, in "Bright Star," wants steadfastness; that, Shelley knew, is not a lover's due. Wordsworth sought continuity, sustenance, or renewed access to joy in time. Shelley, like Wordsworth, considers joy functionally: in terms of what it does and how it does that. He is excited in particular by this song's clarity within darkness. His poet aspires to moving the world "to sympathy with hopes and fears it heeded not." Shelley has a sense of a poet's struggle for authority in an intellectual milieu: poets work behind the scenes. His figure for this is the one of being hidden in the light of thought (36–37)—poets obscured among thinkers. Poets need joy, but most need doubt too, if only to develop their songs.

Why is praise or approval especially important? Shelley also claimed that "poetry is the record of the best and happiest moments of the happiest and best minds."[7] But this is surely untrue; *The Norton Anthology of Poetry* is thick with woe. If poets were so happy as Shelley says, their art would get still less hearing among intellectuals than it now does. Robert Lowell liked to cite Wordsworth's lines: "We Poets in our youth begin in gladness / But thereof come in the end despondency and madness."[8] Despite clear awareness of the melancholy situation of poetry, post-Enlightenment literary theory has only a shallow account of the functions of praise; to get at this subject one needs to consider ancient poems. Ancient Greek poetry proposes a connection between praise and the generality of truth. In Robert Fagles's translation of Bacchylides' "Isthmian Ode for Aglaus of Athens," fame circulates even among the dead.

Fame, Herald of Virtue
Heard through the tribes of man,
Riving earth's black folds
You enlighten the dead
With Glory's names;
Winners of honors
The world can share
Look with eyes serene as sea
On the staid rest from games
Their golden triumphs earn.

Now the mate of Aglaus' sister
Stirs this seaborne bee
To build with his clear song
A work for the deathless Muse,
A joy in common to men
That sings your skill among them,
Sings how Triumph repeatedly
Wreathed your tawny head,
As you planted splendor
Through Athens' breadth,
And renown for Oeneus' race.[9]

One reasonably thinks that fame brings to the living a memory of the accomplishments of the dead; "songs . . . make the names of the dead sound again in time," as Andrew Ford says of Simonides.[10] But here the contrary is the case. Fame enlightens the dead concerning the achievements of the living. This is important because fame is not only renown; on this account, it is a rich, magical medium of life itself. The dead, in some sense, live vicariously through the achievements of the excellent living.

The dead are told of these achievements and presumed to envy the living, for the living face with equanimity a rest after their wins. The dead instead face oblivion. Fame provides a means of sharing life—success, renown, and envy—and this is the poet's concern.[11]

The heart of this traffic in praise is a complex notion of representation. Glorious athletes are "Winners of honors / The world can share" (7). Their achievements represent their families, their cities, and finally "A joy in common to men" (15). That is exactly the poet's business: representation. Bacchylides refers to himself as a "seaborne bee," a busy intermediary who transports and pollinates. In the second strophe, he addresses Aglaus directly to say that his brother-in-law commissioned the song. That matters: the maker of the song and the poet's benefactor are not directly involved in Aglaus's activities. The benefactor is no blood relation to Aglaus, but he cared enough to commission the song. The one praised is merely the athlete; the song travels a circuit of representation, lending vitality to many, even the dead, whose need for word of life itself must be most intense.

Leslie Kurke brilliantly analyzes the social function of praise, what *kudos* (an ancient Greek term that survives in modern English) actually does. It is naive to think, as Pound did, that Pindar merely flatters his athletes and tyrants; this is a shallow modern misunderstanding of praise. Emile Benveniste argues, as Kurke notes, that *kudos* is given by the gods and enables an athlete or warrior to succeed brilliantly.[12] Pindar corrects misrecognitions of excellence and lapses of memory, and he crafts poetic artifacts to stand for the talismanic power given by the gods to individuals. His poems produce power by giving an athlete, a household, and a city recognition from outside the city's boundaries. An athlete's family or patron commissions a choral praise poem and bears the expense of its public performance, but the recognition expressed by the poem must come from elsewhere in order to produce symbolic capital.[13] Pindar is thought to have traveled to the home cities of the victors for the staging of his lyrics. He accepted commissions as gifts that required repayment, as athletic excellence in itself warrants recognition. The production of the poem, Kurke argues, is part of a system that transforms power into community.[14] An athlete demonstrates extraordinary power, which is generally disruptive and hazardous to the status quo, but a choral poet reintegrates that exceptionality into the community. "The poet's intent," she writes, " . . . is to make the entire polis feel that it participates in the victory won."[15] Bacchylides too directly addresses the *general* value of praise (15). Praise poetry is not adequately understood as referential statements about particular people, events, or things. This poetry instead sets out to produce general value for a wide audience to share. The particular occasion of praiseworthy action is a magical instance of something larger that poets in particular can see. Kurke analyzes the political circulation of praise; but the opening lines of Bacchylides' ode are especially important in articulating the claim that the value of praise is not merely political. This is the significance of Fagles's conjectures: fame circulates even among the dead, who are certainly beyond political and social communities altogether.

Pindar explicitly identifies the advantage of praise over blame in poetry, and Kurke quotes this passage from Pythian 2, translated here by Frank J. Nisetich:

> [God] curbs the man
> whose thoughts soar on high
> and gives to others ageless glory.
> But I must shun the crowding bit
> Of bitter speech;
> For in the distance I have seen
> Bilious Archilochos often in distress,
> Swollen with harsh words of wrath.
> To prosper in accord with heaven's will,
> Is wisdom's finest flower,
>
> And such is yours to display
> With a free mind,
> Lord of an armed host,
> Ruler of cities draped in garlands.[16]

Pindar argues that the satiric poetry of Archilochos produces only suffering. A better art praises the achievements of others, for that makes peace. The alternative is the routing of cities by "an armed host." The display of wealth and power at the games is a competitive potlatch. By accepting a commission, a poet "transform[s] the 'war of property' into community, for . . . the obligation to repay [in this case, athletic excellence with poetic excellence] represents a choice against war."[17] "There must be nothing mean," Kurke says, "in the response to victory. . . . The poet extends the obligation to praise to the entire aristocratic community."[18]

The casual modern view is that praise is a gift to a deserving or undeserving recipient. The ancient one was rather that praise circulates through a culture, justly binding people in a network of obligations. A poet recognizes value and accepts an obligation to praise as a consequence of that recognition. "We should be fucking dead," Jules Winnfield (Samuel Jackson) says to Vincent Vega (John Travolta) in *Pulp Fiction* after an adversary has emptied a gun directly at them, without a single bullet touching either of them. "Yeah, we was lucky," Vincent responds. "Nah, nah, nah. That shit wasn't luck. This was divine intervention," Jules says. ". . . What just happened here was a miracle, and I want you to fucking acknowledge it." Jules has had "a moment of clarity," and understands, as though he knew Rilke, that he must change his life. At the heart of the Greek understanding are two principles that are actually not remote from a thoughtful modern sense of praise, such as Quentin Tarentino's. The first is that praise follows from a recognition of value in the world and fulfills an obligation to others. The circulation of *kudos* illustrates the fact that praise is not a discretionary gift, but instead an acknowledgment of obligation. Second, praise songs acknowledge and help in overcoming the difficult fact that one only intermittently recognizes value. Praise, like song, is not constant; it is needed so that one can believe in not only the presence of value but also its recurrence. Jules intends to give up the life of an enforcer, he says later in the closing sequence, and wander the earth listening for demonstrations of God's will. Vincent asks, "What if He doesn't do that?" "Well, if it takes forever, then I'll walk forever," Jules replies. The inconstancy of the experience of value is what requires explanation. Can one generalize about experience on the basis of intermittent revelations of value? Is there sufficient ground for a claim that experience itself is generally valuable? Is song enough to get one through the darkness? Praise songs express wonder more than admiration. Wonder is felt when ordinary human agency has been exceeded. When an achievement is too great to attribute to human agency alone, one sings of wonder. Pindar celebrates divine agency, just what Vincent refuses to acknowledge. Their debate breaks off and Vincent says, "I'm going to take a shit," and leaves the table. This is ominous for Vincent's side of the argument, because viewers have already seen, earlier in the film, that he is killed with his own gun as he emerges from a later squat on the john. Mundane skepticism comes to a bad end.

Praise rejuvenates. Athletic excellence is understood as hereditary, but time erodes the achievements of one's predecessors; a championship renews the authority of a household. A choral praise poem reminds its audience of the stability and endurance of a particular household; its past is renewed by a new victory and a new poem.[19] The victory odes are especially instructive exactly because they are so abstract; the excellence they celebrate is entirely symbolic, because athletic victories have no utilitarian value, in a straightforward sense. Pindar stands between eras, according to Kurke. In the archaic world the *kudos* won by an athlete could be given to a king to fortify his power. The performance of a choral lyric was an expensive spectacle, as the games were too, demonstrating the power and magnanimity of the ruling class. In the classical era such power went to the cities that claimed the athletes, not to the kings.[20] Historical development is toward more general and comprehensive payouts of prestige and authority. Whole regions and nations are now the beneficiaries of poets like Miłosz, Ginsberg, Plath, and Celan, whose works migrate across political and linguistic boundaries.

The work of a choral poem is achieved when a poet convincingly attains a level of general, universal discourse. The objective is not admiration of the particular qualities of an athlete, but the articulation of an individual with transpersonal, transhistorical values. Bacchylides' "Isthmian Ode for Aglaus" is distinctive in its account, in the third strophe (22–43), of the actual physical activities of the athlete. But the last strophe of the poem is a discursive statement of features of universal life.

Striving to reach unique success,
Men light out on myriad branches.
Here they climb on precious hope
In the lores of mind and art;
Here is a seer in his hour, another
Who strains his crafty bow at gold,
Still others exult in herds and harvest.
Though the future bears inscrutable fruit,
And fortune's scales are fickle,
Still finest, one among all
Who thrives on special skill.
I know the pressure of wealth
That makes the blunt seem keen—
But why swerve song so far afield?
Let this enlighten man:
Concord is the crown of conquest.
Over blended reeds and lyres
Lift Aglaus' rising roll of glory.[21]

Bacchylides works to the point where he can plausibly assert the nature of life itself. The language of representation is itself deeply affirmative. Every sentence expresses a collaborative relation among people; that such collaboration can succeed predictably justifies some hope in mutual assistance and the resolution of conflicts. One's worst fear is that no terms might be found to reconcile individuals. All representation resists the darkness of solitude and estrangement. The most general language concedes least to the slippages that produce isolation. The definition or even the invocation of transpersonal or transhistorical values expresses idealism, not complacency. A choral poet's objective is not only to speak for others, to put praise in circulation, but further to encourage others.

›››‹‹‹

The Hebrew Psalms, known as the Book of Praises, have been performed in English-language churches and chapels by communities of believers since the seventeenth century; much translated and imitated, they live in memory and in the forms of Christian worship. The Psalms and the hymns they inspired are the closest poems we have to the choral lyrics of Pindar and Bacchylides—though the Greeks danced in recitation, and the Psalms are performed in place. Greek praise poems are so willfully assertive of the excellence of this athlete or that tyrant that they seem not to answer to skeptical intelligence; doubt is remote from the genre itself. For that reason, praise poetry seems compromised, in a secular literary culture where intellectuals are expected to speak truth to power. Pound failed entirely to see the value of Pindar's odes; Harold Bloom has recently done no better.[22] The Psalms, though, do express resistant doubt; they sing out of a recognizable struggle between faith and despair. They are a poetic presence still, as Pindar is not. One hears in them a dark pressure beneath declarative praise. Praise is not merely a report on things-as-they-are; it may well be a song of hope that events will turn around. The Hebrew Songs of Praise express doubt, even anger. The psalmists knew, as Pindar surely did too, that an idealist's aspiration is not to ignore skeptical thought but to pass through what only seems an Everlasting No, as Carlyle's Professor Teufelsdrökh did, on the way to an Everlasting Yea. "The ability to praise," Stanley Cavell says, "guards against the threat of skepticism—as in religion the acceptance of God may be attested less in the reciting of creeds than in the singing of psalms."[23]

Psalm 92, gorgeous in itself, is programmatic in its explicit refusal to doubt; other psalms are unambiguously doubtful. It begins with a blunt assertion of the value of praise: "It is a good thing to give thanks unto the Lord, and to sing praises unto thy name, O most High." That claim is contested, though, by the recognition that God's justice is problematic. The psalmist asserts, as though it were incontestably true, and deservedly axiomatic, that God's justice deserves praise. The remainder of the psalm makes a case for praise, but the opening expresses the outcome in the form of a wish stated as a truth. Christopher Smart drew on the undercurrent below the praise of praise:

> To tell of thy stupendous grace
>   Before the rising morn betimes
> In pensive night thy truth to trace,
>   When thought itself sublimes.[24]

The darkness that tests faith is pensive; thought exalts and terrifies." As Hopkins says, "O the mind, mind has mountains; cliffs of fall / Frightful, sheer, no-man-fathomed. Hold them cheap / May who ne'er hung there."[25] Smart also nudges the language a bit out of shape: "sublimes" was a working verb in the eighteenth century, but the rhyme to "betimes" registers a little strain across grammatical categories. What is a poet to do in the face of prevalent misery and grotesque oppression? Over the corpses of children, can one praise? "It is good to sing praise to you, Lord . . ." How is a poet to affirm the orders of the world? Look away from the victims and praise the rest? Or affirm always with ironic reserve? According to this psalm, the end of thought and doubt is willed faith, the assertive mode of the song's opening. After a dark night of thinking, praise Him, the poem says. Hopkins commends the relief of sleep.

This mode of song is appropriate, the psalmist says, to a ten-stringed instrument, a psaltery, or a harp. Or even "the damnable steel guitar," Donald Davie adds in his 1988 imitation.[26] Praise overrides all choice of instruments. Any notion that praise is one among several modes of song, or that it better suits one moment than another, is undercut by the verse about diverse instruments. Praise is the mode of song, always, without qualification; affirmation is essential, that is, to song itself. What then of the ascendancy of evil? How praise what appears iniquitous?

O Lord, how great are thy works! and thy thoughts are very deep.
A brutish man knoweth not; neither doth a fool understand this.
When the wicked spring as the grass, and when all the workers
  of iniquity do flourish; it is that they shall be destroyed for
  evermore.

(King James Version; 5–7)

Stephen Mitchell translates this passage inventively, by summoning Emerson and Rilke too:

How great is your goodness, Lord;
  how unfathomable your justice!
It can't be seen by our eyes
  and can't be grasped by our thinking;
but every secret is told,
  every crime is punished,
every good deed is rewarded,
  every wrong is redressed.
Though chaos rules on the surface,
  In the depths all becomes law.[27]

Critical intelligence questions whether praise is appropriate in the face of suffering and wrong. The psalmist attributes doubt to the minds of brutes and fools, though acknowledging that god's thought is very deep, that is, obscure. The lines of Rilke—"Though chaos rules on the surface, / In the depths all becomes law"—assert the resolution of doubt in intellectual terms: principle prevails.[28] Mitchell's claim (and the psalmist's too) is not that worldly justice and rationality do not matter but rather, in the last strophe, that in the fullness of a mortal life recognizable justice prevails. The aged wise thrive as the wicked do not. Although one's enemies triumph, in the long run, as the psalmist says, "there is no unrighteousness" in the Lord.

This psalm engages the modern question whether celebratory praise song suits the lives of thinking people. Just when the psalm praises the profundity (or obscurity) of God's mind—"How deep thy counsels! How divine!" (Isaac Watts); "Thy thoughts from infinite above, / To infinite beneath!" (Christopher Smart)—the psalmist turns to the figure of a fool who cannot fathom God's truth. The psalmist reckons the cost of intellectual failure to comprehend God's deep thoughts: incomprehension, or intellectual doubt, displaces one from the benefits received by the faithful. The psalmist draws on the traditional resource of this mode by declaring claims boldly, but an intellectual argument ultimately emerges from the skeptical analysis of God's deeds: that within the course of a human life justice prevails for the wise, though in the short term things often go badly.

The difficulty faced by believers, or celebrants, is that evil appears to triumph. In modern letters, this is a metaphysical issue, but in the ancient poem the issue is simpler. The passage that Mitchell takes from Emerson expresses a more direct passage that the Anchor Bible has as follows:

> When the wicked sprouted like weeds,
>   And all the evildoers thrived,
> He completely destroyed them for all time!
> But you, Yahweh, are the Exalted from eternity:
> For see how your foes, Yahweh,
> For see how your foes have perished,
>   How all evildoers have been scattered!
> But you exalted my horn as if I were a wild ox,
>   I have been anointed with fresh oil.
> My eyes have seen the rout of my defamers,
>   Of my evil assailants.[29]

As Yahweh has been exalted for all eternity over his enemies, rival gods, so the royal psalmist has enjoyed victory over his evil enemies. That is God's perfect justice: the trouncing of one's foes. Tribal justice is a shallower matter than the metaphysical adversity and frustration that concern modern writers, yet the psalmist's stark demand to see justice served in his own political terms is profound: not ascendance in eternity, as Yahweh has it, but victory now in this one mortal life. That is a severe demand, and the psalmist insists that it be met. The Psalms resist despair: praise of God is thrust forward out of painful adversity. His justice is not apparent; if perfect, it is certainly mysterious. The sufferings of the chosen people make the mind of God appear not only deep but dark too. To praise his justice and this profundity is to push back with one's spirit against the way of one's world, and just this makes the poems compelling.

Some poems seem found; others, clearly made, worked. Praise poetry is all too obviously worked. This was Pound's feeling about Pindar: that his poems are puffed-up products of will. According to Pound, poets do better to assess value in human affairs less aggressively; they may instead acknowledge value that manifests itself, as John Adams's or Sigismondo Malatesta's does. Pound's poet makes only poems; other thinkers (such as Confucius) formulate accounts of value. His poet finds value floating in the air, or more likely in a library book. Nor is that so different with Pindar. He proposes recognition of the value of athletic achievements.

> . . . in return for his deeds of glory,
> we must remember the noble man,
>   and as he celebrates
>
> we must embrace him in soft folds of song.
> (Isthmian 3.7–9)[30]

Pindar does not present himself as an instigator of high assessments of particular individuals: he speaks from within a network of conventional and religious obligations. Only rarely does he posit an independent assessment of someone, and then never of the living. He moves effortlessly back and forth between singular and plural versions of the grammatic first person and singular third person; his own distinctive agency pertains only to poetic craft. The obligations that bind person to person and persons to the gods are his constant context. One action calls for another; neither acts nor agents are isolable. Marvell chooses to celebrate Cromwell; Yeats, Major Robert Gregory; Pound, Malatesta and Adams. These choices are acts of individual intelligence, discernment. Pindar takes payment for his poems, and thereby accepts an obligation to celebrate his athletes. He understands victorious athletes to be entitled to a poem, and not just because their sponsors paid. To praise an athlete or a god is to acknowledge the order of things. All his athletes are presented as recognized champions; he records no disputed calls. The one declared victor is always the true champion. There is no allowance for controversy about such things. Everyone is obligated to acknowledge the victory; it is unjust not to honor a champion, and imprudent. A victory is an affirmation of a network of social and metaphysical relations, and so is epinician poetry generally.

Isthmian 3 begins characteristically with the formulation of a general law:

> If a man, fortunate in the enjoyment
> of glorious prizes or the might of wealth,
> keeps his thoughts above restless ambition,
> then he deserves
> the praise of his fellow citizens.
> O Zeus,
> mortal man's prowess springs from you.
> Greater the span of his happiness
> when he reveres you,
> while for perverse minds
> it is not so—their joys
> neither prosper nor abide lifelong.
>
> (1–6)

Pindar's ready resort to general propositions is instructive: he does not hesitate to connect the actions of a named individual to principles about behavior. As Mark Payne puts it, "This is the ancient world's most celebrated lyric poet making first person assertions about the world in which he actually lives, eye-catching truth claims placed at the beginning of his poems for maximum effect." Payne makes a cogent argument for the universality of Pindar's poetry resting on the very detachability of his gnomic propositions.[31] When possible, Pindar formulates a proposition, as though that were the heart of his project. He wants to express just what his local admiration logically entails; details are understood as instances. Nothing specific is isolated from general rules; no exceptions. That intellectual economy is strongly enabling for him and utterly foreign to modern readers; since 1912 poets in English have treasured exceptions, extraordinary occurrences. Pound warned the young Robert Creeley that generalization is a greased slide. What do poets forego when they renounce generalizing language? Poems that fortify social bonds—nor can a nominalist poet wield the authority that Bacchylides and Pindar enjoyed.

The obligations that Pindar identifies in the opening of his poem are presented as rational, not arbitrary. If a particular condition is met (a winner transcends ambition), a certain consequence (social recognition) is due; in this economy praise is an obligatory payment that a community renders to an individual. Silent admiration is unjust. The premises are clear: that mortals rarely transcend self-interest, especially when they are doing well for themselves; that acknowledgment itself cements the social order. Even religious reverence is proposed for a practical reason: one's good fortune will last longer if one acknowledges the source from which it comes. The gnomic and the narrative passages of Pindar's poems cohere well, though the gnomic passages come at diverse points in the poems; his general claims plainly suit the stories he tells. Not all gnomic poetry achieves such coherence. Pindar writes as an exegete of a system of obligations that bind everyone. No one is particularly free in this system; the prudent, according to him, submit to its exigencies.

Pindar's rhetorical procedures highlight an enduring problem of praise poetry: how far should poets go in justifying praise? His celebrations are intriguingly vague. He names specific champions, their ancestors, their hometowns, their sponsors, but otherwise his accounts are quite general. This is fascinating: analysis and affirmation were counterforces, even twenty-five hundred years ago. There is a sharp boundary between what he will and will not discuss. I noted that he ignores athletic controversies, close or disputed calls. He states, but does not represent, the athletic prowess of his champions. How they won their laurels is not pertinent. They won; he celebrates the scores more than the games themselves ("Melissos has for his portion / not one but two successes"). Athletic activities get the briefest summaries; they are not the important thing. The champions have been touched by the gods: all prowess springs from Zeus, he says. The poems at base are religious, even in their praise for the athletes themselves. Repeatedly (in other poems), he speaks of athletes as radiant; their glow indicates the intervention of a higher power. Artemis and Hermes provide Hieron with such a glow as he prepares for a chariot race:

For the maiden of showering arrows
    and Hermes, god of contests,
        together make a radiance
            glisten about him
                when he yokes his powerful team
                                (Pythian 2.9–10)[32]

Radiance does not inhere in a particular feature of a person, nor in one manner of activity. It is an extraordinary but indefinite effect of divine power.

A few have won joy without effort,
    a radiance on life
        outshining every achievement.
                (Olympian 10.22–23)[33]

Creatures of a day!
What is someone?
                    What is no one?
Man: a shadow's dream.
                            But when a god-given glory comes
a bright light shines upon us and our life is sweet.
                                        (Pythian 8.95–98)[34]

A poet's skill, like divine power, fits song to the object of praise. At the outset of Olympian 6, Pindar says,

As when we build a shining palace,
    Raising its portal on golden columns,
        So now we must make radiant
The entrance to our song.
                        (1–4)[35]

The radiance of poetry imitates the sign of a god's presence, and Pindar asserts his own agency in the achievement of this quality. In the closing lines of Pythian 3 he distinguishes between poets who achieve this quality by mastery and others who must labor longer at it.

> It is radiant poetry
> That makes virtue long-lived,
> But for few is the making easy.[36]

The radiance of a star awakens admiration, but also impresses on the mind the fact of distance. Pindar speaks of poetic radiance as an adornment of a threshold. His listeners are encouraged to contemplate the glory of the victors and to enter into an understanding of social and religious order.

Yet that radiant temple is set, as poetic praise is generally, against a dark backdrop. The powerful conclusion of Isthmian 3 is anything but radiant. Melissos has won the chariot race, and is suitably praised. He is descended from Kleonymos, a more ancient charioteer, whose descendents "have lavished their wealth on the toils of team racing." But this is the family of Laios, Oedipus, and his children. The chariot itself becomes a figure of fugitive success, when the wheel takes a final turn in the last lines:

> But life, as the days wheel past, overthrows
> all things in their turn.
>   Only
> the children of the gods are unwounded.

Your children, that is, *will* be wounded; a grim, harsh prophecy. Songs of praise are always heard against an understood background of defeat, disappointment, loss, impotence, and oblivion. No genre is further from complacency. But the darkness here is blank terror, not corrosive intellectual doubt.

Skeptical analysis, though, the modern rival of praise, is just what Psalm 92 keeps in view, through implication. There is a complaint beneath its strenuous praise. I have discussed praise and doubt as alternatives, with justice; but they are closely connected by the concept of power, as the Psalms repeatedly reveal. Consider the etymology of the verb "to suspect," a synonym for doubt. The word derives from the Latin *suspicere*, to look up to, admire, esteem—which is surprising. But one may well expect trouble from those one must look up to see: to suspect is also to dread. Psalm 92 praises an overwhelmingly powerful God whose justice is dreaded. To praise, to doubt—they are both responses to power. Psalm 92 meets a modern reader, who comes to praise with great difficulty, on his or her own terms. Pindar does not, and his writing is harder to admire. Singers of the psalm sense a struggle to praise, and this feature of the poem is certainly moving. The psalmist seeks divine authority; Pindar claims to have just that. Pindar's assurance allows him to focus steadily on the objects of his praise, whereas the psalmist writes always of the difficulty of praising, that is, of himself as well as of God's glory. Which is the richer resource for poetry? Pindar surely presents forms of expression beyond our contemporaneity. We have praise poets, but not many, because praise generally—not only in poetry—is not the discourse of mainstream, secular intellectuals, and they comprise poetry's audience.[37] Neither Lowell's "For Eugene McCarthy" nor Pinsky's "In Memory of Congresswoman Barbara Jordan" successfully revives praise poetry.[38] Pindar formulates positive values and celebrates their adequate fulfillment by mere mortals. The rhetorical differences between Pindar and our contemporaries are profound. Robert Pinsky calls Pindar a poet for bar mitzvahs. A translation of Pindar raises a question about the place of affirmation in our intellectual culture. Are we better off than Pindar's contemporaries for having confined our articulation of affirmative judgments to social and religious rituals—wedding and retirement toasts, or bar mitzvahs? Is affirmative judgment plausible only among those who know each other? Or should intellectuals cultivate a richer account of affirmative judgment in impersonal settings? Does praise poetry still live? Consider Thylias Moss's "Glory."

›››‹‹‹

Glory survives after the flesh is gone, according to the traditions of praise poetry from archaic Greece to Renaissance Europe. The contrary notion, relevant to the poem, is that one's life, all achievements, may instead go up in smoke. Moss's poem begins not with the issue of longevity, but rather with analysis of the notion of burning.

> The sun does not really rise; the earth turns and leans
> into that perception as it circles a sun busy burning
> for the sake of light.
>
> That's what I'd like God to do, burn himself again
> for the sake of light. Commit to the bush instead of vacating
> when it got too hot, berries burning the hands picking them,
> picking Him, Moses suffering heat as they suffer in a Chicago
>   August,
> five hundred dropping, no rapture to sustain them, members
> of Star of Hope. There should be more hot etching of stone,
> more coal-dark hair burning to gray ash for descent
> from Sinai and ego, more wheels to take us for a hot time
> in Ezekiel's town of exile along the river Chebar.[39]

Her objective is accurate knowledge (1–2). When she refers to the sacrifice of immolated people being understood (17–18), she is guided by an intellectual's aspiration to analyze properly the reasons why the victims were burned (22–24). At the core of these syntactic patterns is the distinction: not this but that. What does this have to do with the praise that constructs glory? Her presumption is that analysis is itself a kind of praise. An inclination to description and analysis shows not only in her syntax but more generally too in her readiness to engage a large number of things, people, or incidents: her attention moves all over, as if one more range of reference—another allusion, say—might move the analysis to an ampler understanding. Hans Ulrich Gumbrecht, thinking of the praise of athletes, explains:

> Since the early nineteenth century, Western readers have come to mistrust hymns or odes of praise. In our present-day culture, I will place my bet on an analytical perspective. Secretly, somehow, I sus-

> pect, analysis has produced a new epideictic genre. The best critical appreciations of . . . literature . . . lay open how complex on many different layers individual works are and how their function and effect depends on such complexity.[40]

Literary intellectuals commonly hold that analysis *is* praise; even that the idioms of intellectual analysis constitute a contemporary equivalent of the religiously based language of praise that Pindar and Bacchylides produced. Emerson confirmed Gumbrecht's analysis in 1841: "Every earnest glance we give to the realities around us, with intent to learn, proceeds from a holy impulse, and is really songs of praise."[41] But Emerson's account of praise is thinner than Pindar's because the Greek sense of obligation, or simply of reverence, is wanting. It makes contemporary sense that Moss frames her poem in praise of the conviction of faith as a critical, interpretive oration. Traditional praise poems celebrate individuals, but Moss, more abstractly, celebrates fire as a sign of faith. Abstraction is now necessary to the credibility of praise poetry. Gumbrecht explicitly acknowledges that analytical language is an instrument of praise exactly insofar as complexity is the overriding evaluative criterion of our time. What variety of complexity deserves this esteem? The complexity revealed by elaborate descriptive accounts of texts with many coordinated parts has been altogether routine in professional interpretation for decades, but it rarely penetrates to principles of value. Intricacy is a technician's value, and a disregard for simplicity is a common sign of evasiveness. Moss's poem does not obviously reward formalist analysis: her language is fluent, ample, even repetitive and prosaic; its form is straightforwardly rhetorical. But the kind of complexity that unsettles one's thinking is indeed a considerable value in that it enables thinking differently from oneself, from others; it encourages, that is, intellectual change. Moss presents a surprising, heterodox line of thought concerning faith and suffering.

Outrageous, to prescribe what God should do. Praise singers customarily restrict themselves to what He has already done, and that's plenty. Pusillanimity is her charge against Him: He should show greater conviction, stronger spirit, as we all should too. "Commit to the bush," she says, "instead of vacating / when it got too hot . . ." (5–6). She is impious, as Pindar never was, but she manages to turn loose on a religious topic the autonomy and wit of secular intellectualism; impious, then, and impish as well, as Donne and Glück are too. But one who philologically corrects the common idiom "sunrise" must be understood to mean what she says, not to speak merely for effect. There is an engaging tension between her literal advocacy, or realistic narration of a Chicago heat wave without sublimation, and her extravagant flights (70–75). She imagines things well beyond realism—other lives, say, after the flames (15–16)—but holds her focus on actual sacrifices, willing and compelled, of the only apparently weak: Jews of Central Europe, Hindu widows, lynched African American boys, condemned Salem witches. The vitality of her style is there in its instability: the literal gives way quickly to a fancy or an irony. Reasonableness, despite all her analytical distinctions, has no lasting grip on her. How ordinary it would be to observe that incinerated Jews, charred widows, and black boys were horribly victimized by abuses of power, that we owe them an ethical understanding of their adversity. Instead, she declares that these spirits taken in fire were marvels of metamorphosis, figures of luminosity. Free-thinking, without sanctimony, and even offensive, Moss asserts that the burnt ones chose to burn, and that their choices reflect enviable, imitable strength and freedom.

Blame is the usual antonym of praise, but Moss's resistance instead is to doubt. She sees that strength comes from refusal to hesitate in the face of uncertainty. She alludes to the story of Shadrach, Meshach, and Abednego, whom Nebuchadnezzar cast into a furnace because they would not fall down and worship the Babylonian god at the sound of "cornet, flute, harp, sackbut, psaltery, and all kinds of music." But they do not burn; instead they walk in the flames with a fourth one, the Son of God. Their faith is recognized because of this marvel, and their God is praised, even by Babylonians (Daniel 3:22–29). Daniel's famous test is another version of this: he was locked in a lion's den because he continued to pray to his God, despite Darius's decree that no one should make a petition for thirty days. When Daniel emerged unscathed he too was recognized by Darius and the Medes as a witness of a true God (Daniel 6:7–27). Flames prove faith, as lions do too.

Give yourself to the glory raging
if the moment comes in your lifetime.
Give yourself to the astronomical temperature where there's
instant outburst into flame, the warmest, the ultimate hospitality.
I don't mean to say embrace it, but if it looks when it detonates
like glory, then take no chances, fellowship
with what little colored boys know
lashed and gasolined on the branches, imperfect crosses
with all the limbs intact, the wood undisciplined, the boys
a wild offering and given to God who could use them
since he's not the God he was in the past when he rejected certain
burnt offerings, clad his favorites in asbestos, outfitted the others
in salt; now he takes whatever he's given, revision into neuter
in the Oxford *inclusive language* new testament
without old biases, without tradition, and without passion.

Praise is unreasonable. A reasonable approach to life involves discriminating causes and effects, adjusting actions to objectives. The phrase "for the sake of light" (3) is revealing. The sun burns, that is, for no earthly reason. All that one might think of as a reasonable response to the spectacle of the Shoah, the Salem trials, the lynching of Emmett Till is irrelevant. Her praise is not of God but of a life of faith in God's rightful determination of the consequences, reasonable or not, of all actions. One does not enter fire expecting not to burn; St. Joan was turned to ashes at the stake (19). Flames and utter uncertainty concerning all that follows a fiery metamorphosis must be accepted. Praise may serve one's interest, or not; one doesn't praise as part of a bargain. But in the face of adversity, it demonstrates fortitude, spirit, and indifference to a cost-benefit calculus. A contract may require reparations for damages, but not praise.

African American literary tradition is rich in praise poetry partly because it is not so thoroughly secular as the mainstream modern U.S. literary tradition; but also because the civil rights movement called citizens to the defense of universal ideals. Modern intellectuals have had good reason to turn their skepticism on political leaders; few poets have written with distinction about social leaders of the twentieth century. African American poets, however, have written strong poems on political and social leaders of this period, and on musicians too. Margaret Walker wrote a remarkable sequence of poems, *Prophets for a New Day*, in 1963; the second poem from that sequence is called "Jeremiah."

Jeremiah, prophet of Jerusalem
Is now a man whose name is Benjamin
Brooding over a city called Atlanta
Preaching the doom of a curse upon the land;
His native land of Georgia.
Preaching the downfall of an accursed system
Preaching to the righteous of all creeds and colors
And his words are wonderfully wrought
Like the powerful prophets of old:
"Yet I say unto you, verily, not one of these stones shall remain.
Not one rock of this rock of hatred shall remain.
This city destroyed by fire a hundred years ago
Rising like a phoenix bird from ashes
To build a mountain of materialism to Mammon
This city must pay and pay and pay
For the horsemen of this city shall be our God's.
My God we are still here. We are still down here Lord,
Working for a Kingdom of Thy Love.
We weep for this city and for this land
We weep for all the doomed people of this land
We weep for Judah and beloved Jerusalem
O Georgia! Where shall you stand in the Judgment?"[42]

The power of these extraordinary biblical pastiches is in their naming. The opening lines (1–3) assert an identity of Benjamin Mays and Jeremiah, of Atlanta and Jerusalem. Mays (1894–1984) was an intellectual leader and pioneering critic of segregation before the civil rights movement. He completed graduate degrees at the University of Chicago, then went to live in India in 1936 and met with Gandhi. In 1940 he became president of Morehouse College in Atlanta, where he remained until 1967; his most famous student was Martin Luther King, Jr. After leaving Morehouse he led the peaceful desegregation of the Atlanta public school system. Walker does not argue the closeness of the resemblance of the two people or cities; terms of measurement would not suit the poem. The relationships of then and now, of the distant and the nearby, are not open to measurement and analysis. The poem boldly folds these dichotomies into identities by announcing a wonder: that Jeremiah is in Atlanta. The forms abide. The work of the prophets is to identify the forms where they are not apparent, and the work of this poet is nearly the same. Hers may seem merely a rhetorical, not an intellectual, task. The point of this rhetoric of naming seems in part to be just this refusal of intellectual justification; the enabling act of faith is to say it is so, not to adduce persuasive reasons or arguments. If you're committed, say it now and say it loud. The authority of naming nonetheless has direct intellectual consequences. The fourth line describes what Jeremiah is saying in Atlanta: "Preaching the doom of a curse upon the land." A curse is another strong form of naming, so strong that it entails unavoidable fulfillment, not partial, not in some measure, but full. This goes to the heart of the intellectual work of the poem.

In political disputes, antagonists may look to their common interests for a workable compromise. Intellectuals often help to identify ways of collaborating with an adversary to benefit a common objective. The discourse of naming, instead of measuring issues that might fit a compromise, identifies the issues that cannot be dissociated from a conflict and encourages faith in the inevitability of a righteous, not just an acceptable, outcome. "Not one rock of this rock of hatred," Jeremiah says, "shall remain." Jeremiah-Benjamin is

> Preaching the downfall of an accursed system
> Preaching to the righteous of all creeds and colors.

The diction is an amalgam of the biblical and the sociological, and Walker's implicit claim is that these two very different orders of thinking and speaking overlap neatly. Cities and families are cursed in the Bible, but Walker substitutes the term "system" which played such a large role in 1960s social theory. The biblical category of the righteous translates through the famous phrase from the Fifteenth Amendment to the U.S. Constitution: "regardless of race, creed, or color." The point is not only that it is not righteous to preach only to one race, creed, or color, but also that righteousness can now be reconstituted through the mechanisms of legislation and litigation. Although these biblical idioms are intended to transcend the ordinary discourse of citizens of Georgia in the early 1960s, they nonetheless imply enormous optimism concerning the power of civil reform. They express so much faith in the political process that they promise a polity and economy transformed by legal reforms of the civil rights movement. The implicit model of social stability here is contractual: restitution shall be paid and symmetry established (15). Or the principle may be called talion punishment. Politically, this is entirely different from Moss's poem, also drawn from the Old Testament, more than twenty years later. It is easy to read "Jeremiah" and other poems in this series and imagine their significance as in some limited sense religious, more than political, prophetic more than intellectual. Yet they are extremely ambitious poems in political and intellectual terms: they propose categories for imagining change and community, and reject compromises that were feasible and contested widely at the time. They were in fact just what they seem not to be: realistic.

There are surprising connections between Pindar's art and Walker's. Both poets define value by articulating heroes with very generally sanctioned terms of divine expression. She connects a contemporary social and intellectual leader with the ancient authority of the biblical prophets. Eliot, reviewing Joyce's *Ulysses*, referred to the modernist "mythic method," which comparably joins contemporary and ancient figures, but Walker leaves no room for an ironic interpretation of the comparison. Benjamin Mays is a wholly adequate Jeremiah, and the Old and New Testaments adequately articulate values that need no modification in the twentieth century. This is the confidence of a poet willing to summon without apology ideals that claim universal authority.

›››‹‹‹

Of places and plants, we have celebrations aplenty; but far fewer of people or abstract values. Poets have taken to heart a counsel of doubt, and with reason. Adam Zagajewski asks, "What are the primary charges against poetry?" His pointed answer: trivial praise. A desire for rapture, he says, inclines poets to hypocrisy; they pretend that things are better than they are.[43] He means to foster ardor among writers, but nonetheless concludes that "poetry and doubt require one another."

> Through doubt, poetry purges itself of rhetorical insincerity, senseless chatter, falsehood, youthful loquacity, empty (inauthentic) euphoria. Released from doubt's stern gaze, poetry—especially in our dark days—might easily degenerate into sentimental ditties, exalted but unthinking song, senseless praise of all the earth's forms.[44]

Poetry is now securely, if not exclusively, situated in intellectual culture, right where skepticism is most constraining. Doubt approves only faint affirmations and modest praise; this is not what Descartes had in mind. Intellectuals especially fear being caught unawares in a contradiction, and worst of all: in public. E. M. Cioran, Zagajewski explains, shunned all forms of affirmation after he saw his error in supporting Romanian fascism.[45] Think how dismal is the political record of twentieth-century poets: Yeats, Marinetti, Pound, Benn. . . . The conspicuous failure of literary intellectuals to see their times clearly has enforced a regime of irony: intellectuals routinely convey the message that all causes deserve to be lost. Poets are now masters of doubt, novices of hope. However, "We don't go to poetry for sarcasm or irony," Zagajewski admits, nor "for critical distance, learned dialectics or clever jokes."[46] How then does the affirmative voice of poetry survive the skepticism of contemporary intellectuals?

Praise is a devotional practice in the optative mood. One may praise, as ecstatic poets do, out of felt joy in spring, a lover, or some other wonder; or another may be moved by doctrinal devotion. The Psalms show that one praises in order to find or retain conviction. Song, like prayer or magic, certainly has this power. To praise noble power encourages the powerful to act nobly. Saying that God is just, or a leader wise, again and again, singing it in perduring form, is a means to make it so. A declarative voice is a magical resource. Is it merely accidental that Moss and Walker assert the living authority of ancient texts, or is the declarative magic of this poetry inherently restorative? Have these ardent poets doubted at all? They have pressed back against the skepticism of their intellectual contemporaries. Moss doubts the abjection of victims of fire. Doubt the doubters is their policy. It's striking too that their optative poetry is not particularly songlike. With prose rather than verse models before them, they have composed formal orations. The language of these poems is "wrought," as Walker says: rhythmic cadences and musical phrases; but not prosodically wrought. The important form for them is public address, the speaking of the words. One must be fully present to take responsibility for praise. Bacchylides, a sea-bee, traveled. An encomiast needs the courage that comes of convictions and sanctions. An avowal is a statement of belief that bears too the root of a promise. Praise poetry uses conviction to serve a hope. The power of praise, and of orphic poetics generally, should now be evident, though the dominant, rhetorical line of literary criticism serves other ends. It is the sociality of language that reveals the limitations of orphic poetry.

3

Civility

In 1952 director Russell Rouse made an unusual film noir about hostile infiltration of the United States. *The Thief* opens with an expanding silhouette of a cloaked man marching toward the camera, as the Capitol rotunda behind him becomes obscured—an allegory of national peril. Ray Milland, who plays that figure, is a physicist employed by the U.S. Atomic Energy Commission in Washington. This thief is passing scientific secrets through a network of spies that extends to Cairo. The plot follows the FBI pursuit of him until, tormented by guilt, he eventually turns himself in. The unusual feature of the film is that it lacks dialogue altogether. United Artists released a technological throwback to the silent era—a bold Hollywood effort to declare that true citizenship is linguistic. Milland lives in the administrative heart of the nation, but estranged from his compatriots; his muteness is represented as a metaphysical condition. No attention whatsoever is devoted to his motivation; the film represents him as he simply *is*: an intellectual outside the national language. The telephone rings repeatedly in the film, and that torments Milland, but there are no conversations. The health of the nation is indicated by linguistic exchange, among individuals and in Congress too, and the psychic health of citizens depends equally upon conversation. A silent life entails isolation, shame, and betrayal.

The dominant tradition in lyric poetry presumes the distinctness of poetic language—its diction and syntax—from the ordinary idioms of contemporary speech or prose. This sense of poetic language as not bound to social usage suits the orphic poetics I have examined in chapters 1 and 2. Yet obviously many ambitious poems are indifferent to orphic traditions; they instead derive authority from a civil order. They signal the roots of their authority by drawing on the resources of recognizable speech. Orpheus threw his head back and uttered sounds that moved animals, plants, and even stones. His music was not keyed to social order. Most of the language one reads or hears is recognizable in relation to a social context or practice; in a sense, one already knows such language. The various poems I discuss in this chapter exemplify a counterpole to the orphic mode. My argument in this chapter is that, whereas vatic writing derives authority ultimately from a religious order of experience or belief, the speech-based poetry under discussion here instead rests on a rich understanding of secular social relations. The significance of these relations in particular poems is easily overlooked because the particular relations under examination often concern intellectuals—the class that includes literary critics and scholars—and their ambition to represent the lives of other classes. Just this ambition is understandably invisible to intellectuals, though the poets I discuss here see this matter clearly. Poems that proudly invoke the idioms of common parlance imply a definite wish to speak with others, even when no dialogue form is constructed. The commonest locutions are signs of civil readiness to communicate within conventions set by many anonymous acts of public collaboration.

The term "speech" is admittedly too comprehensive: all the semantically meaningful phrases that one might plausibly utter with the voice can count as speech. Even that broad usage, however, has significance, because it insists on the participation of the body. Much language, all writing, is voiceless. As Barthes said, "writing is the destruction of every voice, every origin. Writing is that neuter, that composite, that obliquity into which our subject flees, the black-and-white where all identity is lost, beginning with the very identity of the body that writes."[1] Without a human voice, no speech. Disembodied speech, as from a loudspeaker, registers as dubious, sinister, a violation of some uncertain kind. Speech is an ethical category: someone should be present to assume responsibility for what is spoken. This is where plausibility matters. A loudspeaker cannot respond; it merely imitates incarnation. Speech depends upon mutuality or, in this context, dialogue: where that is impossible, speech cannot answer to another. To count as speech an utterance must be iterable in the presence of a listener who might respond with a rejoinder or query. In a sense, such an utterance allows for a critical response. The ambiguity of the term is here: one speaks to another in dialogue; one "answers for" what one has said. Responsibility: the capacity to answer. But one may give a speech, a formal discourse, that may well not initiate dialogue. One gives a speech in hope of getting in return applause or a fee—an inarticulate form of assent—not another speech. We say "give" a speech, but a speech is not part of an exchange of gifts. Or it is a gift to be kept, not returned. One who gives a speech is a public speaker, removed from interpersonal relations to some extent, not a conversation partner. Poems inevitably straddle this ambiguity. No matter how colloquial their diction and syntax, they are more like speeches than dialogues. Their claim to incarnation has more to do with the bodies of readers than with those of poets. The mnemonics of the art seek a place for a poem in the bodies of readers. They are faux speech, composed in reaction against the condition of writing, or not speech at all. "The main fact is," Pound observed in 1929, "that we 'have come' or that 'humanity came' to a point where verse-writing can or could no longer be clearly understood without the study of prose-writing."[2]

Practical literary critics may complain that one poem is insufficiently probing of the spirit, or (more commonly) that another is insufficiently alert to the language. Poetry gains vigor, it is said, by approximating spoken usage. The conventional idioms of poetry are notorious for atrophying as they evolve away from speech—Wordsworth's view. J. L. Austin refers to the etiolation of language in poetry generally; this art itself is not, in his view, sufficiently serious about language use.[3] The vice of writing that is remote from speech is evasiveness or even dishonesty, a distance from human presence and plain fact. "All that is needed for quickly rendering a language cold," Rousseau said, "is to establish academies among the people who speak it."[4] Conventionally governed discourses, such as academic prose, respond poorly to straightforward questions: Is this what you believe? Do you know this to be true? Conventional expressions conceal as much as they reveal. Speech is misleadingly considered an antidote to conventional discourse (for it is highly determined by conventions), though it is often a source of resistance to conventions generated within special fields. The situation of a speaker addressing a listener, who might respond, seems to promise a revitalization of discourse. This is true even though many discourses, not just poetry, do not admit of immediate response, as speech does. (Bakhtin imagined that lyric poetry aims at a delayed response "in the subsequent speech or behavior of the listener.")[5] Conversation is a figure for straight dealing. Dryden, Wordsworth, Frost, and Eliot all sought rapprochement between poetry and speech. Eliot famously argued that, aside from prosodic construction, poetry "remains, all the same, one person talking to another. . . . Every revolution in poetry is apt to be, and sometimes to announce itself to be, a return to common speech." "Common" in the sense of *shared*, of course: that is the appeal. "Common" in the sense of *ordinary* is another matter. "No poetry, of course," he went on to say, "is ever exactly the same speech that the poet talks and hears: but it has to be in such a relation to the speech of his time that the listener or reader can say 'that is how I should talk if I could talk poetry.'"[6] He must have sensed that there is something frivolous about the mimicry of "talk poetry."

Eliot's nativist English line of thought captures an aspiration at the heart of U.S. poetry. But before turning to its articulation in contemporary poetry, it is worth recounting the idealist, utopian, and certainly nonrealistic stylistic ideals to which a rhetorical poetics is opposed. The Prague School theorist Jan Mukařovský formulated this view in sharp terms:

> Poetic language is . . . not a brand of the standard. This is not to deny the close connection between the two, which consists in the fact that, for poetry, the standard language is the background against which is reflected the esthetically intentional distortion of the linguistic components of the work, in other words, the intentional violation of the norm of the standard. . . . The violation of the norm of the standard, its systematic violation, is what makes possible the poetic utilization of language; without this possibility there would be no poetry.[7]

Where Mukařovský speaks of a distortion of ordinary usage, Bourdieu uses the term "deviation," but the point is the same: that poetic language is antithetically related to ordinary usage; one recognizes poetic language because of its discrepant relation to ordinary language. Eliot's friend Pound, for example, argued that the imitation of speech brought no life to the art.

> There are few fallacies more common than the opinion that poetry should mimic the daily speech. Works of art attract by a resembling unlikeness. Colloquial poetry is to the real art as the barber's wax dummy is to sculpture. In every art I can think of we are dammed and clogged by the mimetic.[8]

The conspicuous features of poetic style—figures, extraordinary syntax, archaic terms, rhyme—identify an effort to write beyond the language as it normally is. "Create a language," C. D. Wright has said, "the unborn might be unashamed to speak."[9] Valéry was hopeful on this matter: "One could imagine that the language of poetry might develop to the point of constituting a system of notation as different from practical speech as is the artificial language of algebra or chemistry. The slightest poem contains all the germs and indications of this potential development."[10] Just as diction can locate a poem in a social context, so it can indicate a wish for a milieu where strange structures might be normal. According to Bonnefoy, "However distorted, however transformed our syntax may be, it will always remain merely a metaphor for the unachievable syntax, signifying only exile. And what a sentence reveals is not the Idea, but our aversion from facile speech, our reflection so to speak, the confirmation of exile."[11] For such poets, speech is no great resource. Whatever can be spoken is not the idea that generated the poem. Adorno admired just such idealism in Hölderlin: "The alien quality stems from something objective, the demise of its basic content in expression, the eloquence of something that has no language."[12] The spoken language assumes the adequacy of current conventions of expressing thought and feeling. Most poems begin in the conviction that just these conventions are unworkable. Speech in a poem is a sign of a poet's light touch: when he or she seems merely to talk or to quote someone else. Such passages are taken as a break in the maker's poetic, for a maker makes every detail count. Coleridge praises Shakespeare for "the same perfect dominion, often *domination*, over the whole world of language."[13] An approximation of speech in poetry is contrapuntal to the unavoidable idealist tradition.

Valéry understood that the greatest intellectual aspiration of poets leads them away from the imitation of recognizable speech, or any ordinary language. "Disorder," he wrote, "is the condition and promise of the mind's fecundity, which depends on the unexpected rather than the expected, on what we do not know (and because we do not know it) rather than on what we know."[14] He did not mean that poets might provide ideas or propositions to illuminate the darkness. He proposed that the resources are not of ideas at all but of a "strange discourse, as though made by someone *other* than the speaker and addressed to someone *other* than the listener. In short, it [the formality of verse] is a *language within a language*."[15] Poets grope among words, phrases, clauses, and sentences, not among ideas. "When poets repair to the enchanted forest of Language it is with the express purpose of getting lost; far gone in bewilderment, they seek crossroads of meaning, unexpected echoes, strange encounters; they fear neither detours, surprises, nor darkness."[16] The echoes in the woods may be rhymes, homonyms, or resonant phrases, but they are far from what ordinarily crosses one's lips. Instability, incoherence, and inconsistency are "treasure houses of possibility, which the mind senses almost as soon as it begins to look within. They are storerooms where it may expect to find anything it needs, reasons for hoping that the missing solution, signal, image, or word is closer than it seems."[17] Formal devices, such as rhyme, narrow distance between zones of significance; they suggest that the solution is, as Valéry says, closer than it seems.

Pound objects to fluency, because his is an art of nonconformity; each line formulated in the face of an absence or negation: these particular words, or no others. Geoffrey Hill has said, "A poet's words and rhythms are not his utterance so much as his resistance."[18] A poet pushes back against circumstantial pressure to utter that which is recognizable, the one thing that will stand. Lyric poetry does not allow for on-the-other-hand revision: the blockages come first, then the poem. If it continues, as Poe said, a poem does so at a low intensity. For Pound and Hill, a poem should be utterable without obscuring the struggle with language that preceded its making.[19] Extended poems are verse or, worse, mere speech, an expression of compliance that the Portuguese poet Fernando Pessoa maligns as feminine. "All coarse minds adore speech. To be wordy is itself vulgar. The only thing that renders wordiness interesting is profanity and obscenity, for these things are 'in character' therewith. Wordiness without dirty words and coarse phrases is feminine and therefore vulgar."[20] Speech has too little edge to be a productive medium for poems; it is complacent. Allen Ginsberg, famous as an exemplar of speech poetics, used to say to poets, "First thought, best thought." When he met with the aged Pound in the mid-1960s, he was struck by the slowness with which Pound recited poems. Hill argues that this slowness was "the necessary ethical and physical preparative for that 'quality of a sudden vision of intuition or glimpse into things,' that 'inevitable swiftness and rightness in a given field' which, for Pound, was the essential *virtu* of 'genius.'"[21] Modern critics expect poets to resist their times;

to create art in recognizable contemporary idioms seems accommodating to the status quo. Colloquial speech comprises forms of compliance between what is commonly thought and said and what an individual might wish to say. Fluent speech expresses easy agreement, on received terms, or intellectual conformity. (Pessoa was drawing on Dante's sense that the vernacular is the medium of women; the idioms of power are formal, and women were excluded from the institutions of power.)[22] A fluent, colloquial poet foregoes powers of resistance in order to maintain momentum. Nor is that the last sacrifice taken by the river god Fluency.

Still, the aspiration to say it all is at the heart of U.S. poetry, and even Pessoa admired that enormously. What lyric powers are lodged there? Mark Strand has said that Whitman's achievement is less the composition of one or another poem than the invention of a voice. Not that the voice is personal or authentic; the personhood of Walt Whitman is irrelevant. This voice remains so steadily resourceful that it exceeds any recognizable sense of personhood. Fluency is what it demonstrates: it rarely stops. Objections present no impediment: "Do I contradict myself? / Very well then I contradict myself, / (I am large, I contain multitudes.)"[23] Not all poets wish to contain multitudes. Many try instead to construct one plausible person: speech, evoking an audible, coherent character. Strand's point is that Whitman's voice is a language machine: it produced heterogeneous statements—repeatedly. An orphic poet looks back, stops, loses the beloved, and sings a deep song because of that loss. The language machine keeps moving forward, like Pinsky's figured wheel, over cities and villages. . . . Its power is its momentum and range, not depth. On this view, a single coherent voice is not what a great poet should want. It is no advantage to produce many poems that resemble one another. Hill observes that a true poet "cannot have a 'career' but as a lifelong apprentice-master" who fumbles and fights toward a resistant masterpiece.[24] Such work comes intermittently, and a single voice cannot help that poet.

Here is a remarkable and fluent poem by an exceptional

craftsman, August Kleinzahler's "Green Sees Things in Waves" (1998):

Green first thing each day sees waves—
the chair, armoire, overhead fixtures, you name it,
waves—which, you might say, things really are,
but Green just lies there awhile breathing
long slow breaths, in and out, through his mouth
like he was maybe seasick, until in an hour or so
the waves simmer down and then the trails and colors
off of things, that all quiets down as well and Green
starts to think of washing up, breakfast even
with everything still moving around, colors, trails,
and sounds, from the street and plumbing next door,
vibrating—of course you might say that's what
sound really is, after all, vibrations—but Green,
he's not thinking physics at this stage, nuh-uh,
our boy's only trying to get himself out of bed,
get a grip, but sometimes, and this is the kicker,
another party, shall we say, is in the room
with Green, and Green knows this other party
and they do *not* get along, which understates it
quite a bit, quite a bit, and Green knows
that this other cat is an hallucination, right,
but these two have a routine that goes way back
and Green starts hollering, throwing stuff
until he's all shook up, whole day gone to hell,
bummer . . .
Anyhow, the docs are having a look,
see if they can't dream up a cocktail,
but seems our boy ate quite a pile of acid one time,
clinical, wow, enough juice for half a block—
go go go, little Greenie—blew the wiring out
from behind his headlights and now, no matter what,
can't find the knob to turn off the show.[25]

The syntax is distinctive here: the placement of the second word—"first"—raises this category of style to prominence. "First" initiates a clause that might well be put first in this sentence, rather than second: First thing each day Green sees waves. That is a more direct statement than Kleinzahler's, and it says the same thing. But the poet interposes an interruption. The motive of interruption is an intellectual's inclination to qualify an assertion, if only to acknowledge temporal limits. Kleinzahler is making a speech here—not initiating a conversation—but he does imagine an auditor who presses for concessions. That auditor remains silent; the poet merely conjectures responses: "which, you might say, things really are" (3); "of course you might say that's what / sound really is, after all" (12–13). One response, rather, repeated, but it's an important one. The auditor is imagined to recognize the physical accuracy of Green's perceptions. Green is not wrong, but he lives within forms of intellectual analysis that are meant to govern discourse, not daily perception; there are limits to what intellectuality can manage. To get out of bed in the morning, it does not help to know that all things flow. I stress the intellectuality of Kleinzahler's syntax, because analysis is the poem's deepest function. But the syntax becomes conspicuously colloquial, first, in line 6: "like he was maybe seasick." (The diction becomes colloquial in line 14 and grows more insistently so thereafter.) This clause is subliterary; its grammatical form might be: as if he were seasick. Kleinzahler begins at this early point (6) to move the poem toward colloquial expression, as though speaking in a low fashion were a survival skill.

Remember Pessoa: vulgar, he said, of fluency. The German poet Gerhard Falkner agrees: "The more a poem tells, the less it has to say."[26] Speech keeps going, always, whereas lyric poems seek a point where talking must stop. Lyrics love limits, blockages even. The talkers, though, push on. The deep problem with fluency is the equanimity or imperturbability it conveys. Kleinzahler here speaks of a man who lives in such adversity that he requires an hour to get out of bed, and then hollers and throws things at the air, imagining a single adversary where there is only the indefiniteness of life itself. Kleinzahler's is a smart style, clever, worldly, untroubled. If Green were an actual permatripper, this style could not pass in his proximity: it's too cool to accommodate the suffering of a berserk man. Green, however, is a type, an innocent pursuer of experience. Kleinzahler's style is abstract, but appropriately so in that he examines the extensions of scientific analysis and chemical construction of consciousness. What he cannot manage in this talky style is humane consideration of Green's pain and loss. Brisk blank verse is utterly at odds with Green's paralysis. Any reader moving through the clauses and lines here is far removed from the quality of Green's experience, if typical experience can be said to have such quality. That is a limit more of the fluency speech permits than of speech itself, but it is nonetheless the case that the momentum of a spoken style is ill-suited to those topics that properly unsettle one, to the subjects of lyric, that is. Moreover, Kleinzahler's poem shows that, despite the common notion that speech is a humane resource for poets, talky poems are clever and hard as often as they are humane. The poet who gladly imitates speech accepts an observer's role and foregoes that of the stunned or transported. This is why speech poems must be especially penetrating, or else they are mere verse. But the rationale behind Kleinzahler's poem is that he can observe closely much that is otherwise overlooked, exactly because he does maintain curiosity and composure while renouncing not only transport but compassion too. He means to dissect and preserve city life, not to transform it, and certainly not to transform himself.

Kleinzahler has made a compelling speech poem within a heterogeneous linguistic medium. He has woven together elements of prose syntax and colloquial syntax—the ordering principles of conventional intellectual explanation and those of colloquial speech. The poem demonstrates the range of linguistic resources that intellectuals have at their easy disposal. They are at liberty to move from the analytical and expressive orders of one sector of the language community to those of another. To just the extent that the speaker ranges widely, he proffers credentials to speak generally for others, to represent experience across boundaries of social class. This style asserts the justness of the poet's general representations. To speak from the positions of diverse social classes—a politician's dream—is a practical warrant of authority. There is too a thematic warrant of poetic authority. Kleinzahler is taken by the nexus of scientific correctness and madness. Green instantiates the analytical categories of physics, and a chemical laboratory has altered his mind to see as a physicist reads. One might suggest that Kleinzahler sees the madness of scientific explanation at the practical level of daily consciousness, but no one thinks otherwise. Green may, though, be a sort of Colin Clout or green poet who represents doubts about the value of accurate, close perception—just what poets claim for themselves. A comparable figure, Anthony in James McMichael's *Four Good Things*, counts the steps across the room, once he has been released from an asylum. Poets who closely examine things may be constructing only their own estrangement from the concerns of their contemporaries. Tennyson stopped, knelt, and inspected a flower. Kleinzahler's lines move on at a colloquial clip.

›››‹‹‹

The representation of speech, even vulgar speech, establishes insistent temporality, locality, and separateness, and yet paradoxically it provides poets a resource for generalizing their statements. In "High Windows" (1967) Larkin conjectures the equivalence of venial envy from one generation to the next.

> When I see a couple of kids
> And guess he's fucking her and she's
> Taking pills or wearing a diaphragm,
> I know this is paradise
>
> Everyone old has dreamed of all their lives—
> Bonds and gestures pushed to one side
> Like an outdated combine harvester,
> And everyone young going down the long slide
>
> To happiness, endlessly. I wonder if
> Anyone looked at me, forty years back,
> And thought, *That'll be the life;*
> *No God any more, or sweating in the dark*

About hell and that, or having to hide
What you think of the priest. He
And his lot will all go down the long slide
Like free bloody birds. And immediately

Rather than words comes the thought of high windows:
The sun-comprehending glass,
And beyond it, the deep blue air, that shows
Nothing, and is nowhere, and is endless.[27]

Larkin's speech in the first two quatrains is just as mean as that of his imagined predecessors. The difference of subject matter—sexual intimacy or religious faith—is of no consequence. Low-down meanness abides. The two speakers (romanic and italic) are congenial through nearly four stanzas, as if human nature were small, nasty, and brutish for one generation after another. The response to the italicized lines of hypothesized speech is benign erasure, a relieving eloquence that wipes away all identity: Larkin's voice and that of his predecessors. He is a master of conclusions, as Christopher Ricks sees him; he certainly favors strong, memorable closes like this one, and cannot be accused of fluency.[28] But the last stanza, while it makes the poem, does raise a problem: who utters it? Literally, the speaker of the poem, whom I refer to simply as Larkin, speaks all but the italicized lines. But the diction and syntax of the last stanza are unimaginable in the mouth of the speaker of the first two quatrains. Yes, this is a matter of coarse diction, but the differences go deeper. The initial speaker thinks in terms of objects in the history of various technologies—pills, diaphragms, harvesters—and guesses and wonders his way to interpretations of what he sees. The speaker of the last stanza thinks far more abstractly, and boldly asserts a metaphysical perspective. But does it really matter that the speaker of the first stanza is at odds with that of the last one? Dialogue and reciprocity presume a coherent agent behind the words of a poem, a speaker who answers for what is said. The effort to represent speech in poetry entails a constraining sort of mimesis and, according to some poets, misrepresents the construction of poems. One might hypothesize some psychological development—this is what Charles Bernstein objects to—and one *would* do that if the lines were part of a play to be staged.[29] But as a lyric poem, this level of stylistic variance is not destructive, because the illusion of a particular or coherent speaker is unnecessary to the poem.

"What we call a *poem*," according to Valéry, "is in practice composed of fragments of pure poetry embedded in the substance of a discourse."[30] There is much testimony to the brokenness of poetry. Language is a resistant medium, not given to easeful resolutions. Lyric poets rarely seek a unified, coherent style. Some prefer to convey the diversity of a quilt. "If a poem seems to require a hierophantic phrase," Stevens said, "the phrase should pass. This is a way of saying that one of the consequences of the ordination of style is not to limit it, but to enlarge it, not to impoverish it, but to enrich and liberate it."[31] Even a conservative poet such as Larkin, when representing distinctively spoken language, is free within the dominant conventions for reading mainstream lyric poetry to shift from one stylistic register to another without difficulty. Lyric poems are traditionally comprised of smaller units: striking phrases, lines, shapely stanzas; lyrics tend to break down into their parts, and their parts even to move away from each other toward enigmas. The pressure on lyric poets to chisel memorable phrases, lines, and stanzas entails a corresponding compromise of the coherence that critics have misleadingly called organic form. A lyric poem is a thing of parts. "In poetry . . . every whole can be a part," as Friedrich Schlegel said, "and every part really a whole."[32]

But just what does Larkin gain by imitating vulgar speech? The particular phrases here establish a strong and insensitive version of individual agency. Consider the coarsest words in the poem: "he's fucking her" (2). Putting the matter just this way views the boy as an individual agent doing something to someone else. Had Larkin written "they're fucking now" the sense would be that they mutually constructed their sexual intimacy. Even the phrase "he seduced her" would preserve male agency, but imply the existence of intimacy within sexuality. The actual words of the poem instead assert a predatory view of sex as distinct from intimacy—the savvy view of the locker room. Strong agency is also attributed to the girl, though. The important term is "wearing" (3): to say that she is "using" a diaphragm might be less aggressive. Larkin wishes to assert instead a physical, even anatomical sense of the girl's evasion of the adverse consequences, as his generation understood them, of sexual intercourse. Larkin's low vernacular in these two lines represents the young harshly and superficially (one contraceptive or another is all the same): the young are not just free; they are also tough and pragmatic. The last line of this first quatrain—"I know this is paradise"—is wonderfully incongruous with lines 2 and 3. What has Milton's word for the biblical Eden to do with this pair? Or Milton's poem, with Larkin's? The humor of the line reveals an incidental resource of speech in poems: this speaker shifts zones of discourse radically, without scruple, as one does often in conversation, revealing of course what is really on one's mind. Both zones remain incongruously in play in a poem. Whether the high windows are those of an urban high-rise or of a church, the speaker remains imaginatively inside a Christian structure of expectation, however diminished by time; the windows comprehend the sun itself, not the son of God, and figure no eschatology. But both structures (high-rise and church) are there in the poem, invoking each other with allusions and homonyms. The issue is framed explicitly in terms of temporal development, as though Christianity had simply degenerated to a form of disappointment, resentment, and base fantasy as time passed.

The notion that the Christian God had begun disappearing in the nineteenth century, and by the mid-twentieth was reduced to nostalgia, was an ideologeme of secular intellectuals of Larkin's moment. Now in the early twenty-first century the Christian God has not disappeared; English-speaking believers continue to invest their spirits in the forms that Milton celebrated, though intellectual discourse has not reckoned well with the survival of Christianity, and religiosity more generally. Larkin's representation of vulgar speech helps him to present the historical perspective of secular intellectuals as if it were that of the classes with their feet most plainly on the ground, which is what Wordsworth claimed for the rustic poor. A poet imitating speech seems to be tapping the statements of those who do not write poems, who merely speak; the resources of speech allow poets to propose the interests of the literate as those of another class. Poems are not speech, in no sense natural. As Bernstein says, "Every element is intended, chosen."[33] When they sound like speech they represent another mode of language; when they quote, they speak for others, and that always entails, not only for critics, a judgment of justness.

The speech of individuals remains, however, an attractive norm for poetic language. As Susan Stewart suggests, conversations entail an expectation of reciprocity.[34] One imagines speech as a medium of egalitarian exchanges; in the abstract, this seems more desirable than a style suited to everlasting objets d'art. Yet in lyric there is one overriding voice, not two. Even when two voices are represented, one poet, not two, constructs the exchange. There is no formal guarantee of equity; true reciprocity comes from an intellectual commitment to finding the wisdom of two perspectives, not from a poet's choice to imitate the idioms and rhythms of the vernacular. Consider Langston Hughes's ballad against race-mixing, "The New Cabaret Girl":

> That little yaller gal
> Wid blue-green eyes:
> If her daddy ain't white
> Would be a surprise.
>
> She don't drink gin
> An' she don't like corn.
> I asked her one night
> Where she was born.
>
> An' she say, Honey,
> I don't know
> Where I come from
> Or where I go.

That crazy little yaller gal
Wid blue-green eyes:
If her daddy ain't fay
Would be a surprise.

An' she set there a cryin'
in de cabaret
A lookin' all sad
When she ought to play.

My God, I says,
You can't live that way!
Babe you can't
Live that way![35]

The structure is plain concerning the male poet's control of the female subject's speech: I said; she said; I said—not an even exchange of utterances; the poet openly manages her speech. He wants to know her parentage, but he doesn't dare ask the intrusive question he has in mind. He rather broaches an adjacent topic, hoping to get her started talking about her origins. His contrived indirectness becomes the major figure for the poem; her lack of orientation is understood to stand for a broader confusion about her cultural identity. The poem fortifies the cliché that people of mixed race lack a secure place in either white or black culture. Stewart speaks of speech as a counterterm to the predatory gaze of a voyeuristic culture. Isn't this actually, for all its commitment to vernacular speech, a voyeuristic poem—as most barroom poems are? The speaker begins as a captive of the girl's allure (1–6). Rather than establish a frank and mutual relationship, he ends by trying to channel her charm into his understanding of the constraints on her life (21–24). He patronizes her. The scene of seduction one expects becomes instead a scene of instruction.

Discussion of the role of speech in poetry moves easily toward metaphysics, as though speech were universal, more or less the same by virtue of the voice (Stewart speaks of the "immediacy of speech").[36] Wordsworth argued that speech, because it arises out of "repeated experience and regular feelings, is a more permanent, and a far more philosophical language than that which is frequently substituted for it by poets."[37] But Hughes's poem shows on the contrary that the representation of speech is instead a matter of specific social positioning. He makes this point not only by writing in a black vernacular, but also by moving from that vernacular to standard English (7–8) and then back again to vernacular. Speech among black people is a category of discourse, as standard English is too. Speakers do not live entirely in one sector of a language; they migrate among idioms, more or less widely, to suit their speech to their listeners and to their statements. The girl too speaks an idiom close to standard English (10–12). It is not important to maintain a perfectly consistent use of one dialect; the point is rather to mark shifts that signal a speaker's identity and range of experience. Hughes's theme is the value of cultural stability, or roots in one culture; references to black vernacular stand for that value. The vernacular also underwrites the notion that sexual segregation is advocated by race men as well as by the Klan. Racial segregation of any variety is objectionable, no matter who its advocate. Hughes tries to foreclose objections to black racism by framing the question with awareness of the fact that white men have abused black women for centuries: maybe her mother, not her father, is white; but that raises the familiar and unwanted issue of black men pursuing white women, so it remains a suppressed possibility. Hughes asserts the viability of black culture by writing in dialect, but he demonstrates his own mobility within the English language; the girl of mixed ancestry has less mobility, even though she speaks standard as well as African American English. She has no social stability and no access to joy, because she is neither entirely black nor white. Critics tend to think, as Evelyn Nienming Ch'ien does, that socially specific language is particularly valuable in literature, and that dialect is a resource for progressive art: "The dialect of *Trainspotting* restores energy to English," she writes, "remaking the profane into a musical language and training the reader to be open to new speech."[38] "The New Cabaret Girl" is one of Hughes's very best poems, but it is nonetheless a molded bit of rhetoric, and the use of vernacular is crucial to its intended effect. Hughes's artistic success here shows that there is no sense in which writing in a vernacular is inherently progressive or liberating; a vernacular provides distinct resources of social identification, and these may be used to progressive ends or not, as a poet chooses.

The advocacy of a vernacular basis for poetry draws on two distinct features of speech. The first is its social setting; the second, its physical utterance. Social setting: speech is not only produced but also heard in space and time; it is local language. One can imagine almost anything being uttered, but there are constraints on what one imagines someone listening to. Standards of plausibility, comprehensibility, and reasonableness pertain to a listener's access to an utterance. Despite the local quality of speech, understanding speech requires generalizing interpretive methods. A poem presented as speech usually bears markers of social structure: who might be speaking to what sort of listener? What might such people share? What might seem controversial to one or both? Where might they meet? Is that location inevitable, or contested? A poet representing speech without irony—Hugh MacDiarmid or Kamau Brathwaite, for example—may well be understood to affirm the political interests that enable a kind of social setting to exist and survive. Such poems reasonably seem to affirm the political forces that create or underlie their enabling situations. They preserve speech, and that itself is a value. Affirmation is entailed too in the making of art within the dialect of an identifiable social group, as Dante understood. Vernacular art legitimates the political conditions of its survival. To produce art in the idioms of a rising class, as Hughes and Baraka understood, is an act of political as well as literary invention. To produce art in the idioms of an established class is no less an act of political affiliation. Great poems inevitably honor the idioms in which they are composed, and the social relations that underlie those idioms too. Critics judge not only the inventiveness of poets, but their justness too.

Where is the institutional site of the authority to which a secular poet aspires? Is there, in our language community, a collaborative future worthy of the poems we now read? Patterns of speech allude to social orders that bear on a poem's likely consequence. Allen Grossman believes that strong poetry needs a social institution to realize its aspirations; different poets, different institutions. Eliot and Pound certainly felt a need to declare their affiliations with institutions that might have realized (they thought) their aspirations, one to a church, one to a regime. Langston Hughes, Louis Zukofsky, Pablo Neruda, Tom McGrath, and many others affiliated their poems with particular social movements. Lowell did too, and Adrienne Rich, Gary Snyder, and Baraka as well. But what of those poets who joined no parties—surely the majority? Have they shorted the art's ambitions? No. The stylistic register of a poem expresses its greater objectives, if one listens properly. "Only one who hears the voice of humankind in the poem's solitude," Adorno remarked, "can understand what the poem is saying."[39] Well, no, that is not what I mean by proper listening. Poetry that approximates speech leaves the universal aspirations of poetry to others. One listens instead for voices from definite places. Speech comes off the tongues of people living in some sense together. To craft art in a socially determinate medium is to decline an address to remote communities. Poets and linguists both recognize an American English—like Williams's "American idiom"—though one knows too that within our national borders speech varies enormously. Most versions of plainly American speech make no assertion to national hegemony, to a standard American English. African American dialects, for instance, assert instead their difference from any such norm. To make art with such a dialect is to promote removal from the linguistic norms of standard American English, but not only from linguistic norms. Only a college-educated, propertied social class now claims national normativity. Marjorie Perloff believes instead that the national media proffer a bland, classless language. She argues effectively that the electronic media, particularly television and radio talk shows, have so drained common speech of significance that, in her words, "Poetry . . . has moved elsewhere."[40] The avant-garde poets she appreciates have relinquished the Eliotic aspiration to purify the language of the tribe, and instead construct their art out of sonic and visual resources that bear no particular relation to spoken usage. The avant-garde, as she sees it, has moved beyond class. But the idioms of the national news shows are still quite exclusive; they express the desire of a broad and yet also distinct social group (my class, and Professor Perloff's too) to represent the norms of the nation.

Poets affiliate themselves with this social group when they craft their art from the medium that effectively represents the nation. Louise Glück, Jorie Graham, Robert Hass, and Robert Pinsky all deliberately situate their art at the point where the college-educated, northern, metropolitan class of the intelligentsia asserts its authority to explain the world. Pinsky and Hass read poems on the *Lehrer News Hour*. A photo of Graham gets a full page of the *New Yorker*. "The audience, the constituency, or if you will, the *allegiance* of the cultural elite belongs to the cultural elite," C. D. Wright acknowledges. "One would show little thought to expect otherwise."[41] There is a national intelligentsia, including professors and the citizens who remember their college years (and professors) fondly. We read the *New York Times*, *Salon*, and listen to NPR. The poems of Hass, Pinsky, Graham, and Glück demonstrate the flexibility, exactness, and vitality of standard American English as an artistic medium. If gorgeous or acute art can be made in this medium, one may have faith that just legislation, judicious litigation, and progressive social policy can also be crafted from this general social position.

Most poets affiliate their work, without extensive reflection, with the literary language more than with the speech of their moment—and that is a good thing.[42] Conventionally poetic language participates in the political culture by registering dissatisfaction: no class deserves the adornment a poet like Robert Duncan, for instance, meant to provide. Pound felt the attractions of poetic diction; his early poems also came from the idioms of Rossetti. He admired Laforgue for writing "not the popular language of any country but an international tongue common to the excessively cultivated, and to those more or less familiar with French literature of the first three-fourths of the nineteenth century."[43] A specialized literary language, familiar to coteries, is displaced from civic institutions, and without any prospect of changing anything public, and yet not idiosyncratically peculiar (like Berryman's *Dream Songs*). Such an alternative milieu had broad appeal in the late nineteenth century; Pound felt it still in the early twentieth century, and some poets now do too. Pound eventually saw the necessity of a speech-based poetic, but he came reluctantly to the advocacy for which he is known. Lionel Johnson's language, he said,

> is a bookish dialect, or rather it is not a dialect, it is a curial speech and our aim is natural speech, the language as spoken. We desire the words of poetry to follow the natural order. We would write nothing that we might not say actually in life—under emotion. . . . I do not, however, contradict it when I say that the natural speech of one decade is not the natural speech of another. . . . In 1600 people were interested in painted speech. It was vital. It was part of the time. For a later age it is rank affectation.[44]

"Curial" is a telling term. Regimes pass, but the church abides. Its business is conducted in Latin. The priestly orders, whether of art or of Rome, are an alternative to the current speech that Pound and others called natural. That contestable term "natural" matters: Pound meant to esteem the vitality, not the inevitability, of particular styles. At one point a curial tongue is more vital than any widely spoken idiom, and long afterward Pound still felt its allure.

›››‹‹‹

I have spoken of affiliation as though it were a state rather than an activity, as though poets took a loyalty oath: ambitious poets not only select their audiences; they analyze them too. To affiliate one's writing with a class does not restrict one to apologetics for that class: affiliation is not so determinative. Moreover the intelligentsia is a large and diverse group. The differences between a particular poetic style and the norms of usage with which it affiliates itself are a measure of the plausibility of an actual realization of a poem's values. The pertinent norms may be the usage of a social class—as they are in Robert Hass's poetry—or the usage of a range of literary practice, as they are in Pound's most visionary cantos. Hass, in this sense, is far more pragmatic, less utopian than Pound. One comes to understand the particular values of the intelligentsia that engage Hass's project. "Faint Music" is a case in point; it begins in midconversation, as if recoiling from the coarse concerns of other poems in *Sun under Wood* (1996), like "Shame: An Aria." "Maybe you need to write a poem about grace," his low-key muse or confidant says, straightforwardly naming the poem's thematic project. In Luc Besson's *La Femme Nikita* (1991), after the title character has witnessed and perpetrated senseless brutality, she is asked, "What is your definition of grace?" The poem is presented from the outset as an effort both to respond to an interlocutor and to resolve a conceptual problem. Grace seems an answer to an unasked question. What grace is available to a poet who writes of the "body's fluids and solids, its various despised disjecta" and more generally of cruel and recurrent selfishness?[45]

When everything broken is broken,
and everything dead is dead,
and the hero has looked into the mirror with complete contempt,
and the heroine has studied her face and its defects
remorselessly, and the pain they thought might,
as a token of their earnestness, release them from themselves
has lost its novelty and not released them,
and they have begun to think, kindly and distantly,
watching the others go about their days—
likes and dislikes, reasons, habits, fears—
that self-love is the one weedy stalk
of every human blossoming, and understood,
therefore, why they had been, all their lives,
in such a fury to defend it, and that no one—

except some almost inconceivable saint in his pool
of poverty and silence—can escape this violent, automatic
life's companion ever, maybe then, ordinary light,
faint music under things, a hovering like grace appears.[46]

Hass affiliates his poems vigorously with one sector of the intelligentsia: those educated in the humanities. The analytical categories of a literary education, on his view, bear directly on personal relations among friends and lovers. The economic needs of people in Hass's poems look after themselves somehow; affluence achieved, their real lives are outside the economy. The great affection and trust expressed by this paragraph are directed toward a mode of expression and investigation. This periodic sentence is remote from colloquial speech, reminiscent of meditative blank verse, and yet so paced over the lines as to summon a character to utter it. Lines 2–5 hold firmly to the structure of the lines: clauses close at line end. But with the sixth line the sentence tugs against the line endings. From that point on the sense of the sentence is wholly suspended, and the uncertainty of its completion is more pressing than anything else the sentence says. This long sentence manages two weighty achievements: this manner of expression is shown to be capable of ambitious generalization ("everything," "every human blossoming," "all their lives," "no one," and "ever"); and of bringing complexity to resolution. Sweep and closure: enviable intellectual strengths. Coleridge recognized that the language of a class is known not only by diction but by syntax as well. Specifically, educated speakers have access to "greater *disjunction* and *separation* in the component parts of that, whatever it is, which they wish to communicate." He attributes to the educated classes an advantageous "prospectiveness of mind, that *surview*, which enables a man to foresee the whole of what he is to convey . . . as an organized whole."[47] The important point is not just that the educated classes express themselves with more elaborate syntax than the working class does; but rather that the educated classes claim, by means of elaborate syntax, to see to the ends of things. The assertion of grace at the end is qualified, and many turns are needed before even that can be asserted. Nonetheless the vigor of English prose syntax has been convincingly demonstrated. One can complain of diffidence—the softening qualifiers are designed to make it easy to agree with the speaker ("almost inconceivable," "maybe," "like")—but the paragraph is a sumptuous realization of literary confidence. Even the diffident touches are a way of refusing to acknowledge this style as anachronistic: exactly these hesitations mark the contemporaneity of this style.

> As in the story a friend told once about the time
> he tried to kill himself. His girl had left him.
> Bees in the heart, then scorpions, maggots, and then ash.
> He climbed onto the jumping girder of the bridge,
> the bay side, a blue, lucid afternoon.
> And in the salt air he thought about the word "seafood,"
> that there was something faintly ridiculous about it.
> No one said "landfood." He thought it was degrading to the
>   rainbow perch
> he'd reeled in gleaming from the cliffs, the black rockbass,
> scales like polished carbon, in beds of kelp
> along the coast—and he realized that the reason for the word
> was crabs, or mussels, clams. Otherwise
> the restaurants could just put "fish" up on their signs,
> and when he woke—he'd slept for hours, curled up
> on the girder like a child—the sun was going down
> and he felt a little better, and afraid. He put on the jacket
> he'd used for a pillow, climbed over the railing
> carefully, and drove home to an empty house.

The curious feature of the anecdote, in my professional estimation, is the regenerative role of philology in the friend's crisis. The word "seafood" is the turning point in the healing process; it comes more or less reasonably from the scent of the salt air on the bridge, and brings with it memories of personal accomplishment. (To understand the distinct class orientation of Hass's poem, one has only to recall Hart Crane's "bedlamite," "shrill shirt ballooning," about to jump from the Brooklyn Bridge in

1930; that figure in that poem could not have thought of "seafood.") Although Hass does not say that the effort to understand the perceptions preserved in words is corrective or medicinal, the proper naming of things is shown to matter even in moments of excruciating loss. Why that is so is not obvious, but the fact that the senses are not separate from the understanding of language is forcefully registered. The particular words involved here seem impertinent to the friend's loss—"seafood," "rainbow perch," "black rockbass"—but they do recall another portmanteau term that governs the theme of the poem: "self-love." And the most plainly poetic line of the poem (22) demonstrates the power of feeling one thing in terms of another: passions represented by little beasts; that line provides instruction in how to read lines 25–31. The friend is alert to the distinction between literal and figurative language. His recovery after a nap is evident because he demonstrates prudent care for himself (35–37). The rocks and rainbows he senses in the salt air (presumably before his healing nap) sustain him with a self-approval precious to one on the edge of a suicide platform. His philological analysis serves a larger effort to define very general, abstract terms: this is how we come to recognize grace; these are the features, some surprising, of the concept of self-love. The poem, all of it, stands behind my deictics. It is not analytical as a dictionary article is, but it nonetheless dissociates senses of these abstract terms.

Hass defines secular grace as a cold music of the natural process: that after loss and pain and the sun itself have run their course, the sound of trees responding to the cooling air with little breakages and contractions is heard as a blessing, an austere but encouraging and surprising adjustment to change (58). One understands too that self-love is an incentive not only to survival but to deception of self ("I really tried so hard" [45]) and others ("Guatemalan weavings from his fieldwork on the wall" [50] of this sensitive-seeming professional intellectual), and to petty sentimentality. The friend, his girlfriend, her new lover all enact a pageant of veniality and dishonesty. Their life crisis is provoked by mere promiscuity. The ethical temper of the intelligentsia, of Hass's constituency, as Wright puts it, is admittedly low. Who understands the force of self-love? None of these characters from the anecdote; only the hero and heroine understand the mirror's revelations (4–6). Self-knowledge is here a literary experience: the texts that still have heroes and heroines dare to look at mean truth; Hass's contemporaries instead lie to themselves and to one another. He writes often of friends, and he seems an especially genial and companionable poet. But the values he expresses are not grounded in social relations. There is a darkness to California bucolics, as one knows from Jeffers. The eloquence of Hass's writing is greatest in the first long paragraph (2–19), where he interprets a literary text; it is much weaker in the third long paragraph (38–52), where he narrates the rationalizations of his friend's unfaithful girlfriend. Hass's own literary resources are not fully marshaled by satirical writing; this paragraph is too close to sarcasm. But grace abides in the weeds and trees. The behavior of the characters in the poem is ignoble in various degrees. The hero and heroine in the poem's first section try to understand the internal lives of other minds and fail: "likes and dislikes, reasons, habits, fears" (11)—all, so many vague motives. The successful general term is "self-love . . . the one weedy stalk / of every human blossoming" (12–13). What another mind may really think or feel is unknowable in this poem, but stalks, blossoms, fish, and bark are knowable and sustaining. Hass's skepticism of the avowals of others, even of friends, is great, but the perceptible orders of nature have his full faith.

There is a sense in which all poems instruct one in understanding general terms, insofar as poems have themes. But some poems explicitly invoke specific general terms and avow too the interpretation of words as a poetic project; "Faint Music" does this. An ambitious modernist account of the function of literature, one that continues to serve distinguished poets like Hass, derives from a claim that writers cleanse less the speech of their time than the prose of the center. Such poetry is fully affiliated with the classes that control not only their syntax and diction but the political institutions that thrive in a unified system of social control. Has literature a function in the state? It has, according to Pound.

> It has to do with the clarity and vigour of "any and every" thought and opinion. It has to do with maintaining the very cleanliness of the tools, the health of the very matter of thought itself. . . . The individual cannot think and communicate his thought, the governor and legislator cannot act effectively or frame his laws, without words, and the solidity and validity of these words is in the care of the damned and despised *litterati*. When their work goes rotten—by that I do not mean when they express indecorous thoughts—but when their very medium, the very essence of their work, the application of word to thing goes rotten, i.e. becomes slushy and inexact, or excessive or bloated, the whole machinery of social and of individual thought and order goes to pot. . . . One "moves" the reader only by clarity. In depicting the motions of the "human heart" the durability of the writing depends on the exactitude. It is the thing that is true and stays true that keeps fresh for the new reader.[48]

Pound held to the Whorfian (or Humboldtian) view that language determines the structure and substance of thinking. The modernist idea is not only the uncontroversial one that great writers assist clear thinking, but further that poor writing, unnecessary obscurity, is poison to a people. Valéry wrote: "I maintain that we must be careful of a problem's first contact with our minds. We should be careful of the first words a question utters in our mind. A new question arising in us is in a state of infancy; it stammers; it finds only strange terms, loaded with adventitious values and associations; it is forced to borrow these. But it thereby insensibly deflects our true need."[49]

Pound and Valéry presume the circulation of literary language through civic institutions. That circulation may be complicated, or mediated, by other institutions (the press, the universities), but for Pound's claim to hold, the literary language must not be isolated, as Milton's and Rossetti's surely were, from the idioms of the administrative classes. This is the allure of what Arnold referred to as the "tone of the center." Eliot felt it in his *Four Quartets*; Hass, Pinsky, and many others feel it now. Such poems alter the language that circulates in their wake by combining with general terms the complicating, refining features of more specific language. Edmund Burke understood this as a necessary ethical and intellectual function: "No body, I believe, immediately on hearing the sounds, virtue, liberty, or honour, conceives any precise notion of the particular modes of action and thinking, together with the mixt and simple ideas, and the several relations of them for which these words are substituted."[50] Stanley Cavell, following Wittgenstein, argues that "forms of life" are "held in language and gathered around the objects and persons of our world."[51] These forms are joined to one another by grammatical rules already known by those proficient in the relevant language; an analyst risks banality in explicating their operation in terms of ordinary experience. Valéry notes that such poets negotiate banality in order, as Wordsworth proposed, to sharpen "the discriminating powers of the mind."[52]

> Just as the everyday use of our limbs makes us almost forget their existence and neglect the variety of their resources, and just as it happens that an artist in the use of the human body sometimes points out to us all their suppleness, at the cost of his life which he consumes in exercises and which he exposes to the dangers of his addiction, so the habitual use of language, the practice of reading at random, and the use of everyday expressions, weaken the understanding of these too familiar acts and banish the very conception of their power and of their possible perfection, unless some person survives and dedicates himself who is particularly disdainful of the easy ways of the mind, but singularly attentive to what he can produce that is most unexpected and most subtle.[53]

The surprises yielded by Hass's analysis are subtle, and they have a special gravity for those who think that generosity is close to human nature.

> He went out onto the porch, and listened
> To the forest in the summer dark, madrone bark
> Cracking and curling as the cold came up.
>
> It's not the story though, not the friend
> leaning toward you, saying "And then I realized—,"

> which is the part of stories one never quite believes.
> I had the idea that the world's so full of pain
> it must sometimes make a kind of singing.
> And that the sequence helps, as much as order helps—
> First an ego, and then pain, and then the singing.

The term "grace" is complex and beautiful: it refers to an enigmatic element of Christian theology; to a quality of social interaction, and of physical movement. Christian grace is a benefit given unpredictably in excess of deserts; it exceeds theological explanation. Grace is not merely given, Hass suggests; it is ultimately taken, even by selfish people who seem thoroughly graceless (and undeserving). It is extracted from bitterness and pain, not munificence, and taken, as medicine is, for healing. The cosmic music one senses now and then is not of harmony but instead of massive suffering. Pain added to pain does not unendingly resolve into more groaning and suffering; there is a point at which more pain, defying logic, flips into well-being. The sum of all suffering is imaginable as a universal song. With that song, heard in the cracking of trees (the curling bark conforming to the curled sleeper on the girder), we go on selfishly giving our friends and lovers more pain, and taking more in return. The point of his refusal of a moral to the story (61) is that logic will not yield grace (as theologians always said) or well-being. Why the contraction of tree bark should sound like consolation or encouragement, why the sounds of suffering should seem musical, why the arrangement of events in time should turn the spirit around—all of this is mysterious; none of it logical. But it answers how secular people of Hass's class and region might know what Christians have described as grace.

Hass is properly understood as a poet of personal experience, even of domesticity; he's a master of the scenic mode so despised by critics like Bernstein and Silliman who claim that speech is the basis of this corrupted poetic. His subject, though, is the representation of personal experience by a class that intends to control the means of such representation. One understands the civic project behind his poems once one recognizes the affiliation of his style with the aspirations of the class closest to the academic literary culture. He writes in a familiar style, but its basis is only intermittently speech. Prose, discursive and narrative, instead provides the matrices for his diction and syntax, and that makes lasting problems for a lyric poet. Prose is especially attractive because he is writing for an educated class that aspires to speak with the composure and generality of prose; intellectuals like to think that their speech is as economical as published prose. Familiar prose is the fair face of the intellectual class. Pound quoted Ford Madox Ford's mistaken claim that "good prose is just your conversation."[54] The clarity and economy of prose do not roll off anyone's tongue; stammerings, redundancies, and non sequiturs do. Spoken rhythms actually disrupt the narrative movement of the poem in lines 30–31, when "mussels" are asserted as a "reason." The tempo of spoken thought or disputation is quick, because it flies over gaps. There is logic to the "reason" here, but it is asserted before it is explained; excited speech is enigmatic. Prose moves more slowly, taking readers through the logical steps of an argument. One weakness of Hass's prose basis is that, without a traditional metric, it is hard to hear a musical line emerge from this style; the continuity of the prose paragraph is overwhelming. The music here is faint. This is a problem for anyone urging poets to exploit the resources of speech or prose. The structural units of poetry are the line and the stanza; of speech, the complete utterance, as Bakhtin explains; of prose, the sentence and the paragraph.[55] Speech and prose, that is, accrue large orders; the words do not stop at the end of the line. The musical resources of verse are at odds with the orders of both speech and prose.

When a passage of speech has a distinctive musicality of its own, this conflict is especially clear. Here is a passage from C. D. Wright's *Deepstep Comes Shining* (1998) that illustrates the structural problem well:

> Don't touch that dial. Here's the rest of the story: These three
> ladies they had been into all manner of wrongdoing. They
> were wearing the evil one's varsity jacket. They were hot for

> god and they were on fire. That night they were thrown to the ground under the power. That night the glory cloud filled the church. The prayer line stayed open that night. A real hard light, sharp, cold as a nail, split right through the boards. Angels went to banging around in the rafters like a sackful of birds. We'll pick up at the next chapter, dearly beloveds.[56]

Wright's language is vital, forceful, and extravagant; its musicality derives directly from the play of speech rhythms. This text, reprinted in her selected poems, *Steal Away* (2003), evokes a voice to articulate it, a human presence to answer for the language; in that sense it seems a conservative piece of writing. Wright begins with the directness of imperative address, as though there were an auditor, with a mind of her own, who might just tune out entirely. The disengaging auditor, or reader, is promised "the rest of the story"—characters, a social setting, and closure. Wright conveys the menacing exuberance of the three women by archly calling them ladies and saying that they wore Satan's varsity jacket. At the same time and not altogether coherently the women are said to have been "hot for god." Which team these women wished to serve is ambiguous. The idioms invoke the messianic rhetoric of charismatic churches. The evangelical sentences one hears in tents or on the radio stress one or two syllables out of all proportion to the others in a sentence. In the second through the seventh sentences, MANner, VARsity, HOT, FIre, GROUND, POWer, FILLED, and Open carry just this excessive stress. Thereafter the rhythm shifts away from such oratory toward a calmer, less designing lyric speech. Wright's words effectively evoke styles of utterance and social context too; exactly because they plausibly track spoken utterance, they seem to invoke the presence of a speaker.

This illusionistic power is the target of poet-critics who, after Derrida, note that there is no there there. Speech is now a degraded basis for poetry. Wright's text first appeared in her wonderful volume, *Deepstep Come Shining*, with one small variant: the phrase "a sackful of birds" was originally "like barn swallows." This matters a little because "a sackful of birds" echoes a phrase—"a sack of birds"—three pages earlier in *Deepstep*. Many of the phrases in this short text echo phrases Wright has used earlier in the book in different poems or passages, which qualifies the notion that the representation of speech in poetry is essentially mimetic and illusionistic: Wright's construction of specific spoken utterances evokes speakers and contexts, but not illusionistically. There is no dial to touch, no three ladies, no sack, no barn swallows: these are all words that Wright employs in diverse contexts in her book; they are the material of her art, but not traces of people or things in time and space. The recurrence of phrases drains ordinary reference from the words. One might reasonably think that strong speech patterns inevitably invoke a coherent speaker to articulate them, but it is not so. The text seems to evoke some moment in a narrative. But several of the phrases here are taken from other passages earlier in the book without any sign of a narrative connection. Wright recirculates phrases like "Don't touch that dial," and with each repetition the phrases move further away from any realistic narrative in which they might count as speech between characters. The passage here sounds like strong speech, but no narrative frames the passage as speech. There is instead a linguistic context in which the words are recirculated sounds first and semantic units second.

Everyone hears the power of vernacular speech, but poets rightly express ambivalence about it. Speech patterns easily overwhelm the prosodic structures of a poem. Pound said that there is a "sort of [speech] which not only makes music unnecessary, but which is repulsive to it."[57] The vernacular is more force than resource. Wright's short text has that power, and it has the musicality of speech that Pound understood. On the page, with a ragged right margin (Wright has printed it twice with an unjustified right margin), it looks like free verse: nine lines of twelve to seventeen syllables. But this is a little prose poem. The unit of the line plays no role in its rhythms: the rhetorical rhythms are more than enough to establish its musicality, and more too than most free verse can handle. Only a very strong prosodic measure will maintain an identity in competition with the musicality of distinctive speech rhythms. The most significant rift in American pronunciation is between northern and southern regions; which is loosely misconstrued as one between urban and rural cultures. The national media maintain a strenuous embargo against southern pronunciation, and northern universities do too; but even in the north one hears southern speech patterns frequently among African Americans and in fundamentalist churches. Southern speech appears in northern contexts as an unpredictable, extravagant guest. It has a special vigor because of its contact with the oratorical traditions of southern churches. The mere articulation of southern speech can raise or allay doubts about the legitimacy of northern secular, civic regimes.

Poets who ground their art in the imitation of speech often derive the authority of their poems from that of a social class, and beyond that from the premise that civil, secular values properly govern cultural life. Orphic lyricism, which derives authority from religious belief or experience, is just what speech-based poetry rejects. The musicality that seems mysterious, or seems to symbolize a transcendent order, rarely sounds in the project of civil poets like Pinsky, Hass, Graham, and Glück. The order of speech, in art, is a sign of secularity. But, as Wright's text indicates, there is a point at which speech can involve not a civil society but a community of believers.

Richard Rorty and others believe that language constitutes truth, that "truth is made rather than found."[58] For Hass, as for Pinsky and Glück, language is instead a fully constituted public instrument. These poets do not invent language practices or make truth, as Rorty proposes; they invent poems by employing their instrument attentively, artfully. They hold to the controversial notion that poetic language is not properly separate from ordinary language, that poets have no special freedom to constitute a language or system of discrimination, on their own, that value is to be found within the constraints of recognizable contemporary linguistic and social practice. These are obviously not the grandest premises of poetic art, but they nonetheless express an admirable courage that should recommend itself to citizens of a secular democratic republic. Rorty praises instead an orphic poet, "the maker of new words, the shaper of new languages, as the vanguard of the species."[59] Hass and these other poets who orient their work on the idioms of their peers are less high-flying and better satisfied with the species of people we live among.

4

Thought

The supreme test of a book is that we should feel some unusual intelligence working behind the words.
«EZRA POUND, "The Serious Artist"»

Whether poetry is a branch of knowledge, or just of rhetoric, is the large question in the background of this chapter. I believe poetry yields knowledge, but this question remains in the background because it is so grand. The more modest question of how poetry asserts knowledge claims is directly addressed here. There is an old, but still live, and truly pervasive association of poetry and wisdom—think of Gary Snyder, Robert Bly, Wendell Berry. Many Western as well as Eastern poets, all the way back to Hesiod, have worked proverbs into verse. In some cases the verse is only an envelope for knowledge; that's not an interesting poetic genre. Yet the nexus of poetry and thought is where the value of poetry must be defined, especially for secular intellectuals. Poetry is criticized almost exclusively in terms of its meaning, as though it were out to do what philosophy does, but by other means. In a sense, this is right.[1] Angus Fletcher speaks of noetics as "occurring when the poet introduces thought as a discriminable dimension of the form and meaning of the poem."[2] There is then a sense in which some poems more than others entail noetics, but do these poems set about their thoughtful task with all the resources that philosophers routinely have at their disposal? Or are the resources of lyric an intellectual advantage that philosophers might envy? Many modernist poets renounced syntax. How far can thought go without grammar? Can thought be developed, refined, without the resources of conventional prose? Raymond Geuss has recently argued forcefully that poetry has no strong claim to being a special genre of knowledge, exactly because its status as propositional language is mostly beside the point of the art.[3]

Poetry and thinking is closer to my topic. Although one feels that poetry and thinking are deeply involved with one another, that no poem is far from thought and that some seem entirely given over to it, there is nonetheless a mismatch here; much great poetry is not thought, or not always thought, or not only thought. "Literature," Valéry said, "is the instrument neither of a whole thought nor of an organized thought."[4] Poems often do not answer to the demands for clarity and definiteness made on thought expressed in prose; poets want partial thoughts arrayed unfamiliarly. Valéry also claimed that the "proper subject of poetry is what has no single name, what in itself provokes and demands more than one explanation" (*AP*, 177). This is a recurrent claim made for the art; it is usually avowed by those who hold most firmly to the essential metaphoricity of poetry. The idea is that poetry is always an approximate, rather than a definite, discourse. Some believe that philosophy can do no better, but the dominant view is that it can adjudicate truth claims with authority.[5] Robert Duncan and Valéry both see not philosophy but music as the sister art of poetry, and they discuss the relationship between poetry and music in ways that reveal the profundity of poetry. Duncan quotes Thomas Carlyle on this topic: "Poetry, therefore, we call *musical* thought. The Poet is he who *thinks* in that manner. At bottom, it turns still on power of intellect; it is a man's sincerity and depth of vision that makes him a Poet. See deep enough, and you see musically; the heart of Nature *being* everywhere music, if you can only reach it."[6] What these writers mean by musicality is a resistance to propositional knowledge within forms whose command of attention and feeling is beyond dispute. This is well within the special resources of poets, but beyond those of philosophers. But what is the knowledge that musical forms can provide?

One wants to know how poetic resources in particular affect thinking. The formulation of lines and strophes is a sonic process but a semantic one too. To follow a formulation in some poems means to trace closely lines of thinking, of analysis, explanation, conjecture. One might infer from the displacement of poetry by philosophy that poets would not invoke the structures of explanatory prose syntax and with them the conventions of intellectual activity that govern philosophy and science. But the contrary is actually the case. Poets do methodically invoke just such conventions of discourse by which to measure their own writing. These are the poems I will focus on, though the topic of poetry and thinking is so broad that it's hard to imagine a poem that might not somehow illuminate it. One recognizes nonetheless that poets like William Bronk, John Koethe, Jorie Graham, Rae Armantrout, and Michael Palmer hold their poems especially close to the rational mode of expression that commonly counts as prose, so I focus on that particular range of the art of poetry.

›››‹‹‹

There are resources at the ready disposal of poets that are conventionally less accessible to essayists, say: figures, dramatic dialogue, juxtaposition, paradox, and all the devices of resonance. How is thinking affected by frequent deployment of these features of poetic language? Do they lead thinking in directions that might otherwise be unexplored, or instead present a sense of wonder in the face of what cannot be adequately comprised in prose? They do both, as I will show in the words of individual poems. The place to begin is with the poets who claim no intellectual license for their art.

William Bronk confronts intellectual issues very directly, and austerely. Here is his "Poem for the Nineteenth of March, St. Joseph's Day."

> Father, foster me as your false son;
> the truth is what we are in our falsity
> and not the intended, not the actual
> —either of which had been easier
> than what we are driven, unwilling, to believe is so.
> Who wants approximations, almost reals?
> It had been easy, suspending unbelief,
> to believe the intended, fool ourselves; or, firm
> and rigid, insist on the proved, the certified,
> in the actual world, knowing the actual
> is not the real, ready to believe it were.
>
> Our ideas are wrong: we think of death, most times,
> as opposed to life as if it were some mistake
> to be rectified by mystic means, one
> means or another. We think of them. But death
> is the nature of life. There are falsities
> which are the nature of life, the truth of it.
> Father, we have had the falsities:
> fathers not our fathers, sons not ours.
> We have despaired; have loved them; and been glad.[7]

The figures that engage poets like Merrill, say, are anathema to him. He writes as though the resources of prose were nearly adequate in themselves, as though poetic apparatus were to be largely avoided. He has indeed a richness of echoic texture that is characteristic of poetry, but that texture is not only strictly limited to parts of the poem, it is actually justified by prosaic elaboration. The poem opens with a magical prayer—"Father, foster me as your false son"—and continues by means of extended rationalization. The line of development is clear, from fanciful consonance and prayer to argumentation in anyone's terms of intellectual discourse: the real as distinguished from the actual; intentions as distinguished from realities; and so on. The development of the poem indicates that magical invocations are to be left behind, and paradoxes (as in line 2) are to be unpacked patiently. Although the title of this poem invokes the most traditional of foster fathers, and most intellectuals of Bronk's generation would not so directly write in a Christian frame, this is an insistently rational poem. It advocates a paradoxical view of human life, but it argues its points, clause by clause, line by line, without any logical gaps; it is a poem that has swallowed an essay. There is little sense of tension between poetry and philosophy or thought in this poem: the poet presents himself straightforwardly as a thinking man, using the same conventional distinctions that others use. Given more to paradox than most essayists, but an honest, exact, respectful citizen of the republic of letters.

Bronk left behind at his death in 1999 an impressively coherent body of work: strong, short, serious poems spanning decades, and they are consistently high in quality. His work frankly faces the traditional, unfashionable expectation that poetry takes its warrant from wisdom. The distinction between thought and thinking pertains here: he has paraphrasable thoughts; the poem does not trace a process of thinking but instead an argument for the validity of those thoughts. There is nothing distinctively poetic about the thinking expressed in this poem; his confidence is in the sounds of syllables and the reasons for his views. Simile, metaphor, irony, character—he wants none of this machinery. Instead he says plainly, as few poets would: "the truth is . . ."; "death / is the nature of life." I admire the courage and honesty of poets who are willing to record their settled thoughts and allow them to stand scrutiny by an audience of intellectual peers. Bronk has refused the appeal of "mystic means," and that appeal is real. The sense of quick movement, of distance traveled—that's the thrill of parataxis, which, as Bob Perelman has argued, is the dominant mode of our time, in terms of poetry and of mass media.[8] Hypotactic writers like Bronk, or Robert Pinsky, are too easily thought to be dull or ordinary because they are understood clearly.

›››‹‹‹

The generation that came to intellectual majority in the first decades of the twentieth century was frankly interested in the processes of ordinary and advanced thinking; the development of psychoanalysis was only part of this current. The Imagist doctrines of 1912–13 were aimed at the presentation of "an intellectual and emotional complex in an instant of time."[9] One of John Dewey's earliest books was called *How We Think* (1910). Ernest Dimnet, a critic of French and English literature, wrote an effective little book entitled *The Art of Thinking* (1928) that enjoyed popular success right away. Dewey returned to his 1910 volume and expanded it in 1933; it too found a popular readership. Roger Caillois wrote a manuscript between 1933 and 1935 that was posthumously published as *La nécessité d'esprit*, and there he analyzes the ideograms that organize what he refers to as "lyrical thinking." (Heidegger published *Was Heisst Denken?* in 1954, but it is not actually on the same topic. The title indicates nonetheless the aspiration of his generation to reconstitute the deep forms of intellectual activity.) The claims of these books help to clarify what later poets have been looking for in the intellectual structure of poetry.

Dewey is an eloquent advocate of connectivity in thinking: what distinguishes reflective thinking, which he advocates, from free association, which he derides, is clear connection between thoughts; reflective thinking is sustained thinking. "Reflection involves not simply a sequence of ideas, but a *con*-sequence—a consecutive ordering in such a way that each determines the next as its proper outcome, while each outcome in turn leans back on, or refers to, its predecessors."[10] Learning from Dewey, one must ask how one thought is connected to the next, and how long and fine a chain of thought is constructed by a thinker. Although he expressly warns against "deadly and fanatic consistency," he insists on the importance of mastery in reflective thinking. Connectivity, consecutiveness, and concentration are names for one process that "means variety and change of ideas combined into a *single steady trend moving toward a unified conclusion*. Thoughts are concentrated, not by being kept still and quiescent, but by being kept moving toward an object, as a general marshals his troops for attack or defense" (*HWT*, 48; emphasis in orig.). Dewey would have liked Bronk, and Pinsky, and Berry.

But then there is the other thing altogether: a quick flight from one thought to another. Dewey derisively refers to grasshopper thinking, but he knows too that sudden perception of connection is a powerful inducement to intellectual admiration. Curiosity, as he acknowledges, derives from a sense that something is missing (*HWT*, 38). Dimnet a little reluctantly recognizes that "rapidity of argument" is commonly understood to indicate "brilliant thinking," though he wants to believe that people argue rapidly not because of genius but because of an extraordinary command of facts.[11] The critical reference to speed actually pertains to disjunctiveness: one speaks of speed because of a sense of distance covered without effort; of a shift from one semantic field or discursive mode to another, without explanation. Dimnet's objective is to explicate the art or craft of thinking, or "to devise a method [of] bringing us all nearer to genius," which, he says, "is primarily power resulting in ease. Genius never plods" (*AT*, 197). A series of clear steps in one direction, or a chain of strong links—these are not the figures of genius. There is a conflict between connectivity and genius, or what Dimnet calls intuition. Intuitions, he argues, "often come in clusters . . . often without any apparent connection" (*AT*, 203). "There is no good or even passable writing," he says rightly, "without some sort of outline destined to guide the pen" (*AT*, 162). But likewise there is no reason to avoid quick leaps over gaps of nonunderstanding, if one is writing within a genre like the lyric that conventionally prizes not discipline but genius. Yes, essayists need outlines, but poets don't. Dewey claimed that "direct immediate discharge or expression of an impulsive tendency is fatal to thinking" (*HWT*, 87), but it certainly is not to poetry:

> The apparition of these faces in a crowd;
> petals on a wet black bough.

The structures of Bronk's thinking are close to the features of mainstream intellectuality that both Dewey and Dimnet explicate, but Bronk's thinking is unusual among poets.

›››‹‹‹

For seventy-five years critics have distinguished poetic from prosaic thinking in terms of the role of figurative language. Eliot discriminates between intellectual and reflective poets in just these terms.

> Tennyson and Browning are poets, and they think; but they do not feel their thought as immediately as the odour of a rose. A thought to Donne was an experience; it modified his sensibility. When a poet's mind is perfectly equipped for its work, it is constantly amalgamating disparate experience; the ordinary man's experience is chaotic, irregular, fragmentary. The latter falls in love, or reads Spinoza, and these two experiences have nothing to do with each other, or with the noise of the typewriter or the smell of cooking; in the mind of the poet these experiences are always forming new wholes.[12]

This famous passage sets out the relation of concrete experience and abstract thought in the eyes of the most programmatic modernist poets, and this view of the matter became academic orthodoxy and persisted for decades. The intellectual poet is one whose thoughts are modified by the sensual and emotional context of their expression. Such a poet brings antinomies into harmony; the project is the integration of heterogeneous thought and feeling. Arnold Stein, for instance, argued in 1962 that Donne's objective was "the rational interdependence of parts" of a poem; he found in Donne's poems a "solid structure of continuous rationality."[13] Eliot's formulation means that thoughts are not adequately paraphrased, and that a poet's thoughts about truth, justice, death, or whatever might well be quite different at different moments, in different poems, and so on. There is no sharp distinction between figures and sense in the language of such a poet: the figures and the prosody alter the thought, phrase by phrase, line by line. Not surprisingly, this poetic gave rise to elaborate analysis of figures and images in poems. Images are constitutive, not ornamental, of thought in modernist poetic doctrine. Figures, though, lead away from a single node of concentrated attention; they bring something new into play, something with roots in an elsewhere beside the point that generated the figure. They are seductive, like distractions.[14] Poets want the pleasures figures give without sacrificing a sense of direction that holds poems together.

Yet one of the greatest poems begins when the poet loses his way: "Midway on our life's journey, I found myself / In dark woods, the right road lost," in Pinsky's translation.

> I'll tell what I saw, though how I came to enter
> I cannot well say, being so full of sleep
> Whatever moment it was I began to blunder
>
> Off the true path.[15]

An accommodation of uncertainty, even error, and vagueness is certainly one of the resources of poetic thinking. My point is not only that poetry is often vaguer or more erroneous than good prose; that alone would not recommend the art. But vagueness and error are inevitable constituents not only of poetry but of analytical thinking as well. I tell young college students who try to use terms and syntactic structures they do not truly understand that they are writing over their own heads. I encourage them to use only terms and expressions they do understand and might be able to read aloud with conviction to their friends. This is the common counsel of freshman composition courses, but it also conforms to the main line of modernist poetics. "In my opinion," Valéry said, "it is more useful to speak of what one has experienced than to pretend to a knowledge that is entirely impersonal" (*AP*, 58). Think of George Oppen's admiration for the knowledge of craftsmen as definite, specific, correct. Pope had been absorbed, believe it or not, by U.S. avant-garde poetics of the 1950s and 1960s: to write but what one understands. There is, however, another view of the matter. Robert Duncan responded to Charles Olson's insistence on accuracy, "I like rigor and even clarity as a quality of a work—that is, as I like muddle and floaty vagaries. It is the intensity of the conception that moves me."[16] He knew that vagueness lies at the heart of the art, that great poets have found a path to artistic success through error. But what did he mean by intensity of conception? Desires, not conceptions, are said to be intense. He may have meant that intellectual desire can be felt not only in austere but also in romantic, lush, indulgent art. A strong desire to think may itself be an admirable feature of a poem, even when its thought does not materialize in anything beyond desire.

Poets often speak about poems coming from an elsewhere; they know that words and phrases anticipate thought. Phrases and clauses open a range of possible significance: Is this what you mean? Try this. When this process works well one can think into that range of significance and move further with one's analysis and explanation. Until one's thinking has caught up with the language, one often knows that one's grip on a subject is still vague and possibly erroneous. Even the didact Emerson recognized that the paths of thought are too surprising to have been blazed by thinkers. "Our truth of thought is therefore vitiated as much by too violent direction given by our will, as by too great negligence. We do not determine what we will think. We only open our senses, clear away, as we can, all obstruction from the fact, and suffer the intellect to see."[17] His point is not the rhetorical one that too much direction of thought renders writing uninteresting, but that too much or too little direction compromises the truth itself of what one thinks. There is, as he put it, a level of "thought above the will of the writer."[18] A mind aspires to see that thought, as one sees a landscape. Thought is not adequately understood as a process of inquiry; it is itself a "fact" external to a thinker. A thinker wants to give a "pious reception," as Emerson says, to truth, and too great or too little willful direction of one's thinking is impious. All writers know this process of negotiating ignorance that is only more or less complete when one publishes a text. One learns later, when the right critic comes along, that terms one thought were firm were actually soft. But in various genres, from instruction manuals to literary-interpretive essays and poems, different conventional expectations prevail concerning the presence of vagueness and error. In poetry the conventional expectation is that terms and structures of meaning are still open to thought, that their apparent signification is not their full significance. This gap between apparent and poetic significance may be attributed to the meanings inherent in language itself or to some relation between language and the intuitions of a poet. Poets expect one day to understand fully all that they write.

›››‹‹‹

How might philosophers analyze the distinctive varieties of thinking represented in poetry? Or is their thinking no different from that of poets? The poet John Koethe is a professional philosopher who has written a distinguished poem on the nature of thought, "The Secret Amplitude." His poem illustrates some poetic resources that might reasonably lure a philosopher away from prose. The first of these is musicality. Bunting says that "a strong song tows / us, long earsick."[19] Musical sequences diverge entirely from the rules and conventions that govern intellectual prose arguments; this is at the root of music's appeal to poets. Some poets think right along musical contours. Not that all song tows us, only strong song. The critical question is whether even strong song has the proper force to govern innovative thought. "The Secret Amplitude" is a deep analysis of a thinking life, and its elaborate verse form reorients the prose sense of the sequence in an instructive way.

The poem is spoken by one who is comfortable in thought and pained in feeling: the first clause discriminates among feelings on the basis not of pleasure but of difficulty.

> Perhaps the hardest feeling is the one
> Of unrealized possibility:
> Thoughts left unspoken, actions left undone
>
> That seemed to be of little consequence
> To things considered in totality;
> And yet that might have made a difference.

> Sometimes the thought of what one might have done
> Starts to exhaust the life that it explains,
> After so much of what one knew has gone.[20]

The structures of analytical reasoning and even of contemporary, professional expository prose have an extremely firm hold on the intellectuality of poets, despite the common and mistaken notion that poets easily leave reason and coherence aside. Koethe notes, however, that poetic resources affect above all the *movement* of thought; in particular, poets do not have to confine themselves, as philosophers do, to progress.

> Poetry is especially suited to engender in a heightened way—the vacillation in viewpoints from moment to moment, along with the larger movement between a personal perspective on the objects of one's attention and an objective view of oneself as part of an impersonal natural world. Poetry has the resources (which it doesn't always draw on) to enact these oscillations: the imagistic and metaphoric potential to evoke perception and sensation; the discursive capacity of language to express states of propositional awareness and reflexive consciousness; the rhythmic ability to simulate the movement of thought across time; and a lyric density that can tolerate abrupt shifts in perspective and tone without losing coherence. This certainly isn't to say that poetry is *uniquely* capable of accomplishing this sort of enactment.[21]

Koethe represents a thinking mind, but the poem does not state his thoughts in an ordinary sense; it dramatizes and generalizes thinking too, as most lyrics do. This particular style has its roots in university culture, an economically supported site of disciplined thinking. This is a shapely form of introspection: the first six lines are eloquent in the idiom of contemporary academic prose. The next tercet, though, pushes this style a little further toward the conventional evasiveness of indiscriminate, hypostasized abstractions like "What might have been" and "what one knew." This is an intellectual low style. The first word of the poem is a hedge, and then the notoriously vague term "things" (1.5), which is not clarified by its complement: "considered in totality" (an intellectual periphrasis for the common locution "all things considered"). Pressure to produce a pointed statement urges the poem onward, but its points are dogged by apprehensive subjunctive imagining of counterfactuals, recollections of moments that may have been either thoroughly representative or entirely exceptional ("Sometimes," 1.7); one just cannot determine the range of relevance these considerations have because a skeptical editor has not yet gathered up the slack. This is still rough prose, though it scans as iambic pentameter. Koethe means to represent accurately a genre of meditation—somewhere in that large gray area between a first and a last word on a subject—known well by institutionalized intellectuals. He conveys the contemporaneity and the situatedness of his own thinking.

The third tercet returns to the A-rhyme, as though to the beginning of the speaker's life, to imagine another way of setting out; prosody elegantly figures the reach of his intellectual conjectures. The point is that a middle-aged intellectual is past the moment when counterfactuals might properly serve self-analysis. The next stanza seems to set these matters to rest in a stunning, banal truism that "all things happen for the best" (1.10). The "yet" (1.13) that sets off the next movement introduces less generalized, admittedly more personal, statements of insistent self-disparagement. (This is the first stanza without a link to a preceding one: its inner rhyme reaches forward to the next stanza, its outer rhyme is without connection to another stanza.) The fifth tercet marks a rupture: the speaker complains of the weakness of comprehensive ideas and asserts the authority of particularity. But, as the rhyme pattern suggests, particular people and places are hard to connect with one another without general ideas.

The language on display at the outset of the poem is worn and inexact, and one wants to read ironically, as one does "Prufrock" or *Mauberley*, say. The one figure asserted in this section is more confusing than clarifying. In line 18 he refers to the "particular movement" of his life "that originates / In the sheer 'wonder of disappointment' / Ascending in an arc that resonates // Through the heavens, before a dying fall." Two problems: the metaphor is mixed (an arc is visual, not sonic); also the word "originates" is misused in that disappointment is not an origin but a consequence of an expectation. The difficulty with "originates" is significant because it is the job of intellectuals to identify causes; obscurity about the cause of the speaker's disappointment is almost a professional error. Koethe is not a slack poet, but he is writing in a style that typifies a social group: this is not a poem of lyric self-exposure. An alternative to secular intellectual inquiry surfaces intermittently in the series: vestiges of Christian linguistic usage and religious belief stand behind this poem, as behind Larkin's "Church-Going," to measure difference and loss. When the speaker refers to a life as "blessed" and to "the heavens," rather than the sky, one infers an origin for his confused disappointment. He returns from churchgoing to a sense of unfamiliar disorientation, as if his secular perspective were undermined by the grand aspirations that built the basilica of St. Denis. His surprise is that he's never experienced vertigo, so far removed are contemporary intellectuals from the religious sublime. The stylistic weaknesses of this section concern the professional conventions of academic inquiry, but also the efforts to formulate general ideas that give meaning to the memories of particular places and people.

The overall theme of the sequence—the function of ideals, or the far side of disappointment—comes into clear focus in section 2, which follows reasonably on the first by examining the bases of disappointment. Koethe wants to know whether esteem for ideals inevitably estranges one from the richness of lived experience, and from the lives of loved ones too. Again his intellectual difficulties are indicated by a stylistic weakness. The speaker sets a take-charge tone, in the second section, with a series of imperatives or directions; he is unable to retain a humane, respectful sense of the existence of others—not a rare pitfall of intellectual explanation. The speaker proposes a mechanical way to formulate ideals: "construct an idea of heaven // By eliminating the contingent / Accidents that make it [the given] seem familiar" (2.3–5). The term "heaven" entails a rich set of concepts of godhead, eternity, and peace, though the speaker imagines ideal-formation as a process of subtraction. He seems strident (2.10–16) because he has simplified the ideals that command the assent of others; no one defends what he hypothesizes. He rightly despairs of such an ideal but says that nonetheless he tries to formulate an ideal that is inward (2.25–30). He begins to speak of "other // People" (3.3–4) in an abstract fashion in section 3, though the suicide of two close friends is the truly pressing subject. (And his phrasing revises, by echoing, an earlier assertion that he thinks of his life as one lived with others [1.13–15].) His style is so hobbled by an intellectual aspiration to impersonality that he cannot speak tenderly of his lost friends. These friends, eventually identified as Geoff and Willy (3.17), are first stiffly identified as "they" (3.5). The "personal details," he says, lost meaning (3.20), when only the memory of having once "lived them" remained (3.22). He accepts as fact that friends become concepts that feel "like a second nature" (3.29). The proliferation of uncertain pronouns in this section (3.1, 25, 26, 30), normally a corruption of prose style, indicates this passage from particular identities into vaguer categories.

Koethe clears a path away from the expository structures of prose in section 4. Prosodically this is the last variation: the fifth section resumes the rhyme scheme of the first section; subsequent sections run the variations through in reverse order. Sections 1, 5, and 9 rhyme ABA CBC. Sections 2 and 8, ABA CDC. Sections 3 and 7, ABC CDA. Sections 4 and 6, ABC DBE. This array of rhyme schemes conforms to a pyramidal architecture: think of a stepped incline from sections 1 to 5, then a stepped decline from 5 to 9; the first four levels of the pyramid have linked sections (1 and 9; 2 and 8; 3 and 7; 4 and 6). Although, like all poems, it proceeds line by line to its end, its musical form, which repeatedly goes from first to last, builds toward a central peak (section 5), not the poem's end. Most sections begin abstractly, announcing a claim to thematic autonomy. Poems follow sequences as logical arguments and narratives do too, but great poems are also, as New Critics observed, networks with each term connected by various paths to all other terms. Koethe invokes this sense of poetic economy by arranging the nine sections of "The Secret Amplitude" to be read as sensibly in the sequence by which they are numbered as in the sequence by which they are rhymed. Prosody can govern the order of one's statements as productively as logic or narrative can, especially in a philosophical poem. Dante's terza rima is designed to weave each tercet tightly to the next; his form fortifies continuity and fluency, even in the face of heterogeneous thematic references. Koethe is less concerned with continuity; he very rarely links more than two tercets within a section. And the linkages between many pairs of tercets are loose and depend on a single rhyme. His acknowledged model was Stevens's *Auroras of Autumn*, with its altogether unrhymed tercets.

One learns only in retrospect, after reading through the sequence from first to last, of the musical principle that links sections 1, 5, and 9, 2 and 8, 3 and 7, 4 and 6. These sections need to be read not only linearly, as one reads an essay or prose meditation from beginning to end, but in a back-and-forth pattern of paired stanzas: sections 1, then 9; 2, then 8; 3, then 7; 4, then 6; and finally 5. When one returns to section 1, having read 9, one notices that the diction is very general, concerning the feel of one's entire life, although paradoxically one very particular subject is generating these words. He mentions the loss of friends (1.20) in an incidental fashion, but this is actually central to the entire sequence. This subject bears directly on the first section, because the locution "Thoughts left unspoken, actions left undone . . . that might have made a difference" (1.3 & 6) speaks to one's feeling after learning (as the speaker does) that a loved one has committed suicide. One discerns clearly, then, returning to section 1, the gravity of the misleadingly casual phrase "particular days // Whiled away with a small handful of friends" (1.15–16). Some particular friends are named in the opening lines of section 9: "Mark" and "John." But the crucial connection is to Willy, who took his own life by wandering "up the stairs / To a 'final privacy'" (9.13–14). These lines give a poignant sense to "the thought of what one might have done" (1.7), and they hold in sharp focus through the reading of the entire sequence the responsibilities of friendship. This issue is complicated by the parallel between the speaker's admitted reclusiveness, his evasion of intimacy (9.7, 10), and Willy's insistence on the privacy of suicide. The life shared with friends has paradoxically included an annihilation of relationship; the speaker, Willy, and Edward Albee all understand that the (literary, intellectual?) values they share include abstention from community. Just below the surface of the ostensibly general language, he asks himself whether he might not have been more attentive to his friends' needs, and whether his friends may not share greater love for their ideals than for each other. In the printed sequence, sections 1 and 9 are as distant from one another as possible, but prosodically and emotionally they are proximate. The sequence is clearer and richer when sections 1 and 9 are read next to one another. The formal brilliance of Koethe's poem is that the line of thought that the numbered sections mark is one of two plotted for the poem. The surprise is not that the poem can be read equally well in any way one wishes, but that it is structured to be read in two distinct ways, in conformity to two different lines of thought.

The peak of his musical structure, section 5, expresses an experience of comforting insignificance, an escape from personal memories ("Everything seemed so mindless and abstract" [5.25]). Mt. Null here: no new thinking in this section; instead a release from thought, and a narrative resolution of the Parisian anxiety expressed at the end of section 1. He begins section 6 with his philosophical topics:

> What is the abstract, the impersonal?
> Are they the same? And whence this grandiose
> Geography of a few emotions?
>
> (6.1–3)

The fifth section relates an anecdote that begins in fear of loneliness and ends in the peace of solitude. These two views of the experience are merely juxtaposed, not articulated discursively. The relevant conjunction, "Later" (5.17), is placed one line off the exact center of this 270-line numbered, plotted structure. First one feeling, then another: a sequence that becomes a transformation, and the thematic turning point of the poem; but the philosopher-poet has no explanation of how it was achieved. In section 6 he means to analyze the terms of the immediately preceding narrative: "the garden," "abstract," "personality" (5.17, 24, 25). His last question (6.2–3) about the garden, geography, and landscape truly turns the poem toward an affirmation of vision. He likens the richness of an uninhabited landscape to the emergence of an indeterminate thought, one without concern for origin or consequence ("causality and death" [6.13]). This productive intellectual dynamic generates not only personal transformation on the order of that narrated in section 5, but cultural transformation too. The imagination of Christ risen on the third day ("the empty desert [turned] to an empty tomb / On Sunday, with the body set aside" [6.17–18]), or the "inhospitable terrain" of North America turned to "an open space, 'a fresh, green breast' / Of a new world" (6.24–26).

What would it mean to know, he asks, how epochal metamorphoses were achieved? He is citing the conclusion to *The Great Gatsby*, when Nick Carraway glimpses Long Island as a Dutch sailor might have: "The last and greatest of all human dreams; for a transitory enchanted moment man must have held his breath in the presence of this continent, compelled into an aesthetic contemplation he neither understood nor desired, face to face for the last time in history with something commensurate to his capacity for wonder."[22] He had described his own mental life antithetically, as beginning in the "sheer 'wonder of disappointment'" (1.23). The sailor sees a new world. The abstraction involved appears just when a concept has reached its own form, and that form alters experience. The material circumstances of experience—North America, Paris, or Barcelona—do not matter. All that matters, he said, is "what a person does / In the aftermath" of a particular experience (4.5–6). The speaker refers to a "private alchemy" (6.22), as though transformation were an occult art, and the last line of the section ends with the title of the poem, but also with a term for only proximate knowledge: "And what that secret amplitude was like" (6.30). Likeness, not definition.[23] Rhymes—here an extra one, and exact, back to line 9—are alternatives to rational structures of knowledge. One might ask what caused that amplitude, or how one might repeat the transformation it enables. Instead he asks an impressionistic question, echoing too the opening of section 4 (4.3), the prosodic mate to section 6. What Koethe's analysis repeatedly addresses is the inexactness of intellectual experience. Causes and consequences are not his objective. He wants rather to characterize vision, to say what it is *like*.

›››‹‹‹

I have illustrated Koethe's repeated indulgence in the habits of poor prose; my point is not that the poem suffers from lapses. Koethe means to undermine the clarity one wants in expository prose, especially in philosophical argument. He disturbs distinctions generated by his own analysis. In the first section of this profoundly self-complicating poem, he puts together two similar words just where he is explaining how reflection undercuts knowledge: "results, remains."

> I guess that all things happen for the best,
> And that whatever life results remains,
> In its own fashion, singularly blest.
>
> (1.10–12)

These two words are used here as verbs to indicate that something remains known after time and reflection have eroded some of what one thought one knew. These words are cognate in their substantive forms: the results of a process of erosion might be called the remains of the process. Although the point of his sentence is to affirm a bit of knowledge that survives erosion, their echo, one word against the other, reminds one that sameness, not distinction, survives the erosion of time. And the "blest" remains can incite little confidence, since they evoke something corpse-like at the end of the process. Koethe, like his master Ashbery, deliberately undoes the very meditative process he charts.[24] Both poets think that the most common and apparent signs of thoughtlessness often reveal something profound. Section 3, for instance, addresses the dynamic of abstraction. The pronoun "it" enters the section without an antecedent (3.1). The topic under discussion is evidently abstracted from some prior statement that was more particular in its reference. This use of vague abstraction is evident grammatically in the first three tercets of the section. The grammatical structure that is repeated here is familiar in intellectual prose: "the thought of places" (3.2); "[the thought] of my distance from them" (3.3); "the measure of another / Year" (3.4–5). Abstracting a quality from a substance is here an automatic intellectual function, a mere tic. An editor excises most of these formulations from academic prose without any loss. The speaker's point in this section, though, is quite serious: that this process of abstraction grows so natural to one that it becomes "hard / To separate . . . the thought of a day // From the day itself" (3.6–7). As one matures one retains memory of indefinite abstract qualities more than of substances themselves. The "pure" experience, then, is the most abstract, the least encumbered by specific reference (3.15–19). This analysis proposes that the mannerisms of academic prose style actually have a purchase on intellectual experience extended over decades.

A poet is not so constrained by truthfulness as a philosopher is, as Koethe says. A poet enjoys liberties, as Koethe does. For instance, his allusion to Wittgenstein is made to bear on life in general (1.23–25), but the original passage in the *Philosophical Investigations* relates specifically to the linguistic construction of sense: "How do sentences do it?—Don't you know? For nothing is hidden."[25] Koethe and Wittgenstein share an engagement with conventions of meaning-making; Wittgenstein's point, as Koethe well knows, is that the semiotic structures of sentences (not the meaning of life) are open to view.[26] The terms and forms of philosophical arguments can be adopted and altered by poets, as Koethe boldly substitutes his terms for Wittgenstein's, as if a philosophical statement were like a metrical grid that absorbs diverse semantic specification. "In the course of a poem's elaboration," Koethe says, "one may entertain and *essay* notions of whose untenability one is perfectly aware—an untenability one may even acknowledge—without being led to abandon them. Indeed the awareness of the futility of a conception may lead to an even greater insistence on it, because the animating force of poetic speculation is always *desire*, rather than an ideal of impersonal accuracy."[27] Poetry is an expression of hope, then. One thinks in a poem not so much *of* a truth as *toward* something unpossessed—maybe lost, like Eurydice, or never fully attained, like Beatrice. This is why the movement of a mind is a poet's concern, why a critic speaks less of propositions than of a poem's development. Helen Vendler makes the point eloquently:

> Living thought must, like ordinary thought, characterize, allegorize, reason, denominate, and analogize—but it must also jump up and down, over and under, left and right; it must swell and contract, leap from register to register, joke and feel pangs. Above all, it must advance too swiftly for instant intelligibility: the reader must hang on for the ride, bouncing to the next hurdle hardly having recovered his seat from the last. It is as if the poet wants to say, "This is what thinking really is like: have you ever known it?"[28]

The movement of Koethe's poem is not startling moment by moment, as Vendler suggests great poems are, but it does use prosodic resources to suggest a brighter outcome than that reached by the numbered sections. Koethe is nothing if not a dark poet. The second half of the poem, sections 6 through 9, proceed under a sign of resignation. Consider section 7, which is as full an expression of doubt as I can imagine. The lives of dead friends are unknowable, not because the living gradually forget their dead, but because the dead had already withdrawn before dying, and more comprehensively because no one's being answers to "the logic of a parable" (7.18). The terrifying clarity is that one cannot hear what is killing one's loved ones (7.21–29). This section is eloquent, thoughtful, honest, and imaginative, a genuine flower of intellectuality; but it is as dark as any of the poems of this dark poet. This is the poetry of contemporary skepticism. But the musical order of the sections lightens the resolution of the poem. Section 6 is the thematic conclusion of the musical sequence. It ends by affirming an ability to see a world in a grain of sand. Intellectually, this is the brightest section of the sequence. As the penultimate section it reorients the entire poem on a hopeful, positive note. The prosodic ordering of the sections does not alter a word of the poem, but it seriously alters its sense by increasing the heft of personal feelings, putting the deaths of Koethe's friends Willy and Geoff into the poem from the start, and by resolving the poem on a brighter note than any found in section 9. Poetic forms, even just a rhyme scheme, can silently alter the significance of ordinary language.

›››‹‹‹

I want to turn now to the most popular of my intellectual poets. The main theme of Jorie Graham's "The Guardian Angel of the Private Life" is the dialectical relationship between one's aspiration to an intellectual life of good ideas and one's mindless plans for busy days. This is a long-ish poem, so I will be schematic. The poem has two main parts: lines 1–37 focus on those mindless plans; lines 38–82 discuss the approach of a good idea. The shift from part 1 to part 2 is marked by an impatient, querulous insistence and an effort to generalize the poem by invoking the first-person plural voice:

> Oh listen to these words I'm spitting out for you.
> My distance from you makes them louder.
> Are we *all* waiting for the phone to ring?
>
> (38–40)[29]

That phone call might disrupt the plan for the day with some unforeseen novelty, like a sudden good idea. But the poem describes the formation of a good idea as a slow process that begins somewhere so far back in the past that Graham speaks of antique, pseudo-Homeric figures, "the greater men," holding their heads as it rises slowly, like a blood clot (58). Everything about the good idea is retro. It is like homesickness (65); it doesn't lead forward to progress. An aneurism lies in its future.

What patterns of thinking are expressed by Graham's accretive style? There is an implicit equivalence of phrases throughout her work: one phrase or figure apparently serves as well as another; she typically includes both: "a *done-deal* or the name-you're-known-by" (67). This can be annoying to one who prizes economy—Graham can't be the poet for such a critic—but it expresses an admirable commitment to a secular style. One phrase or another can serve, because none is indispensable, or of transcendent significance. Neither genius nor vision produces the poems, just fluency. The structures that help her shape the flow of phrases are grammatical: they generate expectations that move writer and reader forward to the next line. She uses grammatical tools to add one item to another closely and plainly related; progress from one phrase to the next is small, based on analogy and apposition. Filigree (72), she says: contiguous, exuberant ornamentation, not architecture. Grammatical orders intended to complete statements within a recognizable pattern are exploited but usually suspended. In the first part of the poem, for example, the grammar of the conditional keeps the lines flowing: if (7), if (12), if (20). This is where Duncan's insight about error counts: the conditional is used incorrectly; no then-clause follows those ifs. Her syntax does reach conclusions, though, and then a complete sentence often marks that turning point:

> (Or is it the sum of what *takes place*?) [6]
> Oh listen to these words I'm spitting out for you. [38]
> Oh look at you. [48]
> Oh put it down. [82]

The goal of this thinking is to move from one thought, eventually, to another. Give up the list—that's the simple point of the poem, its guiding principle, from the beginning. Neither a surprise nor a challenge. If her objective were to refine her thinking, terms like "the mind," "the heart," "the thinking," and "the idea" might be analyzed into closer distinctions. Her lines are driven by an intensity of conception, not clarity but a desire for ideas; this is what Duncan was driving at. The "puffed-up greenish mind" wants an idea but has to work up to that by filling out clauses generated by prepositions or by grammatical structures that can remain fragments of promises. The poem is meant to be more a rhetorical than an intellectual achievement. Graham writes in a line of wit. Although she has no powerful sense of conventional form, her work addresses the literary sensibility of the late New Critical advocates of Donne and Hopkins.

›››‹‹‹

By now poets have fully absorbed Eliot's claim about the constitutive power of figures, and the example of the Surrealists has fortified the point. The challenging elements of poetic intellectuality lie elsewhere. One such challenge to the representation of thinking in poetry came from Pound, who experimented with induction. He held that inductively derived hypotheses rest not only on observations or on experiences but on emotions as well. His effort was to derive intellectuality from the emotions—in Canto 36 he admires Cavalcanti for just this—not to apply intellectuality to the emotions. "Intense emotion," he wrote in 1915, "causes pattern to arise in the mind—if the mind is strong enough. Perhaps I should say, not pattern, but pattern-units, or units of design. (I do not say that intense emotion is the sole possible cause of such units. I say simply that they can result from it. They may also result from other sorts of energy.)"[30] This is a deeply significant claim. It means that the formal features of a poem might best adhere to the structures of an emotional experience—more than, say, to the structures of a line of rational investigation. Surprise, intensity, confusion, awe—these might, for instance, be the qualities that a poet like Pound would want to structure not just a poem but an intellectual poem, a line of thought. If emotional experiences may justly underlie thought itself, the structures of statements of thought may correspond not to syllogisms but to emotions themselves. When is Pound thinking of ideas and when of emotions, when of concepts and when of sensual patterns? These questions are notoriously unresolvable in the *Cantos*; the distinctions do not hold firm for him, exactly because he is imagining an intellectuality in poetry that breaks down customary distinctions in analytical thought.[31]

The intellectuality of poetry now usually shows in implication, in the folding of one sort of statement onto another. Folds of signification are different from articulated joints in a consecutive argument; the folds come—as emotions, Pound might argue—before one has anything so definite as an idea, in Graham's analysis (65). "Poetic thought," Fenollosa argued, "works by suggestion, crowding maximum meaning into the single phrase pregnant, charged, and luminous from within."[32] Prosaic thought may spell out relations between statements, but poetic thought is different: it leaves meaning implicit, loaded not unpacked. Poets condense; critics explicate. Faith in the power of implication ran very high among modernists. Williams said that Cezanne created paintings "so that there would be a meaning without saying anything at all. Just the relation of the parts to themselves. In considering a poem, I don't care whether it's finished or not; if it's put down with a good relation in the parts, it becomes a poem. And the meaning of the poem can be grasped by attention to the design."[33] Meaning for modernist poets was characteristically relational. Propositions or concepts of *x* or *y* were not the point; poetic attention shifted in the 'teens to complicated, enigmatic relations between statements. To implicate, as its etymology suggests, means much more than not to state openly.

Pound got the manuscripts of Ernest Fenollosa in 1913, and that was a turning point for poetry. The essay he carved from Fenollosa's papers, "The Chinese Written Character as a Medium for Poetry" (1919), changed American poetics by undermining the authority of prose syntax—the conventional rules for connecting words and thoughts—not only for his generation but for at least two more. "The ideogrammic method," Pound said, "consists of presenting one facet and then another until at some point one gets off the dead and desensitized surface of the reader's mind, onto a part that will register."[34] He was constructing a revolutionary rhetoric, justified, he thought, by empirical observation of visible natural processes, and by an appeal to fresh neurological paths through the brain. He recognized that his contemporaries in scientific disciplines felt some freedom from logic and grammar. In Fenollosa's manuscripts he found empirical ways to argue for new poetic forms. "In diction and in grammatical form science is utterly opposed to logic. . . . Poetry agrees with science and not with logic. . . . The more concretely and vividly we express the interactions of things the better the poetry."[35] Vivid in the sense of live, always that—for Fenollosa and Pound—against dead convention.

> Aristotle will tell you that "The apt use of metaphor, being as it is, the swift perception of relations, is the true hall-mark of genius." That abundance, that readiness of the figure is indeed one of the surest proofs that the mind is upborne upon the emotional surge.
>
> By "apt use," I should say it were well to understand, a swiftness, almost a violence, and certainly a vividness. This does not mean elaboration and complication.[36]

Pound advocated sudden violence (as Deleuze and Gasché later did), not steady accretion.[37] Both Dewey and Fenollosa regarded the connections between statements as crucial to their normative accounts of thinking. "We do not always sufficiently consider that thought is successive," Fenollosa says, "not through some accident or weakness of our subjective operations but because the operations of nature are successive."[38] Fenollosa and Pound wanted the sanction of nature for poetry. Dewey, on the contrary, was interested only in what successive thought—like a well-marshaled army, according to his figure—might actually do. But all three writers admired successive thought for its force. "All truth," Fenollosa says, "is the *transference of power*. The type of sentence in nature is a flash of lightning."[39] Behind the modernist appeal of juxtaposition in poetry is a hope for sudden transformation and a fascination with violence. One needs to remember that, if one mistakes the patient hypotactic style of Bronk or Pinsky as dull.

The shock of Fenollosa's or Pound's ideogrammic method is gone; this technology has been transformed by more secular poets. Poets and their readers commonly understand that intelligibility is not limited to what can be concisely stipulated. Some poets urge their art into the gap between what conventional discourse comprehends and what readers of poetry may apprehend. As they do so, intelligibility is inevitably spoken of in the subjunctive mood. One asks, poem by poem, how unintelligibility brings gain, and of what kind. Consider one recent and modest poem of juxtaposition. The title of Rae Armantrout's poem, "Overhearing," names the theme intended to hold the poem together, and it's central to English poetics. John Stuart Mill spoke of the lyric as a genre not meant for an auditor; in his sense, all lyrics are unintended addresses, self-colloquies. But there is another sense of the title too: like overreading, "overhearing" might suggest hearing too much. Here is the first of the poem's two distinct parts; both senses are operative:

> The way "The Tennessee Waltz"
> is about having heard
>
> "The Tennessee Waltz"
> before:
>
> an almost floral
> nostalgia,
>
> totally self-
> contained,
>
> is what we call
> beautiful.[40]

The poem's first two words focus on a *manner* of activity—that of definition. This definition comes to seem retrospective or even faintly redundant, like the title of the poem. At the center is this one amusingly musical phrase: "floral / nostalgia." This is the kernel of the poem's definition of beauty, or the quality of being beautiful, and it is flanked by an indefinite modifier and a proud phrase of intellectual conversation, "totally self-contained." I have spoken of the effort at definition in this section, but it would be more accurate to characterize the definition as ironic. There is an implied contrast between "what we call / beautiful" and what may be beautiful. And this contrast invites a counterreading of other terms in the poem: "floral" is a term most frequently used to describe flowers not in nature, but rather in "arrangements": contained, then, in the sense of a florist's shop. "The Tennessee Waltz" is a song of ostensibly local, southern, provincial pride, though it became a big, kitschy national hit (it was adopted by the Tennessee state legislature as the official state song in 1965).

Ironic definition, yes, but the irony is uttered from within conventions of aesthetic explanation: these lines attempt to identify a *quality* of judgment by invoking figures and phrases that echo social contexts of usage without naming them. There is here both an intellectual's commitment to the definition of a core term of aesthetic thought, the beautiful, and an aesthete's effort to explain by analogy and implication, by naming qualities, not kinds or essences. The tone of the first section is cool, like intellectual observation, and the progress of the poem through fragments of intellectual syntax presumes a bond of shared sensibility with her audience.

The poem's second part leaves definition altogether for the genre of the anecdote. As "The Tennessee Waltz" is a song within a song, so the anecdote is largely a dream (hers, 11–25) within a dream (his, 26–29).

> You're in the rocker;
> I'm on the couch,
> long since hauled off, but
> stationed
> like organs
> in this dream.
>
> You're saying,
> a bit too loudly,
> so that I'm afraid
> the one doing dishes

(now dead)
and the one in the bathroom
(now gone)
will overhear,
why you first wanted me,

when I wake up
to hear you
thrashing,
yelling out in a dream

Her dream is the anxious one of having her love life overheard, perhaps by parents. His dream is presumably also an anxious one, which she overhears and imagines as an explanation of desire, in that sense, another definition ("why you first wanted me"). Armantrout has constructed a series of subject rhymes about song, beauty, and erotic desire, though there is no technology of transport here. The dreams of the second part pass over each other like echoes, leaving very little behind. Both sections look back at an imagined original moment, when song, beauty, or desire seemed to begin.

This is an obviously post-Poundian poem: it juxtaposes coherent small units in the aspiration of constructing a large-order figure of a whole, a thematic complex that can go by the title "Overhearing." The order of the poem must come from the relations of the parts to one another. The thematic rhymes on hearing and doubling back are characteristic of Pound in the early cantos. As one interprets Armantrout's poem, one hypothesizes an ideogram of the whole. But Pound continued in the passage on the swift perception of relations to speak of his own poetry as aspiring to the condition of "revelation." His sense was always that the ideogrammic method had a capacity to reveal divine presence in the mundane. Armantrout's ideogrammic method retains no vestigial religiosity. She is thoroughly skeptical, secular. The form of the poem is simply constructed, without any suggestion of extraordinary perception. It is so skeptical a poem that the speaker's dream is a little ridiculous: not just that she fears exposure before those who are dead and gone, but rather this phrase "like organs." She must mean sexual organs, since the topic is the origin of sexual desire, and that is a ludicrous image to contemplate.

The ironic reading that I proposed has a bearing on line 25: "why you first wanted me," in this context, awakens an implicit contrast between then, when the parents were living, and now, when they are dead; between a time of being wanted and one of not being wanted, or of being wanted differently. "The Tennessee Waltz" is a song recollecting a lost lover: "Now I know just how much I have lost." A cornball song keeps this topic in view from the outset. The poem ends with its only moving lines; its affective power is heard there, when the partner yells out in the night. For what, for whom? Who's been lost? She wasn't supposed to hear this. That voice in the night is from another poetic—the call of a less skeptical, more romantic art not addressed so directly to institutional intellectual culture.

›››‹‹‹

Cleanth Brooks argued famously that a paraphrase of a poem, the thoughts expressed by it, can in no sense be taken as "the real core of meaning which constitutes the essence of the poem."[41] He identified as essential the "structure" of the poem, and this was comprised of all the statements of the poem arrayed in relation to its speakers and figures.

> The structure meant is a structure of meanings, evaluations, and interpretations; and the principle of unity which informs it seems to be one of balancing and harmonizing connotations, attitudes, and meanings. But even here one needs to make important qualifications: the principle is not one which involves the arrangement of the various elements into homogeneous groupings, pairing like with like. It unites the like with the unlike. It does not unite them, however, by the simple process of allowing one connotation to cancel out another nor does it reduce the contradictory attitudes to harmony by a process of subtraction. The unity is not a unity of the sort to be

> achieved by the reduction and simplification appropriate to an algebraic formula. It is a positive unity, not a negative; it represents not a residue but an achieved harmony.[42]

This totalizing account of the unity of poems reveals the idealism of the New Criticism: Brooks imagines ways in which poems reconcile differences that elsewhere go unreconciled. A poem makes a complex peace that cannot be reduced to a set of propositions. It promises a peace elsewhere. Something like this notion survives, because it is deeply true, even in poetry that is very far removed from the commitments of the New Critics.

In recent American avant-garde poems there is similarly a sense of a structure, or poem, behind the poem; the words on the page evoke a poem beyond the page, one that isn't there, strictly speaking. The ordinary way to refer to this phenomenon is to say that the words of a poem represent the poet's thoughts, but Brooks rightly discredited that view of the primacy of the paraphrase or the thoughts of a poem. The avant-garde poems I am thinking of—Armantrout's is one—construct gaps between lines, or visual stanzas, or even clauses. Such poems imply that there is a structure behind the text of the sort that Brooks describes, a coherence beyond the surface incoherence or disjunctiveness of the words, lines, or stanzas on the page. This implication is very powerful in Pound's work, where one needs to infer an ideogram for each canto: how does it cohere? Pound's enormous idealism rested on a faith that the structuring powers of the mind are universal, natural, and effective at identifying orders not marked by the conjunctions that conventionally indicate intellectual relations: if, then, but, because, for, although, however, and so on.

Recent poets have inherited that idealism, though without the psychological grounding of Pound. That is, a poet like Michael Palmer does not believe in universal, natural orders that can be inferred by most readers. Here are the first six lines of "Construction of the Museum":

In the hole we found beside the road
something would eventually go

Names we saw spelled backward there

In the sand we found a tablet

In the hole caused by bombs
which are smart we might find a hand[43]

It is not the case that Palmer leaves the construction of inference to each reader, though this naive sort of populism is often adduced to support the poetic policies of Language writing. The lines I have cited pretty clearly invoke an alternative syntax behind these lines:

Something would eventually go in the hole we found beside the road.
We saw names spelled backward there.
We found a tablet in the sand.
We might find a hand in the hole caused by bombs which are smart.

Palmer's readers, as competent speakers of English, know the syntactic structures behind the words he has written on the page; they can all feel the backwardness of his lines. The poem does invoke norms of usage as universal among English speakers. The gap between normative English syntax and Palmer's syntax itself identifies a utopian conceptual space for the poem: there is an order elsewhere, beyond this page. These words might be arrayed otherwise, in keeping with conventions of English usage. Once established, this interpretive horizon affects the rest of the poem too.

It is the writing hand
hand which dreams a hole

to the left and the right of each hand

The hand is called day-inside-night
because of the colored fragments which it holds

We never say the word desert
nor does the sand pass through the fingers

of this hand we forget
is ours

We might say, Memory has made its selection,
and think of the body now as an altered body

framed by flaming wells or walls

What a noise the words make
writing themselves

The notion of a hypothetical elsewhere behind the poem suggests that in some conceptual region these lines might all cohere, as Brooks showed his poems to cohere. The syllables echo each other musically ("hole" [1, 5, 8], "sand" [4, 13], "hand" [6, 7, 8, 9, 10, 14], and then morph into others, uttered ("holds" [11]) and virtual ("whole," as in the whole hand found in the sand). The fulfillment of the musical structure comes in one visionary, lyrical line (18), after which Palmer just backs out of the poem. Fully realized musically, and thereby warranted; but intellectually? Where might that conceptual elsewhere be? At the level of interpretive theory, it resides in the historically established conventions of an interpretive community. Brooks articulates that generic expectation among readers of poetry for the generation of Palmer's teachers. At the level of this particular poem, the conceptual region might well be political-historical. The poem is dated April 11, 1991, during Desert Storm. These were the days when General Schwarzkopf proudly displayed the results of American smart bombs in Iraq, when body parts might well be found in bomb craters, when flaming oil wells blackened the skies. The poem clearly refers to these features of American political history.

Or the poem might cohere allegorically, since Palmer does characteristically invoke an allegorical regime when he indicates that names are given for reasons (10–11). Repeatedly in Palmer's poems allegorical phrases are proposed as names of ambiguous figures; the suggestion is that enigmas are constantly on the horizon of poetry, and that naming entails them. Along this axis of interpretation, the assignment of significance to the signs of the poem—most obviously, the hand—would govern the overall coherence of the poem's structure. This line of interpretation might help to explain the transition from smart bombs (6) to the writing hand (7): the apparently self-guiding systems of the bomb and the writing hand of the author both demonstrate agency; the deployers of the bomb are concealed behind a notion of technological smartness, and the maker of this poem is the most proximate agent here. The predicate of the writer is to dream (8), though he claims that the words write themselves (19–20). In an allegory where body parts are named for explicit reasons, one expects maximal authorial agency and accountability, but the poem focuses on lapses of accountability. "We never say" and "we forget" are phrases that identify failures of responsibility. What might be said and remembered is a common sense of mortality and humility, marked by the traditional figure of desert sands slipping through the fingers. But instead subjunctive predicates—"We might say . . . and think" (16–17)—follow and articulate the euphemisms that displace responsibility onto "Memory." Allegory comes to express not an intensification but an evasion of significance.

The poem stands as a wish for another poem: what if this poem cohered, as poems traditionally have done; what would that coherence signify as a path of thinking? How would we think, if this poem were the expression of a recognizable, comprehensive resolution? One cannot easily answer these questions, exactly because Palmer represents, in a fashion Valéry would understand, what seem plural ways of thinking. He has not drawn the political-historical and the allegorical interpretive perspectives into a harmony, as Brooks would say; that was the project of an earlier generation. The relations between these perspectives are not resolved, and that presents an intellectual challenge beyond any of the other poems discussed. I know no name for the "structure" of this poem, in Brooks's sense, though in the body of its language I can feel the power of its structure. Palmer is at the edge of conventions of thinking, insisting on the distinct intellectual resources of the poetic art, which seem to have to do with resistance to resolution. My notion of a hypothetical coherence behind an avant-garde poem is entirely in accord with Anglo-American and European modernist aspirations. Caillois was close to Pound in more than just his terminology when he explained the structure of lyrical thinking:

> So it is that several irregular rocks put together carelessly leave a certain gap between them, the shape precisely defined, such that the shape of the rock that would fill this interstice is strictly determined in advance, the determinism of this space being as rigorous as any other. Similarly, it seems that an accumulation of convergent representations predetermines all or part of the conditions that the representations they need to present a flawless coherence will have to meet. It follows that this representation exists virtually because of the existence of the previous ones, and at the first contingent prompting, passing from potential to actual, it will impose itself on one's consciousness.[44]

The value of lyrical thinking, and of poetry in particular, is to lead consciousness toward ever more comprehensive ideograms, or ideas of order and coherence.[45] Although Caillois uses a Freudian notion of overdetermination and autobiography to explicate ideograms, he did believe, as Pound did too, that ideograms are universal and based on biological nature. Those are not my beliefs, but I do value the virtual poetry we strain toward as readers, and I look to poetry (as Deleuze, Lyotard, and Gasché look to philosophy) for an extension of conventional patterns of thinking.

Poetry is often spoken of as the most personal genre. Sappho, at the outset of lyric, is certainly personal: she gives a concrete representation of the feelings of her body and no one else's. The genre of confessional poetry is rooted in this central and archaic feature of lyric poetry. This is also one of the acknowledged links between post–World War II and Romantic poetry. But there is a sense too in which poems are understood as inherently representative of other persons, of some general subjecthood. Poets know this, as readers do, and they have no trouble invoking claims to general representativity. Even Shelley easily speaks in a universalizing idiom in "To a Skylark":

> We look before and after,
> And pine for what is not—
> Our sincerest laughter
> With some pain is fraught—
> Our sweetest songs are those that tell of saddest thought.
> (86–90)[46]

The subjectivity he describes is that of analytical thinking and of spontaneous feeling; he has no difficulty using the first-person plural claim to speak for untold others. And it is worth noting that all the poems I have discussed make important use of the first-person plural voice. The intellectuality of poetry seems tied to its generality. In my epigraph, Pound claims that the best books register an *unusual* intelligence. The choice between parataxis and hypotaxis, between prizing one or the other mode of writing, bears on this question. A claim to unusual intelligence may be made obvious by an eccentric method of elaborating statements. Unusual can mean strange or exceptional. "Criticism needs to be able to describe thought," Angus Fletcher says, "occurring under extreme conditions."[47] The poetic aspiration to reveal a distinctive and unfamiliar manner of thinking is a tradition of U.S. poetics. It was Emerson who proposed "a metre-making argument" as essential to the art: "a thought so passionate and alive, that, like the spirit of a plant or an animal, it has an architecture of its own, and adorns nature with a new thing."[48] When Dryden said that a good poet must be "accustomed to argue well," he did not mean that poets employ distinctive manners of argumentation, or of developing thought.[49] Emerson and his successors, like Dryden, consider poets advocates and intellectuals, but U.S. poets traditionally cultivate strange thinking. Gasché observes, following Deleuze, that "true philosophical thought arises from what is peculiar, singular, and private, as opposed to what is publicly established and what everyone knows and cannot deny."[50] Academic interpretation, it should be remembered, is ready for unusual thinking—for Palmer or Pound more than for Bronk.

Only Bronk, among the poets discussed, was unconcerned to elaborate his thinking in an unusual manner. Palmer especially distinguishes his writing from the lingua franca of nonliterary intellectuals. This means, I think, that all these poets except Bronk feel an advantage over other explainers, that they do not wish to accommodate poetry to philosophy. Despite the prestige of political engagement in recent American letters, the symbolist Valéry is closely attuned to the confidence of these poets in their own peculiarity.

> There is something, then, a modification, or a transformation, sudden or not, spontaneous or not, laborious or not, which must necessarily intervene between the thought that produces ideas—that activity and multiplicity of inner questions and solutions—and, on the other hand, that discourse, so different from ordinary speech, which is verse, which is so curiously ordered, which answers no need *unless it be the need it must itself create*, which never speaks but of absent things or of things profoundly and secretly felt: strange discourse, as though made by someone *other* than the speaker and addressed to someone *other* than the listener. In short, it is a *language within a language*." (*AP*, 63–64)

Philosophers pursue knowledge. What poets most want to know is how to write the next poem. Why would they wish to reduce the scope of the unknown? "It has," as Stevens said, "seductions more powerful and more profound than those of the known."[51] My claim about the relevance of a virtual coherence behind enigmatic avant-garde poems is a variant of what Raymond Geuss identifies as knowledge-as-acquaintance-with (*kennen*).[52] Poems like Palmer's or Pound's acquaint readers with indefinite ideals, ways of thinking that are only imperfectly accounted for by the poem, and cannot be reconstructed by a reader. In the end, the rhetorical project gives way. These are orphic calls into the dark for a fulfillment that may never arrive. Even the most intellectual, or philosophical, poets realize that the discourses of poetry and philosophy, as the rational adjudication of rival propositions, are properly separate, that thinking in poetry should remain unlike thinking in any other medium. Exactly these poets present, with musical language and figure, a sense of what will not be brought into propositional prose. This evocation of a "sentiment that something remains unsaid, or muffled" is poetry's most deeply thoughtful, if not most rational, moment.[53] The music leads away.

5

Music

Musicality is crucial to poetry, as mimesis is to drama and narrative, though critics rarely give music its due; they rather explicate meaning. The origin of music, for Nietzsche, is Dionysian joy: a conviction that life is, "despite all changes of appearances, indestructibly powerful and pleasurable."[1] It's true that even the most melancholy music is still affirmative in this way. Which clarifies what is to be expected from the musicality of poetry. Eliot said that his own poems began not with something to say but with a particular rhythm. Nietzsche noted that Schiller had said that "a certain musical mood comes first."[2] Marina Tsvetaeva said the same.[3] Musicality does not properly ornament poetry, nor emphasize its paraphrasable sense. It rather names the origin of art: an order of experience and value unconstrained by particular concepts or reference, and knowable in the flesh. When words cohere musically they allude to significance beyond paraphrase. How is an explainer to clarify that in prose? Just what lies beyond that sense remains indefinite, but nonetheless reassuring, as Nietzsche said, that the power and pleasure of life abides.

For three centuries music has been analyzed in terms of its affective mechanisms more than its metaphysical status. But two generative figures in poems repeatedly invoke a rich intellectual and religious account of the metaphysics of music. First is

Orpheus, again, the archaic poet-musician whose power jumped species boundaries. The second is that of the music of the spheres: the Platonic and then Christian humanist notion that the heavenly bodies, in their ordered movement, produce a harmonic music that humans can no longer hear.[4] These are figures whose moment seems to have passed, but John Hollander has shown that they continued to generate poems, in the late seventeenth century, well after they commanded belief, and they have more recently enabled Rilke and Bunting.[5] They are names and narratives, even clichés, not explanations, of the power of music. That musicality is magical, unaccountably charming; that what musicians produce seems to correspond somehow to something heavenly or cosmic—these notions are needed still. One should remember, before dismissing Orpheus and the spheres as superstition, that modern secular musicology has no convincing account of the power of music. Music seems to correspond to some transcendent order, though one cannot define that order. Musicality is a sign of that order, but in an indecipherable code.[6] Paraphrase certainly won't do. Musicality corresponds *to* . . . It rather signifies the very idea of affective correspondence. Maybe critics wisely avoid poetry's music because analysis cannot get to the bottom of it. Is analysis even instructive? Plato thought so: an education in music provides a measure for assessing "things which are badly made or naturally defective."[7] Poetry's music instantiates norms for relative assessments of poems; but Plato meant that musical understanding enables one to discern defectiveness more generally and profoundly "because rhythm and [musical] mode penetrate more deeply into the inner soul than anything else does."[8] A resonance felt within helps one recognize poorly crafted claims, for instance, as distant or alien. Some poems, we answer with our bodies; other expressions, poems or arguments, we don't even hear at all. Not everything strikes a responsive chord, as we say.

Lyric poetry is a genre of song. When words alone sing, one has it; when they don't, another category of writing may obtain. A song is a series of both sounds and signs. Literary criticism generally works only with semantic signs, and that arouses mistrust among poets. The challenge to a poet is to compose a text that is compelling not so much in two separate ways—semantically and sonically—but in one way that draws sign and sound into collaboration. The challenge to a critic is to recognize and then characterize their interaction. Critics who attempt this almost always use a single model of a successful meeting: Pope's prescription that the sound "must seem an echo to the sense." This model suggests that sense is essential, while expressive sound is ornamental to a poem. All that critics can do with this model is to show how and where sound imitates sense. Yet sound is not merely instrumental to the delivery of sense, and the sound effects that matter most are not merely local to one statement. Meetings of word and sound in song are too various to fit this one model. The musicality of poetry is a topic that invites abstraction: a metaphorical understanding of one art in terms of another leads one away from particular poems and songs. My focus is not only on the meaning of musicality in poetry, but also on the practical resources of musicality for poets and readers now. In order to hold my feet to the ground, I derive almost all of my claims from particular poems. I have two models of musicality to propose: the first derives from the sounds of conventional discourse—particularly literary and social conventions; the second means to express the body itself. Musicality, that is, pushes to one side the categories of orphic and civil that I have been using. Or rather the range of expression designated by those categories is altogether encompassed by the varieties of musicality retrievable in poetry.

My examination of the relations between words and sounds begins with popular poetry, but not doggerel. American poets like Eliot, Pound, Moore, Stevens, and Williams have found readers all over the world, though they had to make their audiences. The most popular American poets have set their verses to melodies and immediately found audiences that are held together by the apparatus of the music industry. The great American lyricists mastered the physicality of words, the sonority of phonemes and syllables, and the resources of rhythm, though modernist poets were inattentive to their songwriter contemporaries. In Canto 81 Pound expresses his admiration of Renaissance English songwriters, but he knew nothing of Johnny Mercer, Yip Harburg, or Ira Gershwin. These songwriters understood the interaction of bodies and words, and they found large, international audiences for memorable poems. My approach to the topic of musicality in poetry is to scrutinize various successful meetings of sound and sense or, as this dyad will develop, sonority and speech. Musicality is known not by itself, but rather in relation to what it is not, viz., conventional speech between strangers. This is to say that speech is always present in some way where vocal music is heard. The first significance of speech in poetry is its communication of social status, not its paraphrasable sense. The significance of musicality, though, is its insistence that speech and social order generally are not the heart of life. That is my argument. My two models of musicality—Tin Pan Alley and doo-wop—establish poles of a continuum, and my other examples, strictly textual, illuminate the elements of poetics that affect special—that is, moving and memorable—meetings of sound and sense.[9]

One small aim of this chapter is to get beyond the Popean musicality of poetry; my larger aim is to understand better the role of sonority, or pleasing sounds, in poetry. Another word here about the songs. Language is a conventional sound system that, for the sake of systems of semantic meaning, puts dramatic limits on the sounds available for use; instrumental music, in contrast, ignores the constraints of semantic meaning and insists on the right to use all sounds. Tin Pan Alley represents a poetic extreme wherein the conventionality of language is accepted, and the limits on the sounds a poet creates are also accepted. Doo-wop, in contrast, represents the opposite extreme: the poet sacrifices meaning to sound, and especially the pleasures of vowels. Once I establish these poles, I explore four contemporary poems that mark out the poetic terrain between these two extremes: David Ferry's "The Guest Ellen," Robert Pinsky's "Poem with Refrains," Jim Powell's "First Light," and Thylias Moss's "Glory."

I have ordered them from the poem that is most accepting of the limits that meaning puts on musicality, Ferry's, to the poem, Moss's, that is least accepting of those limits and most hungry for sonority. Each poem, and the point on the musical continuum it inhabits, renders discernible some particular feature of the complex relationship between poetry and music. So first Tin Pan Alley and doo-wop.

›››‹‹‹

I begin with one great and famous Tin Pan Alley song, "Skylark" (1941) by Johnny Mercer and Hoagy Carmichael. Poets rarely collaborate with each other, but it is common for a composer to produce a melody, as Carmichael did, before a lyricist like Mercer writes a word. Lieder and arias are produced by the opposite procedures; art music begins with the text and sets that to music, as though the semantic text were more determining than the music. Popular lyricists make no such assumption. Mercer had difficulty collaborating with André Previn, because the director of the London Symphony wanted the lyric first.[10] "I prefer having the music first," Mercer said, "because I seem to catch the mood of the tune. If I have any gift at all, that's it, being able to write the mood properly."[11] Mercer has a sense of an emotional fit between melody and lyric; he sees to it that the text conforms to a feeling implicit in the prior structure, the melody. First a "particular rhythm" or a "musical mood," according to Eliot and Schiller, then a poem. This is similar to, but not quite the same as, Pope's fit between sound and paraphrasable sense, partly because "mood" is so much less definite than "sense." There is no suggestion, even by lyricists like Mercer who fit words to music, that the relation is organic, that any particular lyric is implicit in a tune. Other words are certainly imaginable for any melody. He sometimes wrote multiple lyrics for a song and asked his collaborator to choose one. A poem has only one set of words, though they may be set to various stanzaic or prosodic patterns. But both poets and songwriters are looking for a distinctive effect from the conjoining of words and music. "The greatest romance in the life of a lyricist," said Yip Harburg, "is when the right words meet the right notes."[12]

Most songs and poems produce nothing distinctive from the meeting of words and sounds. Sophisticated music audiences recognize failure quickly, and they don't buy it; but poetry audiences, distracted by semantic codes, often overlook the failure of sound and sense to produce a spark. This has to do with money. A song that works especially well usually finds an audience right away. That's the economy that paid Mercer well. He knew the system thoroughly, and he loved it. In 1940 he was elected the youngest member of the directorate of ASCAP, and he served in that capacity through the conflict between songwriters and radio stations that led to the ascendancy of the rival organization BMI and of the rhythm and blues and rock songwriters it represented. He was the founding president of Capitol Records in 1941, the first major label on the West Coast. He wrote in his autobiography about the feel of working on Hollywood scores:

> The buzz around the movie set when you've brought in a "hit" and everyone on the set knows it and is singing it . . . These are the things that mean even more than the big checks that come rolling in when you've got a big one—a song that everybody loves—and all the artists can't wait to sing and record. It really is an exciting, stimulating experience, and like having an adventure in love, it does not pale with time, as each adventure is different and the end result is always pleasant, combining as it does, a sense of prideful accomplishment with the happiness of making other people happy.[13]

There is a thrill in contemporaneity, in being attuned to the appetites of one's exact contemporaries—that's immediate gratification, and it comes even to some poets, though without Mercer's checks. Fellow artists want to collaborate; audiences feel the art and learn the words by heart. It's money, for Mercer, but above all engagement.

Mercer's compositional procedures were unusual. Like many lyricists, he sometimes worked in the same room with his composers. When a collaboration got troublesome, he would always take his work home, and he would often do so anyway. Song lyrics, he said, "don't always come fast, believe me. I remember once Hoagy Carmichael gave me two tunes to set. Well, I struggled over them for a long time. Must have been a year before I got one; I called it 'Skylark.' I called up Hoagy and I said, 'Hey, I think I got a lyric for your tune.' He said, 'What tune is that?' He'd *forgotten* it!"[14] His usual practice, though, looked effortless to others. He would listen to a melody, often only once, then lie down and appear to sleep. "I simply get to thinking over the song," he told his father, "pondering over it in my mind and all of a sudden, I get in tune with the Infinite."[15] But "Skylark," as he said, came slowly:

Skylark,
Have you anything to say to me?
Won't you tell me where my love can be?
Is there a meadow in the mist
Where someone's waiting to be kissed?

Oh, Skylark,
Have you seen a valley green with spring?
Where my heart can go a-journeying
Over the shadows and the rain
To a blossom-covered lane?

And in your lonely flight
Haven't you heard the music in the night?
Wonderful music
Faint as a will o' the wisp,
Crazy as a loon,
Sad as a gypsy serenading the moon.

Oh, skylark,
I don't know if you can find these things,
But my heart is riding on your wings,
So if you see them anywhere
Won't you lead me there?
Oh, skylark,
Won't you lead me there?[16]

This is a thematically conventional poem, one of any number of romantic poems addressed to birds. Mercer incidentally had a special fondness for birds and even some success at summoning them with his whistles.[17] More important (and unlike Shelley's "To a Skylark"), the lyric expresses a romantic yearning to be in the land-of-heart's-desire—fulfillment imagined as a pastoral utopia. Why the speaker is suffering adversity and yearns for delivery is unstated because unimportant. Yearning itself is the thing. It's an impersonal, intransitive sort of desire. The phrase "my love" (3) suggests for an instant that a particular lover has been lost, but the very next sentence corrects this misapprehension:

> Is there a meadow in the mist
> where someone's waiting to be kissed?
> (4–5)

Philip Furia, Mercer's biographer, argues that the song's origin was indeed one person. Mercer was so madly in love with Judy Garland that he asked his wife for a divorce—twice, in fact. Mercer's song, according to Furia, was an answer to Garland's big hit with Yip Harburg's lyric "Over the Rainbow" (1939).[18] Ginger Mercer had a sense of humor: she refused to divorce Johnny until she learned from the paper (before he did) that Garland had married David Rose; then she agreed. But this is extraneous to Mercer's text. The desire in the song is altogether anonymous. Keats and Baudelaire ("Invitation au voyage") stand directly behind "Over the Rainbow" and "Skylark"; there is a long tradition of wanting to get away. Mercer's speaker imagines being free from adversity. A bird is a colloquial symbol of freedom; "like free bloody birds," Larkin says, in an altogether different spirit. Everything about the poem's emotion is abstract, categorical.

The traditionality of this song is stylistic as well as thematic. Its very opening (2–3) establishes a slightly formal, literate (even prosaic) manner of expression. A more colloquial utterance would be: Do you have anything to say to me? Tell me where my love can be. At one point, the diction moves beyond romantic conventions even to quaintness—"a-journeying" (8).

In this song Mercer was deliberately traditional, not colloquial, not contemporary, though he was a master of vernacular. The one and only intellectual issue in the song is expressed directly in the third strophe. The question might be restated as, Is there a reversal implicit in adversity? That is "the music in the night." The will-o'-the-wisp, the loon, and the gypsy are all outlier figures, conventional signs of activity that exceeds normal explanation. I stress the conventionality of Mercer's diction and figures because there is a subtle point to his indifference to freshness of phrasing. "Wonderful music," he says, outside his syntax (13). No phrase could be more banal to a songwriter. The nice point, however, is that a song—the skylark's, his own—for no good reason, just as a wonder, has a power to transform adversity. A music full of wonder is his objective. The only authority underwriting that wonder is the repeated, recorded experience of others. A meadow in the mist, a valley green with spring, a blossom-covered lane—these utterly familiar figures of untroubled peace are lodged firmly in the conventions of romantic sensibility. Exactly their familiarity testifies to—but states no good *reason* to believe in—the transformative music in the night. As Yvor Winters said, conventional language is not always dead; it may be "very subtly living, if well employed."[19] And only a few performances of this lyric that I have heard enhance the delicate life of Mercer's conventional language.

Behind the lyrics as sung is a countervailing norm of social speech, the way the words would need to be articulated to count as conventional interpersonal communication. In some performances that norm is not far removed from a singer's utterance, but in others speech—and with it, the very idea of social interaction as normative—is remote indeed. When a norm of speech is remote, either the individual style of the one singer is overriding, or the instrumentation of the tune dominates the production. If the band overpowers the lyric, the meaning of the performance may well entail social values such as cooperation, competition, and supplementation, because band musicians collaborate to produce, as citizens do too, power and harmony. But a single vocalist who overrides a lyric text moves a song away from sociality altogether. Speech is a discipline. Diction, syntax, articulation—these are coordinates that constrain improvisation, in song lyrics and in poems. When the conventional limits of a living language community are accepted or rejected, an artist implies a position on social authority. Some singers and poets affiliate their utterances with the social practices of particular communities; others distinguish themselves as outliers.

This is an admittedly abstract introduction to a song so popular that well over five hundred performances are on record, but some of the differences between particular performances actually illuminate basic features of poetics. In particular, the one version I think of as the best—Carmen McRae's 1958 recording with Ben Webster—reveals something important about the relations of vowel music, stress, and the representation of speech in poetry.

Mercer's song came out during the ascendancy of the big bands, when great vocalists like Billy Eckstine, Helen Forrest, and Anita O'Day were accompanied by extraordinary dance bands. As soon as the song was available, in November 1941, Anita O'Day recorded her version of "Skylark" with the Gene Krupa band, which then included virtuoso trumpeter Roy Eldridge. The bands kept a bass line steady and constantly audible; that was the necessary heart of the music. A metrical norm like iambic pentameter does the same sort of thing for English poetry. These great band singers oriented their performances on that steady command of the body's attention. They accepted a governing beat and rarely drew out their vowels against their steady accompaniment. They let the instrumentalists like Roy Eldridge and Harry James take the horns on flights of interpretation, but the vocalists' lines were always within hailing distance of comprehensible English speech.

The marked bass line gives Carmen McRae, Anita O'Day, and Helen Forrest easy access to the calm, self-assured, and subtle music of Mercer's lines. As a director of Capitol Records, Mercer himself oversaw many recording sessions. When Margaret

Whiting was recording "Moonlight in Vermont" in 1943, he told her to "talk the lyric out as if it were a poem," his biographer reports.[20] Speech was the basis of song for him: what a song actually says is crucial, and singers are meant to deal carefully with that, even when the referential sense seems slight. Whiting got to the phrase "Ski tows down a mountainside" and admitted that she could not imagine what a ski tow looked like. Mercer wanted her to understand clearly what she was saying in the song, so he phoned the composer and the lyricist to get their approval to change one word. They agreed to have Whiting sing "Ski trails down a mountainside."[21] For Mercer and his contemporaries, lyrics are at base speech, and that base has to be secure. For band singers, the bass too has to be secure and dominant. The distinctiveness of vocal interpretation was constrained by the conventions of speech, by the dance beat, and by the convention that instrumentalists had greater freedom to improvise than singers did. That was Mercer's sense of the poetics of his art, and these priorities were generally dominant in American popular music of the 1940s. This would all pass in the 1950s with doo-wop poetics, and then too with the pop music of the following decades.

Carmen McRae, Anita O'Day, and Helen Forrest all sing "Skylark" with perfect enunciation. One can transcribe the lyrics without confusion or ambiguity. That is the tradition of band singers. They respect Mercer's achievement, and they trust his words too much to improvise at the level of semantic statement. There is an austerity in their performances that a stylist like Cassandra Wilson or George Benson renounces. Forrest and McRae accept the separateness of word and melody; they do not try to overcome the differences between language and instrumentation. Their commitment to the clarity and definiteness of the text is a brake on the impulse to expand the sensuality of the song by employing the voice to imitate or emulate the lead instruments, as Wilson does. Cassandra Wilson draws out syllables without reference to their semantic sense as speech; for her, the song is a series of sounds, not signs, and her performer's body can elongate sounds that suit her auditory sense of the song. Her performance is powerful to the ear, but there is no poem in her song. Mercer's name is nowhere listed in her credits for "Skylark" on *New Moon Daughter* (1995): rather, it is Hoagy Carmichael's song, which was released by Blue Note, a division of Capitol Records.

›››‹‹‹

Critics, like Valéry, frequently distinguish poetry or song from prose or speech. These last two terms are meant to signify the medium in which the world's business is conducted—instrumental language. And this approach to musicality leads one to esteem poetic language and leave prose to the merchants and bankers. But the very musicality of much poetry and song too depends on a poet using both these conventionally contrasted categories in close proximity. One way to assure the flight of poetic language is to set it right next to prosaic idioms, which is what many poets do. Early in the twentieth century Yeats and Pound were awakened to the resources of music and poetry in combination by Florence Farr and Arnold Dolmetsch. Farr was clear about the resources of quick switches of register. "There is no more beautiful sound," she said, "than the alternation of caroling or keening and a voice speaking in regulated declamation. The very act of alternation has a peculiar charm."[22] Yeats and Pound understood this feature of their art, and so did Mercer. In his last stanza Mercer moves his lyric toward a prosaic register in which one expresses not passionate conviction but hesitation and conditional requests. These lines—

> I don't know if you can find these things . . .
> So if you see them anywhere . . .
>
> (18 & 20)

—are written for a speaking voice, one that can move easily and quickly through those syllables. It's an error of interpretation to draw out these lines, as Cassandra Wilson and Aretha Franklin do. A quick-paced speech is needed there to set up the lyrical flight of line 21 ("Won't you lead me there?"). The musicality of poetry is relational, differential: one idiom alternates with another, and by that shift the music is known.

The music that started me listening, the doo-wop lyrics of the 1950s, actually displaced Mercer and the songwriters of my parents' generation (my father was a bassist and songwriter). Mercer made a lot of money because he had a ready market until the late 1950s. Thereafter young people bought other songs. In the early 1950s the youth market for records expanded, as the industry shifted toward younger and therefore less literate listeners.[23] The shift was poetic too. Doo-wop radically subordinated semantics. Even a writer like Mercer with relatively light investment in thematic specificity was left behind by the vowel music of doo-wop and then by rock generally. He gradually lost control of—and interest in—Capitol Records. His managing partner was Glenn Wallichs, who owned the largest music and record store in Hollywood, at Sunset and Vine. In 1947, when Wallichs took over the presidency of Capitol from Mercer, the Capitol offices were moved to the second floor of Music City. On the ground floor were all the records that young people bought and glass listening booths for them to sample the wares. Mercer had an office on the second floor, but he disliked it and is said never to have even sat at the desk. He didn't want to come in the store. Taste, music, and the poetics of songwriting were changing, and by 1974 Mercer was altogether bitter:

> I can't write any more lyrics for this generation. I am so disgusted with what they are calling lyrics and how nasty they are. . . . I rode from my mother's old house to the office, and there was only one tune on the radio. And it was ugly, nasty. And it was just going up and down the scale, up and down. And all it was saying, that "I want it, I gotta have it, I need it." . . . What kind of lyric is that? Why are they letting that go on the air?"[24]

›››‹‹‹

My first poems were mid-1950s doo-wop songs from the radio shows of Art Laboe and Johnny Otis. I lived a few blocks from Scrivner's drive-in restaurant, on Sunset Boulevard, where the *Art Laboe Show* originated: "To the girls in the fine white Chevy . . ." That was one block west of Mercer's office at Wallichs's Music City. Like my friends, I heard the songs on small home radios and then in cars. We knew the lyrics by heart, had taken them into our bodies, trusting their transports entirely.

> There's a moon out tonight
>   Whoa-oh-oh ooh
> Let's go strollin'
> There's a girl in my heart
>   Whoa-oh-oh ooh
> Whose heart I've stolen
> There's a moon out tonight
>   Whoa-oh-oh ooh
> Let's go strollin' through the park
>   ooh-ooh-ooh-ooh
>
> There's a glow in my heart
>   Whoa-oh-oh ooh
> I never felt before
> There's a girl at my side
>   Whoa-oh-oh ooh
> That I adore
> There's a glow in my heart
> I never felt before
>   ooh-ooh-ooh-ooh
>
> Oh Darlin'
> Where have you been?
> I've been longin' for you all my life. . . .[25]

Never before, never before, never . . . What does Aphrodite say to Sappho, at the start of Western love poetry? "Who is it this time?" We were skeptical about a great deal that our parents, teachers, and the police too had proposed in enforcing the proprieties of the neighborhood; but the idioms of conventional romantic love—the ardors, moonlight, and eternal fidelity of our parents' songs and of hyperbolic love poetry since Petrarch—they were deeply ours too. The very first European modernist artists had turned directly against just this romanticism as early as 1909, when Marinetti published "Let's Murder the Moonshine!" Thematically these songs were a good half century behind avant-garde aesthetics. Their conventionality interfered not one bit with our absorption of them, and I listen still.

How did these cornball lyrics get to me so deeply? They were inaccessible to the ironic sensibilities of Mercer's generation. It was the music, mostly of voices: harmonies, resonances, elongated vowels (melisma). "I do not wonder at the miracles which poetry attributes to the music of Orpheus," Emerson once remarked, "when I remember what I have experienced from the varied notes of the human voice."[26] Doo-wop asserted a sense of song addressed directly to bodies. Emerson could hear what 1950s teenagers heard too: a magical power in the nonsemantic sounds that voices make. The elongated vowels and nonsense syllables were plainly excessive by the standards of Tin Pan Alley. Doo-wop proposed a severe subordination of speech in song, and it did so at the end of a period of extraordinarily distinguished writing in the urbane, sophisticated (i.e., social) style of Tin Pan Alley. The music of English verse that we chart with prosodic taxonomy doesn't get at these doo-wop tunes at all. The technical terms used to account for vowel-length in Greek and Latin now signify only stress in English. English renaissance poets knew that vowel music, the play of long and short syllables, constitutes much of poetic eloquence, and poets from Campion to Pound have tried to tap that mysterious source systematically. But still we have no workable analytical tools for revealing the claims of the vowels on our hearts, though we testify now and then to the presence of this deep, obscure music.

Doo-wop lyrics barely count at all as semantic statements. Their paraphrasable sense is hokey, and yet the songs are compelling because the stories of teenage romance themselves are not the source of power. The musicians knew this perfectly. The Jive Five did an earnest ballad called "My True Story" (1961) in which, though the names of the principals are said to have been veiled "to protect you and I," no story at all is told. But the song is delivered with somber, elegiac sincerity, and it lives still. No matter how plaintive a song, its effect was always exhilarating, exactly because its power came more from sonority than from statement or story. Another big hit for four different groups was "Gloria," in which the predication is almost entirely negative. The obvious pleasure of that song comes from the doo-wop annexation of key syllables from centuries of European church music. Nonsense syllables were essential to the genre. There was a great deal of gentle romantic irony in doo-wop. Singers and listeners were at peace with the slightness and unoriginality of the lyrics as propositions. But their sounds—that was not a matter for irony. Mark Halliday's tribute to this music makes just this point.

> "Little Star" by the Elegants (1958)
> is one of those perfect early rock/pop songs
> that radiate confidence in a few
> orderly truths. Above all,
> if you have the right girl as your girlfriend—
> you know, the one who walks that way
> and tosses her hair, the one who dances
> just a little between cheers at the football game—
> if you've got her, you're golden,
> there's nothing else you could wish for.
> Oh, God, do you remember the golden liquidity
> of the lead singer's voice
> as he expresses this shapely truth—
> he could get it across without needing to rely
> on the mere meanings of words—
> he could do everything with golden syllables!

That exhilaration derived only partly from the pleasure of the made song; it was also the thrill of contemporaneity. The music industry recognized this appeal and in 1957 supported even younger groups, like Frankie Lymon and the Teenagers and Little Anthony and the Imperials, to target early-teen listeners. One remembers the plangent but impersonal line from the Students' "I'm So Young" (1958): "I'm so young, can't marry no one"—that eagerness to enter established social structures. The representation of innocence imagined as biological youth was the objective of doo-wop. Tin Pan Alley had already constructed sophistication. In doo-wop those falsettos and tenors led, and the baritones were in the back: big, deep, dumb accompaniment. The arrangements were meant to empower the very young: the leaders were not the biggest, strongest, or toughest. Style commanded power: small dandies—black, Mexican-American, or white—had the highest prestige; they represented, in an allegory everyone understood, the authority of the very young in opposition to an older generation.

In those pre-Elvis days one knew every syllable, but didn't care much about the identity implied by lyrics. The songs seemed almost anonymous, like renaissance lyrics. They were all made things, but scores for the body in a period style. Halliday is right to suggest that the individual doo-wop singers deserve more attention than they received.

> Who was he?
> Can anybody tell me the name
> Of the lead singer for the Elegants?
> In view of that grand confidence
> it would seem a name worth preserving.

The Platters, the Flamingos, Frankie Lymon, et al., were only minor celebrities by today's measure; historians of doo-wop say that then "songs were more important than artists."[27] Doo-wop solicited adulation for collectives rather than individuals. Those starless radio days pretty nearly ended in 1956 with Elvis's appearance on the *Ed Sullivan Show*. Susan Stewart writes of the particularity of voice in poetry: "The voice, with the eyes, holds within itself the life of the self—it cannot be another's."[28] But doo-wop voices are markedly generic: they sound bodies more than identities. This range of the art of song reaches toward universality.

There is a music in poetry that derives from the rhythms of speech, and it is governed by a sense of character and presence, even experience. It establishes or fortifies the illusion of an actual person speaking lines. But doo-wop was different. It had speaking segments in which a male voice uttered earnest, naive sentimentalities, as though directly but very formally to his sweetheart. These spoken bits were particularly important because they staged a direct address that was constantly invoked by references to "you." "You"—who? Simply, the teenage beloved. But as Allen Grossman says, that beloved is at the core of lyric poetry: she or he stands for an ideal of desire fulfilled in an allegory present in all lyric. Doo-wop artists staged an address to this ideal constantly. Its ubiquity and indeterminacy must derive from an understanding of desire's vagueness and promiscuity. Those suited singers on stage pointing in unison at a "you" in the audience were helping everyone to pretend that teenage desires are truly restricted to particular individuals; whereas no one knows better than teenagers that desire moves on with devastating alacrity. "I've been longing for you all my life. . . ." The music that interests me here is not strongly speech-based, more an end in itself. In the early 1950s young audiences for this popular poetry learned to love a lyricism that came from the sonorities of human voices working collaboratively, unrestrained by common notions of language as functional or even meaningful. I might have learned the appeal of vowel music from ancient Greek poems, had I the sense to study Greek. Instead I learned, as so many did, from Art Laboe and Johnny Otis that the body's sounds are the real thing. Those who came of age musically after Bob Dylan have had good reason to take more seriously the role of thematic statement in poetry. Dylan hated doo-wop: "I love you and you love me / ooka, dooka, dicka-dee." He re-established the primacy of semantics and social reference in popular poetry. I take doo-wop as an instance of poetry willing to give almost everything to sound. That seems a silly hedonism to Dylan, but the importance of that music goes very deep.

›››‹‹‹

Valéry starts at the root of poetics in "Poetry and Abstract Thought" (1939), with the distinction between verse and ordinary speech, an instrument of practical communication.[29] "*I ask you for a light. You give me a light*: you have understood me" (*AP*, 64).

Those words serve their speaker's purpose, and then disappear. Ordinary language is ephemeral. But verse is a "*language within a language*" (*AP*, 64). Words do not always disappear once their practical purpose has been served.

> The strange thing: the sound and as it were the features of your little sentence come back to me, echo within me, as though they were pleased to be there; I, too, like to hear myself repeat this little phrase, which has almost lost its meaning, which has stopped being of use, and which can yet go on living, though with quite another life. It has acquired a value; and has acquired it *at the expense of its finite significance*. It has created the need to be heard again. . . . Here we are on the very threshold of the poetic state. (*AP* 64; emphasis and ellipsis in original)

Valéry's request for a match is a conspicuously uncontroversial bit of practical speech. He would have had a clear sense in 1939 of more controversial public requests. Keep it simple, for the sake of theory: a match. The practical uses of language, which he calls speech (though the written language is relevant here), are determined in economic, political, and social contexts. His example is restrictively social. Politics and economics are fenced out, but they too figure large in the semantics of communication. His point is that poetry begins exactly in a conflict between semantics and sound, between social utility and bodily pleasure. As the power of sound grows, when some words trigger a desire for repetition, the practical sense of a statement, or a word, recedes. The words of poems do not disappear, like burnt matches. They return as echoes that close distance, illusions of presence. That, the sensuality of sound, is the origin of poetry: it begins in music. And pleasure. Not in loss, as Heidegger and Grossman claim: the sounds come back.

Valéry pursues his logic to a deeper distinction between noise and sound. A noise, he says, "merely rouses in us some isolated event—a dog, a door, a motor car—a sound evokes, of itself, the musical universe" (*AP*, 67). That universe, "the beginning of a world," is within the auditor, but the repeated sounds of words evoke it. Ideas, propositions, beliefs, opinions, intuitions, visions are all irrelevant. Sounds, and only sounds, do the job. What especially concerns him is that the overlap of the arts does not leave musicians and poets comparably equipped.

> I will confine myself to saying that the contrast between noise and sound is the contrast between pure and impure, order and disorder; that this differentiation between pure sensations and others has permitted the constitution of music; that it has been possible to control, unify, and codify this constitution, thanks to the intervention of physical science, which knows how to adjust measure to sensation so as to obtain the important result of teaching us to produce this sonorous sensation consistently, and in a continuous and identical fashion, by instruments that are, in reality, *measuring instruments*. The musician is thus in possession of a perfect system of well-defined means which exactly match sensations with acts. (*AP*, 66–67)

Poets should be so lucky. They instead labor in a medium that is inherently compromised by its mixed nature:

> The poetic universe is not created so powerfully or so easily. It exists, but the poet is deprived of the immense advantages possessed by the musician. He does not have before him, ready for the uses of beauty, a body of resources expressly made for his art. He has to borrow *language*—the voice of the public, that collection of traditional and irrational terms and rules, oddly created and transformed, oddly codified, and very variedly understood and pronounced. Here there is no physicist who has determined the relations between these elements; no tuning forks, no metronomes, no inventors of scales or theoreticians of harmony. Rather, on the contrary, the phonetic and semantic fluctuations of vocabulary. Nothing pure; but a mixture of completely incoherent auditive and psychic stimuli. Each word is an instantaneous coupling of a *sound* and a *sense* that have no connection with each other. Each sentence is an act so complex that I doubt whether anyone has yet been able to provide a tolerable definition of it. (*AP*, 67–68; emphasis in original)

The musical, or poetic, universe, is Mercer's "meadow in the mist": an expansive elsewhere of desire satisfied—for order and purity. One can imagine birdsong as evidence of its natural existence. Poetry, on this view, is essentially utopian. This is no theory of satire, or of any realism. The poems that pursue this ideal aim to enchant, by repetition and sonority. Their music is meant to be magical, to make of one thing something apparently different in kind, transforming perception by means of charm. Valéry was James Merrill's master. The poet's handicap is that his medium is contrary to the aim of art: words are anything but universal and permanent, or orderly and pure. Valéry's invocation of multiple hypothetical "universes" is a dated but revealing feature of his thinking. One speaks now instead of systems, interlocking and mutually constituting in time, not separate orders. Valéry sought alternative orders, not wiggle room within the given. The dominant social, economic, political, and linguistic regimes produce orders that the novel describes and engages, but poetry takes exception to all that. "Every time words show a *certain deviation* from the most direct, that is, the most *insensible* expression of thought, . . . we conceive more or less precisely the possibility of enlarging this exceptional domain" (*AP*, 184–85). The linguistic density of poetic expression is necessary to its project, which is neither social improvement nor accommodation; this art implies withdrawal rather than engagement. It may be that, as Valéry suggests, the meaning of sonority is withdrawal from social interaction; not that sonorous poetry is necessarily antisocial, but that the social dimension of speech is needed to invigorate sonorous poetry, as Mercer seems to have realized.

Valéry understood that the impurity of usage undermines the coherence expected of rational analysis and explanation. Words move through a language community in surprising, unpredictable ways. A poet must trade in the public currency, as Valéry recognized, rather than construct a private language. But the coherence of an idiom is exactly what obstructs poetry, in his account. A poet should seek out incoherence and deviations from linguistic expectations. Some poets, like Frost and Hass, instead seek coherence in the speech of a class and region; they are realists whose art inevitably confirms the coherence and authority of a social class. They tie their own hands, in Valéry's view. For him, the orders of speech provide resources, but so do books ("traditional . . . terms"); a poet does the work of an engineer to assemble a poem. Mercer begins "Skylark" in the register of very polite social discourse (2–3), and he returns to this at the end (18–21). Like Cole Porter, Ira Gershwin, and other Tin Pan Alley poets, his style was sophisticated and urbane. But the spoken idioms of no one language community can account for the full range of his resources. He charmed by beginning and ending with sophisticated speech; in between he cobbled biblical and worn romantic diction.

›››‹‹‹

I want now to analyze an antithetical musical form: the sestina. Doo-wop's exploitation of the sounds of lyrics, rather than their sense, is extreme by Mercer's measure. The sestina is a form at the opposite end of a sound-sense continuum in that it facilitates the domination of sense. This stanzaic form is particularly revealing, not because of its rigorous prescriptive scheme, but because it derives from exact reiteration of six terminal words, rather than from rhyme. The sestina reveals a lot about rhyme exactly because rhyme is excluded from it. Rhyme is a technique of sound; sense is apparently secondary to it. One measures how far in terms of sense one rhyme comes from its antecedent.[30] Sense is not irrelevant to rhyme but, when a stanza comes together strikingly, with a sense of surprise and inevitability, sense seems to be brought along by chimes of sound. The measurement I mentioned is one of intellectual progress. Can a statement of meaning go far if it is led by sonic fits, or rhyme?

The music of a sestina is thematically overdetermining. The key signs are frozen semantically. Rhymes produce change; a sestina's terminal words must stay the same (except for homophones), though their syntactic contexts can change. The form expresses a fierce will to retain one meaning within an art that characteristically modifies meaning. This is the least musical, the most prosaic, stanzaic form, because it allows so little to the mutability of sense. David Ferry's wonderful sestina, "The Guest Ellen at the Supper for Street People" (1993), is an instructive example.

> The unclean spirits cry out in the body
> or mind of the guest Ellen in a loud voice
> torment me not; and in the fury of her unclean
> hands beating the air in some kind of unending torment—
> nobody witnessing could possibly know the event
> that cast upon her the spell of this enchantment.
>
> Almost all the guests are under some kind of enchantment:
> of being poor day after day in the same body;
> of being witness still to some obscene event;
> of listening all the time to somebody's voice
> whispering in the ear things divine or unclean,
> in the quotidian of unending torment.
>
> One has to keep thinking there was some source of torment;
> something that happened someplace else, unclean.
> One has to keep talking in a reasonable voice
> about things done, say, by a father's body
> to or upon the body of Ellen, in enchantment
> helpless, still by the unforgotten event
>
> enchanted, still in the old forgotten event
> a prisoner of love, filthy Ellen in her torment,
> guest Ellen in the dining hall in her body,
> hands beating the air in her enchantment,
> sitting alone, gabbling in her garbled voice
> the narrative of the spirits of the unclean.
>
> She is wholly the possessed one of the unclean.
> Maybe the spirits came from the river. The enchantment
> entered her, maybe, in the Northeast Kingdom. The torment,
> a thing of the waters, gratuitous event,
> came up out of the waters and entered her body
> and lived in her in torment and cried out in her voice.
>
> It speaks itself over and over again in her voice,
> cursing maybe or not a familiar obscene event
> or only the pure event of original enchantment

from the birth of the river waters, the pure unclean
rising from the source of things, in a figure of torment
seeking out Ellen, finding its home in her poor body.

Her body witness is, so also is her voice,
of torment coming from unknown event;
unclean is the nature and name of the enchantment.[31]

A sestina is a form of obvious excess: six key words used seven times in a one-page poem. Anthony Hecht refers to "the mood of desolation seemingly imposed by the rigid monotony of terminal repetition"; the emotional character of the form is lugubrious and obsessive.[32] He praises Sidney and Merrill for escaping that profile, but Ferry prefers not to elude those qualities, nor the obvious excesses of the form. Three of the six words—"unclean," "torment," and "event"—are repeated in excess of what the form requires, and Ferry repeats two other words—"obscene" and "witness"—to enhance the insistence of the poem. Though their lack of shelter defines them, excess of structure and measurement is the true métier of the homeless.

The music of the poem is obsessive and tormenting. It expresses a desire to know Ellen's mind, so I had thought of that music (wrongly) as more Ellen's than the speaker's; his voice is encumbered by prosaic intellectual discourse. Her utterances are musical in the sense that, unlike speech, they are not addressed to listeners. Ferry observes her; she does not address him. He addresses a reader, but she speaks, as a musician plays, to the air. His voice moves through conventional intellectual dyads, like body and mind (1–2), divine or unclean (11). He invokes the modifiers that routinely afflict intellectual discourse: "some kind of" (4, 7), "possibly" (5), "Almost all" (7), "wholly" (25), "maybe" (26, 27, 32). Some of his terms, like "quotidian" (12), are just markers of his own intellectual habits and social class. He retains, even in the mythographic fifth stanza, the commitments of secular, analytic prose. From his point of view, the music of the sestina is compelling but mad too. And of course Ellen actually has no voice in the poem; the speaker imputes qualities to her voice—and from a distance that indicates that her voice is incomprehensible to him. I realize now that the recirculated terminal words are not hers at all but entirely his: he is trying to conjure with this form an intellectual understanding that can't be had. The speaker calls out repeatedly for an understanding that fails him. He is merely an observer; he cannot explain. The poem begins very abstractly with a generalization that is modified dramatically as the first line develops into the second. What seems like a powerfully general claim about spirit and body comes to be more specifically about one homeless woman. Yet Ellen is made in the second stanza to stand for homeless or just poor people generally. The pressure toward general explanation is great and persistent, though it leads to an impasse. In the end the first line is about all one can say, and it does seem to pertain generally.

The limits of rational analysis are the real issue. In the third stanza, after the speaker has formulated an eloquent account of the socioeconomic significance of homelessness, the predication indicates his strain to fit Ellen's life to rational or historical explanation. He is compelled to seek a historical event as the cause of her adversity. Incest is the "reasonable"—that is, now common—hypothesis. But the implication of this strained predication is that all such reasonable discourse has no firm purchase on the turkey-talk of Ellen, her gabbling, garbled voice. The myth of the animate waters may be just as true as the proposed psychohistorical analysis of her childhood.

Although the sestina is one stanzaic form among an array of forms available to poets, it actually imposes exceptional constraints on poetic invention. Hecht observes that "something about those compulsory repetitions seems to prohibit the possibility of a sestina developing in the way other kinds of poems do. A familiar lyric freedom is curtailed, . . . narrative development, above all, is difficult to accommodate. The resources of the sestina seem astonishingly circumscribed."[33] Ferry reveals that the sestina is essentially a form of rhythm, of timed reiteration, sameness. The words do not change; the music achieves no transformation. It cannot get anywhere. When he speaks of enchantment, he identifies the objective of strongly rhythmic music. Rhythm often subjugates its auditors, sets them to reiteration by enchanting their bodies, as Yeats understood:

> The purpose of rhythm, it has always seemed to me, is to prolong the moment of contemplation, the moment when we are both asleep and awake, which is the one moment of creation, by hushing us with an alluring monotony, while it holds us waking by variety, to keep us in that state of perhaps real trance, in which the mind liberated from the pressure of the will is unfolded in symbols.[34]

Ferry expresses mistrust and disapproval of the music of the sestina. The reiterative patterns of the terminal words are like webs covering Ellen's mind. The two governing key terms are "body" and "event." Ellen's body is the site of her torment, and as soon as the word appears its customary antonym, "mind," is adduced as an equivalent instead; her body and mind are subjugated. She is locked in the music of the sestina. The term "event" stands for the elusive cause of her subjugation; at the end of the poem it remains unknown because her body and its voice are unreachable by analysis. The sestina is a form of chant—the same terms over and over—and, as the last line suggests, an unclean enchantment, because it only recirculates terms without advance. One must ask, with Ferry, whether music can develop analysis or thought.

The exceptionality of the sestina, as a form of repetition, has a special importance: are its limits peculiar to this stanza, or binding on lyric poetry generally? Repetition itself has particular bearing on the meaning ascribed to poetry. Poetry's musicality is thought to be a sign of transcendence: the instrumentality of speech is left behind by the musical passages of poetry, as though poetry could deliver one from the routine constraints of ordinary existence. Vladimir Jankélévitch argues that this traditional view of music is false, because the pleasures of music are temporary. Music has no lasting effect, he argues; claims for its transformative power are grandiose.[35] The elaborate prosodic structures of poetry actually mark boundaries: the symmetries of poetic sonority prevail within the marked lines; but ordinary speech is outside those boundaries. This understanding of prosodic form is unexceptional. The further point, however, is that musical form is known by repetition; the formal elements of music are by their nature repeatable, as are the couplets, tercets, quatrains, and sonnets of verse. The musical language of poetry is available for repetition, as ordinary discourse is not, because music lodges itself in the memory. That is the special power of formal language. It may not alter language permanently, and one may not be permanently transformed by a poem's music; Jankélévitch has a point. But one repeats poems, and their accessibility to reiteration is a deliverance—temporary—from ordinary flux. "Poetry can be recognized by this property," Valéry observes, "that it tends to get itself reproduced in its own form: it stimulates us to reconstruct it identically" (*AP*, 72). The sestina and the refrain are the stanzaic forms that speak directly to this essential feature of musical language.

Ferry's sestina is written with complete understanding of this dynamic. His poem presents a case for the notion that repetition is no delivery at all. How much comfort, he asks, is to be had from an art that celebrates return, repetition? One returns because one seeks something clarifying, some cause that explains the present, or just because one cannot get anywhere. A sestina offers no repose, only one relapse after another. From avant-gardists one heard that conventional prosodies offered illusory repose. Ferry's point is rather that the core element of musicality, repetition, is itself a cause of torment. Valéry's recognition that repetition is at the heart of music and poetry helps one to see that Ferry's critique goes a long way. The celebrated freedom that poetry and music have from the constraints of rationality brings a great deal of frustration and pain to those who truly live in this art. "Poems make nothing happen," Auden said. It may be that poetry just gets nowhere, that it is no art of consolation.

›››‹‹‹

Poe claimed that long poems are comprised of short segments of poetry within a prose matrix, that one feels the difference between poetry and prose within a long poem. This is a premise of my sense that the musicality of poetry is differential rather than absolute. An ear measures differences among sounds and idioms, and between levels of style. An ability to generate such differences surprisingly, meaningfully, and economically is one source of poetic power. Robert Pinsky's distinction has been his consistent ability to write imaginatively in the audible idioms of an American English whose greatest currency is among middle-class educated liberals; these are the people who have the readiest access to the syntax and diction of expository prose. But they have a distinctive investment in the heterogeneity of the American republic. The absorptive capacity of American English—as of the nation—is the just pride of the educated class. "Our greatest achievements," Pinsky has said, ". . . are as mixed, syncretic and eclectic as our inventions in food or clothing."[36] The speech of this language community often aspires not only to such inclusiveness but also to the authority of the printed word—prose. Pinsky's art is always courageously close to the language that, by definition, is not poetry. His detractors say just that, that he writes not poetry but prose. "Pinsky's poems," Marjorie Perloff has said, "are barely poems at all."[37] What possible relevance, one wonders, does musicality have to so prosaic a style of poetry? Eliot said that "no poet can write a poem of amplitude unless he is a master of the prosaic"—which is Poe's claim again.[38] Here are the first lines of Pinsky's long "Poem with Refrains":

> The opening scene. The yellow, coal-fed fog
> Uncurling over the tainted city river,
> A young girl rowing and her anxious father
> Scavenging for corpses. Funeral meats. The clever
> Abandoned orphan. The great athletic killer
> Sulking in his tent. As though all stories began
> With someone dying.
>   When her mother died,
> My mother refused to attend the funeral—
> In fact, she sulked in her tent all through the year
> Of the old lady's dying. I don't know why:

She said, because she loved her mother so much
She couldn't bear to see the way the doctors,
Or her father, or—someone—was letting her mother die.
"Follow your saint, follow with accents sweet;
Haste you, sad notes, fall at her flying feet."

She fogs things up, she scavenges the taint.
Possibly that's the reason I write these poems.

But they did speak: on the phone. Wept and argued,
So fiercely one or the other often cut off
A sentence by hanging up in rage—like lovers,
But all that year she never saw her face.

They lived on the same block, four doors apart.
"Absence my presence is; strangeness my grace;
With them that walk against me is my sun."[39]

This poem includes four anecdotes about his mother (7–21, 24–54, 58–64, and 68–79); they are not joined to one another by any explanation, but each is coherent and continuous in itself. This is the first and most engaging one. It reveals a conflicted, tormented, complicated person, whom the poet regards as enigmatic but somehow heroically grand. Poe's question is relevant: is this poetry or the prose connective tissue of a long poem? The conflicts of her character bear no special relation to the form of the poem's language; its serviceable blank verse is wholly adequate to the task of narrating this episode in her life. The fact that the poem includes three more anecdotes about her indicates that this one episode of her life is not to be understood as uniquely revealing. The poet uses the patient, fluent idioms of prose to tell his mother's story. The writing signals a move to the discourse of poetry in the gap between blank verse and the archaic cited verses of the refrains. The seams of the poem are entirely exposed. Pinsky has stitched together anecdotes, admissions, and verse citations from the seventeenth and nineteenth centuries.

The mastery of diverse rhythms, idioms, and voices provides great pleasure. There are moments of quick shift, stylistic transits, throughout the poem (not only at the refrains): two registers of style are vying with each other. The first is allusive, another voice, from texts more than from authors; the second is Pinsky's own voice, that of educated speech set to conventional measure. The first paragraph is comprised of enigmatic sentence fragments stretched across the blank verse so as to put full stops in the midst of four of these seven lines. The first two "sentences" allude to the opening of *Our Mutual Friend*, then *Hamlet*, then the *Iliad*. This first register is combinatory, but without a strong implication of the principle guiding the combination of allusions: the literary aperçu (6–7) closing the paragraph does not explain the pertinence of *those* three tales of mortality, as distinguished from all elegies, which begin with someone dying. At the outset there is something specifically unexplained about the first voice. The second register begins with the self-assured observation of a professional interpreter, and it is the dominant style of the poem (6–21, above). Pinsky artfully composes in the idioms of contemporary intellectual discourse without embarrassment or dissimulation. His writing resolves the question as to whether a contemporary American intellectual sensibility is a poetic resource or liability. The two registers collide; the music of the books against the sounds of speech. They come into mutual relationship in line 15, when the figures of lines 2 and 4 provide a nonidiomatic way of saying that his mother looks for trouble, and then that he does too in his art. But this melding of the registers is not really productive for the poem; he has to change the subject in order to continue (17). The first register becomes prominent in the refrains that give the poem its oddly impersonal title. They are opaque insofar as they relate only obliquely to the lucid narratives he tells.

The refrains are musical articulations of the poet's inability to understand his mother's motives sympathetically, and moreover to write an elegy planned for his mother. The essential feature of a refrain is that it is repeated. None of these "refrains" is repeated, not in his source poems, not in his. A refrain, Debra Fried shows, is like an epitaph, a voice from the other side that repeats and repeats in the ear.[40] Any of his six citations might be a gorgeous refrain and give his mother's voice a fixed site (or grave), but Pinsky's "Poem with Refrains" is a poem without refrains. His citations are instead calls to a music elsewhere. They sound from another country and from other centuries; theirs is the language of canonical English poetry, and it is a foreign tongue.[41] This poem suggests that the effort to transform recognizable contemporary speech into poetry calls forth a countervailing poetic, that the presence of speech provokes a need for recognizable song. Why that provocation? Because educated speech is lucid; it expresses only what the educated understand, and that is not enough. The range of thought, feeling, and experience that is obscure to the educated is where the interest of poetry lies. This poem is clever, even funny (58–64), and humane, but its depth lies in what is not well understood—in the mystery of his mother's character. Pope urged poets to write but what they understand, and then Arnold called him a "classic of our prose." The easeful fluency of the verse—eighty-five lines of it—summons an offsetting brevity of refrains. Fluency and anecdotes are problematic in lyric: they are the stuff of prose. The closing of paragraphs with musical citations—especially of fluent prosaic verse paragraphs—invokes the idea of another discourse that moves beyond the questions that rational inquiry raises—why does his mother withdraw from her loved ones?—without resolving them. The wisdom of Poe's claim is not just that readers of long poems expect variety of intensity, but that the aspiration of poems—and of music—to a transcendent discourse is something that is not to be sustained at length. There is doubleness at the heart of poetry because it distinguishes itself from prose, and musicality is one recognizable sign of that difference.

Pinsky's refrains are *trouvailles*: musical goodies found in old books. They challenge a critic to say how they alter or complete the sense of the lines Pinsky wrote, but I want instead to consider the relation of musicality to discovery. The term "musicality" summons thought first of scansion and then of alliteration. The arrangement of stresses is the dominant musical resource, but it is only one: metrical poets move the rhythms of speech into more or less conformity with conventional verse patterns. And the ore of alliteration goes back to the earliest Anglo-Saxon verse: this is an essential, now permanent, resource of poetry in English. But the music that is discovered by an ear, apparently happened upon by a poet—certainly so by an unsuspecting reader—this is what means most to the art, and best justifies free verse. That justification rests first on the value of discovery, and then of imitation, for the music comes from somewhere. Consider these lines near the opening of Basil Bunting's *Briggflatts*:

A mason times his mallet
to a lark's twitter,
listening while the marble rests,
lays his rule
at a letter's edge,
fingertips checking,
till the stone spells a name
naming none,
a man abolished.
Painful lark, labouring to rise!
The solemn mallet says:
In the grave's slot
he lies. We rot.[42]

That Bunting wishes to link his words by the ancient technology of alliteration is plain: mason, mallet, marble; and the liquid l's run through all but two of these lines (19 and 21). The mason begins with an iambic beat—through three feet of line 14—but the birdsong resists that beat in the next line. An iambic beat reasserts itself in line 16, after a headless start, but the innovation comes in the next one: LAYS his RULE. That little unit of three syllables resurfaces repeatedly in this strophe ("letter's edge" [18], "naming none" [21], and "Painful lark" [23]) as a kind of suggestion of some natural unit of structure. But after all the various play of stress through this strophe, it will come to rest in final iambs (26). That comes as a discovery. Bunting's conformity is not to a metrical norm, but to the beat of a mason's arm. The mason, like a poet, labors at memory's monument, tracking, as Mercer did, a little bird that can't be seen.

The doubleness of literary kinds—the way the idea of poetry entails that of prose—is obvious, almost allegorical in Pinsky's poem. Musicality often produces doubleness at a deeper level (before the idea of a kind arises), one that inheres more in the words and lines of a poem. Here is a recent poem by Jim Powell (once a student of Pinsky):

FIRST LIGHT

Graying chest hair emerging from his apron-top in tufts
dusted with a snow of flour
above the swelling rondure of his oven belly,
sleeves rolled, arms folded, at ease on the porch steps
outside the back door of the bakery

in the lively air of the early hour taking a break
while the bread cools on racks inside
and a breeze picks up off the bay: the mist lifts
and the swarming dust of starlight reappears,
the constellations that were given names

beside the hive-domed ovens of Chaldea and of Ur—
near first light, thick arms cradling rolls
and crusty loaves, a gift for late-returning revelers,
for the derelict who washes in the creek
under the bridge his daily bread at daybreak.

The figures of the poem appeal strongly to the eye, and to the fingertips too. The scene is palpable. But there is as well a strong sense of time, especially in the second and third stanzas, and that is an abstract dimension of the poem. The first lines are devoted to the baker's time: his aging body, and his break from timed labors. That much worldliness is implicit in stanza 1. The second stanza focuses instead on the landscape's changes in the times of a natural day; this is the slow pacific time that plausibly evokes the archaic origins of the constellations. The eleventh line changes the poem entirely with exotic proper nouns. The last stanza suggests that bread-baking in California is indistinguishable from that of ancient Babylon. The making of bread is at the base of an archaic economy. The revelers (13) and the derelict (14) come to their bread from different social classes, but from the same (dactylic!) region of the language (3); they evoke the experience of medieval French and Latin. The symmetrical last words of the poem, "daily bread at daybreak," put biblical and Anglo-Saxon idioms side by side. The claim implied is that feeding people, all people, is a universal act that transcends economic systems and social structures. The making and taking of bread underlies survival and also celebration. The trade in consumption is extraneous to the viewpoint of the poem. The politics implicit here are California digger: labor with nature; free distribution.

How does the poem render a political position that gets virtually no play in current political discourse? Not by statement. Powell makes no direct statement in the poem, which is comprised of one long quasi-sentence with no main predicate. Figures make his viewpoint attractive, comprehensible. It is not extraordinary for figures to make a political statement. But it is the music of his lines that gives the poem credibility and authority; the lines get their sanction not from logic or ideas but from compelling sounds. The sonic shape of the poem is masterful, well beyond what I can analyze or explain here. And that control of the bodily experience of language gives a convincing sense that he is right about the archaic orders of production and consumption. Moreover the powerfully shaped sounds suggest that chaos or disorder of any kind is irrelevant to this anarchist expression. That—the severing of anarchism from the threatening specter of disorder—is one more neat rhetorical feat. It doesn't follow logically that music validates a political claim, but in fact sonic resources do just that. Music warrants belief not only in particular claims, but more importantly in the existence of an authority other than, even superior to, reasonable explanation. The musicality of poetry is a site where rhetoric and religion often meet.

The absence of syntax, of a statement directed toward a recognized point, is crucial to the poem. The words, phrases, and clauses gather into units of sound as much as sense. The first stanza displays a pattern of linked sounds that holds lines together: it begins with "top" and "tufts," then reaches over to link "tufts" with "dusted." In the third line "above" and "swelling" are linked to "oven" and "belly," then "sleeves rolled" to "folded" and "ease." "Back" and "bakery" complete the web of echoes that recalls Anglo-Saxon alliterative linkages. The technology of the first stanza allows Powell to describe his character, an unnamed baker, in a relaxed, apparently undirected fashion; yet the lines cohere and take sound-shapes without strict adherence to a metrical norm (or so I once plausibly thought, when its variety led me to think of it as free verse).

The second stanza is on another level entirely. Just let that ninth line pass over the tongue, and Powell's achievement can be felt. I am happy to think about the baking of bread, but the truth is that the powerful substance of this memorable stanza has almost nothing to do with semantics. The dramatic shape of the stanza derives utterly from its sounds. Its resolution, in line 10, is a perfectly regular line of spoken (or prosaic) blank verse, following the most conventionally eloquent line of lyrical flight in the poem; this is the principle of differential music at work. Before that tenth line can sound like a resolution of a drama, there must be a struggle for sonic dominance or order in the lines that precede it. In terms of stress, the contest is between anapests and iambs, which sounds like a pygmy war, as of punctuation marks, but in the reading of the poem the contest is rich. Listen to the sixth line:

x x /	x /	x x /	x /	x /	x x /
In the live	ly air	of the ear	ly ho	ur tak	ing a break

The alternation of these two feet—anapests and iambs—makes for one level of contest, but there is also a contrast between the long liquid syllables of the first four feet and the short, stopped last two feet of the line. These two contrasted segments of the line are coherent in themselves: "early" obviously echoes "lively," as "hour" does "air." "Taking" and "break" nearly rhyme. And there are other, overlapping echoes that reinforce the structure. The rhythm of the line is easy to hear at the level of speech: uttered, it's felt. But the structure is subtle in that the arrangement of metrical feet does not coincide with word boundaries. The semantic pace of the words does not coincide with the prosodic rhythm. In the spoken line, whose pace attends to semantics, there is a caesura in the middle of the penultimate foot: that is where the line splits in two, just before "taking." This tension between semantics and prosody is evidence of an inconspicuous counterpoint—a second contest—in a line that is obviously lyrical.

Powell's use of two metrical norms (iambic and anapestic) produces the effect Pound intended when in 1912 he urged poets to compose in the sequence not of the metronome but of the musical phrase. There is regularity and difference in Powell's rhythm, and this pace suggests that the poet is not imposing order but responding to something distinctive. Yeats said,

> We would cast out of serious poetry those energetic rhythms, as of a man running, which are the invention of the will with its eyes always on something to be done or undone; and we would seek out those wavering, meditative, organic rhythms, which are the embodiment of the imagination, that neither desires nor hates, because it has done with time, and only wishes to gaze upon some reality; some beauty.[43]

The "musical phrase" is a sign of attentiveness to something, "some reality," and in Yeats's view a refusal of utility. There is a sense of deference and of accuracy implied by the unpredictable beat.

Counterpoint between two metrical schemes was a source of pleasure in Latin poetry, according to Eliot; those audiences would have heard prosodic contest but not been able to describe it.[44] The purpose of Powell's intense attention to the sound structure of the line (and of the poem)? Mere pleasure. The imitative principle recommended by Pope ("the sound must seem an echo to the sense" accounts well for only three syllables in this exceptional stanza: "the mist lifts" (8). On a first read, "mist" seems to take stress, after the obviously unstressed definite article. But the next syllable, "lifts," does raise the stress above the level of "mist." What seemed an iamb develops into an anapest, as the stress level, like a mist, rises further than expected. The phrase "taking a break" (6) breaks the rhythm of the preceding feet in that line, but the shift is from a languorous, flowing rhythm to a quick, clipped one—just the contrary of what might be expected of a formal imitation of leisure. The music of the stanza is not instrumentalized by its thematic sense. Its doubling sounds are their own justification. The music has consequences, but not purposes.

The music I hear in this poem hews closely to speech; Powell has found extraordinary richness of rhythm and sonority in words that feel welcome on the tongue. One senses on first reading that this poem has to be read aloud. I have analyzed the rhythm in terms of two familiar feet—iambs and anapests—because they register themselves on my ears, as do trochees, spondees, and dactyls. There are, however, other metrical feet, as I know from correspondence with Powell, but these feet are unfamiliar to me and to most contemporary readers, so they register as metrically obscure or as free verse. Line 7 is a good example. The first four syllables are hard to reconcile to an iambic or anapestic norm: the first two are unstressed and the next two are stressed; and the eighth line begins similarly. The repetition of what seems a metrical irregularity calls the pattern out to the ear, and a reader like me hears a musical phrase. What I do not hear is exactly what Powell intends: an Ionic (xx//) substitution for the first two iambs in each line. To an ear trained by Greek poetry, this substitution is recognizable and entirely legitimate. But to one trained by English poetry, it is less audible as a substitution. Powell writes with a deep sense of Greek, Latin, and English prosody; the metrical rules and precedents that shape his practice are far more elaborate than a contemporary reader is likely to recognize. The sound-shape of a phrase, a line, or a stanza may seem anomalous when it is in fact deeply traditional. (His stanza here is unknown in English: a heptameter, a tetrameter, a hexameter, and two pentameters.) To whom do poets write? This one addresses the illustrious, impractical dead; there are moments when the living only overhear.

This prosodic difficulty brings into focus a special feature of poetic artifice: the musicality of poetry shows that the boundary between natural speech and poetic convention wavers in time. All that I hear in Powell's poem comes from my ear for speech rhythms, for the familiar metrics of English poetry, and the feel of syllables in my mouth and throat; the music he composed with ancient Greek and Latin templates in mind is almost silent to me. The rhythms of speech are audible in ordinary experience, and the feel of syllables in the mouth is common, but these other sonic structures come from conventions unknown by most contemporary readers. I am not Powell's ideal reader; maybe you aren't either. But that is not fatal to the poem, or even to its music. The conventional structures of an unknown system do make themselves felt to some degree; one hears some music in very foreign poetry. Leibniz said that music is "an unconscious exercise in arithmetic in which the mind does not know it is counting."[45] Some of the musicality of poetry is just felt as sound, like doo-wop; some is recognized. I heard compelling music in Powell's poem well before I understood its structure, let alone its source. What is that music? Where is it coming from? A listener who can pose the first but cannot answer the second question may be an acute reader of poetry. The critic Alvaro de Campos, one of Fernando Pessoa's heteronyms, says, "Poetry is that form of prose in which rhythm is artificial."[46] Rhythm in language, he means, is extensive and usually natural. Much of the music we hear in poems and some we don't is constructed—in no sense inevitable—but it seems natural. Poets want always to find a basis for their art that is wider and firmer than that of specialized knowledge. We like to notice that the dominant structures of poetic sound systems—that of blank verse, say—inhere in the language itself. Some artifice, that is, conforms to natural language and thereby seems inevitable, though it is not. Artifice and the medium itself produce that sense of sounds addressed to bodies.

›››‹‹‹

But then there is the other thing: a spectacle of artifice. Our critical language is deeply wed to the principle of organic form, to formal structures whose roots are in the sounds of syllables, words, and phrases—deep form, as in Bunting and Powell. What are the terms for appreciating inorganic form—I mean here not mere conformity to externally imposed formal structures, like the termini of a sestina, but a musicality that is not in the text itself? Here I am circling back to Tin Pan Alley, where the words and the melodies were generated separately.

Thylias Moss's "Glory" seems on the page far from song, and instead close to the essay: the strophes begin in ways that are familiar to readers of analytical expository prose (1–2, 13–14, 36–38, 76–78), and each coheres semantically, as paragraphs do. Like prose, it was written for the page.

> The sun does not really rise; the earth turns and leans
> into that perception as it circles a sun busy burning
> for the sake of light.
>
> That's what I'd like God to do, burn himself again
> for the sake of light. Commit to the bush instead of vacating
> when it got too hot, berries burning the hands picking them,
> picking Him, Moses suffering heat as they suffer in a Chicago
>   August,
> five hundred dropping, no rapture to sustain them, members
> of Star of Hope. There should be more hot etching of stone,
> more coal-dark hair burning to gray ash for descent
> from Sinai and ego, more wheels to take us for a hot time
> in Ezekiel's town of exile along the river Chebar.
>
> (1–12)[47]

The words gather in syntactic units and paragraphs more than in lines; the line is more a typographical than a structural unit. (Read across the line breaks and very little is lost.) When asked to read it in Chicago in 2002, to her son's accompaniment on piano, Moss quickly moved into song, evidently, to her own surprise; she recorded a similar version on CD a year later. This is the obverse of Mercer's procedure. He composed lyrics to suit a melody given him by Hoagy Carmichael. Moss's son Ansted played chord progressions, and she improvised a melody to suit a text that had already been settled. There is nothing natural or inevitable about either procedure. Yeats objected to performances of his poems that render the voice too musical. "No word of mine must ever change into a mere musical note, no singer of my words must ever cease to be a man and become an instrument."[48] He insisted that a manly spoken voice restrain the temptation to render the body too obviously musical. He too would have preferred Carmen McRae to Cassandra Wilson (presuming that not gender but disciplined conformity to a semantic code was the issue). The music of Moss's voice is imposed on the text, artificially, as Alvaro de Campos says. Wagner held that "the human voice is the practical basis of Music," and that is certainly Moss's view too.[49] The music of "Glory" derives from her body rather than from the words and lines. Her argumentative manner suggests the conventions of expository prose, the preferred genre of intellectuals. And her lightly ironic tone invokes social protocols of language use. But the performance of the poem that supplements the text with music comes from her body and expresses desire. She mixes the resources of social discourse, which Mercer and Yeats mastered, with those of body music, the line of doo-wop and Cassandra Wilson, in my genealogy.

Her performance of "Glory" makes audible a gap between the language of her poem and the aspiration of her music. In no sense does the music inhere in her words; she sets out the music as another thing, not just the realization of the words on the page. Her song expresses a longing that reaches beyond her words. The gap between the words and the song renders the hopefulness of her project. Nathaniel Mackey speaks of the way that music anticipates fulfillment; it implies a narrative reaching into a future. "Well, isn't the pathos, the ache we hear in certain music a longing for kin? Isn't that what [Anthony] Braxton means by 'vibrational affinities,' that no sound exists of itself but as a leaning towards others?"[50] There is a sense in which the physicality of music generates an ambition to represent others; musicality and representation are intertwined. Insofar as a voice can be heard as a body, it calls out to other bodies to reproduce its music. Songs summon performance. The musicality of all lyrics summons assent, not the assent of belief but that of performance. Can you hear the poet's voice? Let me represent you, it seems to say.

"Glory" is a religious poem advocating zealous commitment, a reaching beyond reasonableness. Musicality generally signifies a wish to move expression beyond the constraints of rationality; this much was clear in Ferry's sestina. There are ancient traditions connecting music and religious devotion; since the early nineteenth century, German music theory has specifically pursued the connection between listening and devotion. Carl Dahlhaus referred to "the quasi-religious function of listening, whereby proper hearing of sublime music can afford the listener a glimpse of the infinite, or of the Beyond, or at least produce an esthetic experience above mundane ideas, images, and things."[51] Dahlhaus shows that for Herder and many other German writers the religious dimension of music has everything to do with the authority of music as distinguished from lyrics, absolute (or instrumental) music "separated from words and gestures."[52] Roland Barthes has argued that listening itself, not only to music, entails a devotional model: "*To listen* is the evangelical verb par excellence: listening to the divine word is what faith amounts to, for it is by such listening that man is linked to God."[53] Moss sees the sense in which musicality expresses incompleteness or desire and awe as well. She goes beyond Mackey in recovering the religiosity of musical poetry. One knows that musicality is a pleasure in itself, but her poem suggests that the music of words is a sign of what is not satisfyingly present in words; musicality is a trope of *impossibilia*, particularly suited to devotional writing.[54]

When a poet makes so much of the performance of a text, one needs to speak of her voice or implied personhood, which is not always at issue in poetry. There is an energy in Moss's diction that comes from tension, often operative between what she says and the proximity of colloquial claims that resemble what she says. "There'll be a hot time in the old house tonight" (11); "before their time" (17). Her language is full of reference and social presence that is politely acknowledged (as these proximate phrases are) and then declined. The poem's vitality is in the range of tones that affect her explanation. She presents an engaging voice, a convincing sense of a person: humor, playful teasing, ranging imagination, and wit. There is an element of authority earned by registering the discriminations that intellectuals are trained to make, but still greater authority comes to those who inhabit the physical structure of the language. Her individual voice is so strong and willful that she can afford to tap these passing currents of usage that will not be explored. The feature of willfulness bears directly on the musicality of her performance. She moves to song at will, and then back again to speech. She chooses when to invest her words with the audible commitment of her body. This is so obviously a matter of her autonomy exactly because the music does not inhere in the language on the page. What she performs is a freedom to choose the sociality of speech or the sensuality of body. This idea of freedom is essentially one of mobility, of changing categories—poem to song; prose to poem. She performs a persona, but is her personhood involved? Her shifts of category are themselves quite general. The question is less "Who is she?" than "What can she do?" Her allusion to Irving Berlin's *Annie, Get Your Gun* (59–60) is not trivial: "I can do anything better than you."

Her performance of this poem is controversial: one may reasonably dislike this kind of performance quite strongly. Literary critics inherit some skeptical views about performance from music theory. Wagner went to a rehearsal in Paris in 1840 and was seated behind a partition from the orchestra; the music seemed to come to him, as Lydia Goehr says, "from nowhere and thus from everywhere."[55] Thereafter he tried to conceal the orchestra from view. The actual production of the music by musicians seemed distracting. Stravinsky much later spoke of a need for performers to render themselves transparent or invisible as a "moral responsibility."[56] The staging of a personality in performance can seem so deeply wrong largely because it interferes with the most general claims of poetry, the sense that the significance of a line or poem extends far beyond the context of its production. To what extent is a poem available to the generalizing or idealizing interpretations of its audience?

›››‹‹‹

At the outset of this chapter I criticized Pope's model of musicality as an aid to particular thematic utterances. I have instead read musicality, variously, as a sign of a discourse that is different from ordinary prose, or speech. The musicality that has most importance for poetry is extensive: it distinguishes kinds of discourse. Poets who seem to me importantly musical move back and forth between sonority and the sociality of speech. Musicality in these poems is a sign of a range of experience that pulls against speech and the situations of ordinary discourse among strangers. I wish that I could have said more about the pleasures of sonority that are not instrumentalized in any particular way by thematic discourse. I have in the end put music to work, as Pope did, though my account of its work is less constrained by a particular linguistic context. Those pleasures of sound keep one reading and believing in the special power of the art, the power one cannot explain without spoiling. There is a Wordsworthian or retro dimension to my argument. Language writers launched a powerful critique of speech-based poetics thirty years ago. But the critique of illusions of personal presence does not directly damage the critical perspective I have been proposing. Even Moss, who does come before her audience as a person, not just a voice, let alone a text, focuses attention not on her actual person so much as on general features of her persona, on ideals of personhood—autonomy, freedom, energy, mobility are the features I have named. Musicality, in my view, is persistently idealized: it summons another place or discourse—a meadow in the mist. It's an ideal that is recognizable in relation to its opposite, speech or prose. It seems always to ask how to move on to a next step, beyond foreseeable discourse.

6

Universality

Is lyric poetry universal? If any art aspires to universality, surely lyric does. The consequence of attending to musicality as a source of lyric power (as in chapter 5) is that one must then also confront the issue of universality, since poetry's musicality and its figures resist the particularizing reference of ordinary discourse. Although for two centuries poetic theory has stressed the particularizing power of poetic language, a wide range of poets have sought universality, or generality, or impersonality, or disinterestedness. My argument is that poetic language, regardless of whether it is written in an orphic or a civil mode, aspires to general truth. The value of generality is in a poem's capacity less to appropriate the subject position of others than to render indefinite subject positions, those not fully realized or not sustained by historical circumstances.[1] The generality of poetic language derives from an intellectual aspiration to know more than one does, more even than one can, in particular. This chapter will extend the reach of my analysis of musicality and also encompass translation. Contemporary literary culture is ambitiously committed to the particular poetic functions that effectively join diverse literary communities into large, transnational groups—in ways that Wordsworth appreciated. Western poets and general readers have consistently turned to translation for a sense of the abiding same, or of the deeply true. The history of poetic translation records the actual efforts of poets and readers to overcome the linguistic and historical differences separating language communities from each other.

Are the best lyric poets world poets, like Petrarch, Shakespeare, Baudelaire, Whitman, Eliot, Miłosz, and Celan? Are they distinctively, or only accidentally, or intermittently universal? Wordsworth in 1800 was convinced that the power of poetry derives from its universality: "The Poet binds together by passion and knowledge the vast empire of human society, as it is spread over the whole earth, and over all time."[2] Goethe similarly told Eckermann in 1827, "I am more and more convinced that poetry is the universal possession of mankind."[3] By 1950 not Carnap but Heidegger asked, "Does . . . talk about immortal works and the eternal value of art have any content or substance?"[4] When the universality or even the survival of texts is the topic, literary criticism and theory are notoriously vague, and now fainthearted too, even though poetry and history were sharply severed at the beginning of Western literary theory; there has been time for a coherent universalist criterion to be formulated. "Poetry is concerned with universal truths," Aristotle said; "history treats of particular facts."[5] For centuries then, temporal and spatial specificity were subordinated to the eternizing idioms of poetry. In the sixteenth century Jacopo Mazzoni questioned whether historical subject matter, treated figuratively, might not after all nourish poetry, and these two poles of writing be connected: "To the text of Aristotle, in which he writes that the history of Herodotus spread out in verse would always be history and thus unworthy of the name of poetry, we reply that it is true: but it does not follow that history cannot in some way be a poem when it represents the marvelous as credible by means of idols and particularized images."[6] Mazzoni is careful not to claim too much for historical subject matter, "in some way," he says. He imagines that particularity is not a source of knowledge but an instrument for beguiling the credulous. Since the eighteenth century poetic theory has thoroughly revised this estimation of temporally specific language. For academic critics, historical knowledge is everything; the survival of canonical poets is almost embarrassing. Young poets, eager for intellectual certification, are quick to construct poems from historical documents, and slow to employ the idioms of general formulation. Yet paradoxically mutations of a universality criterion continue to support practical literary judgments—the ones that are not discussed at length—throughout the literary culture.

Poetry is certainly appraised as an expression of specific times and places—its contemporaneity; both criteria, universalist and historicist, operate widely, sometimes even in collaboration with one another. Stephen Owen has analyzed the fascinating case of contemporary Chinese literary opinion. Although the composition of classical poetry thrives in China still, and it is published by many journals devoted to this genre, Western libraries do not archive these journals. "Writers of modern Chinese classical poetry," he observes, "can get no grants; universities will not support them so that they can continue writing poetry. In the world of poetry, they [modern classical poets] are invisible." A young poet, Owen notes, cannot be "recognized as an 'important young poet' if he [or she] writes classical poetry. The literary establishment reserves fame for those who write the new [vernacular] poetry."[7] The paradox is that Chinese poets who get attention in the West (Bei Dao is Owen's example) and even in China seem in fact to be transnational (or universal) poets, and yet they are appreciated exactly because they seem to represent their moment in a national culture. Even the contemporaneity criterion itself, in a pluralistic transnational context, assists the construction of a narrative of global development. But in nonacademic literary culture the contemporaneity criterion has less authority and currency than the universality criterion, even though for over two centuries most poets have agreed with Thomas Gray that "*circumstance* ever was, and ever will be, the life and the essence . . . of poetry."[8]

Western poetics might have been constructed differently from the start. Sappho records in concrete detail her body's responses to her blocked love of another woman. Her situation as a same-sex lover of younger women headed for heterosexual marriage might have been the basis of an historicist appraisal of sixth-century lyric. Instead, she has been celebrated as a type of all lovers, or as witness of the pathos of maturation. Aristotle seems to have been less taken by Sappho than by gnomic poets like Mimnermus who had constant recourse to general idioms that propose laws.

> But what life would there be, what job, without golden Aphrodite? May I die when I be no more concerned with secret love and suasive gifts and the bed, such things as are the very flowers of youth, pleasant alike to man and woman. And when dolorous Age cometh, that maketh a man both foul without and evil within, ill cares do wear and wear his heart, he hath no more the joy of looking on the sunlight, to children he is hateful, to women contemptible, so grievous hath God made Age.[9]

Sappho invokes Aphrodite from within her own distinctive life; Mimnermus on the contrary moves quickly from the pleasures of the bed to proverbial Age in general. For Aristotle, the generality of gnomic poetry, not the particularity of a racing body, seemed essential to lyric.

Although the supposed universality of poetry is easily confused with generality, the distinction between these qualities is enormously significant. Generality can be defined statistically; some texts, such as Mimnermus's, refer more widely than others. And poets who mean to address a large number of readers are rightly said to be looking for a general audience. Universality has traditionally been a definitive feature of poetry, not prose, and measurements of generality of reference or address have no particular bearing on the distinction between poetry and prose. In contrast to generality, universality is an intellectual, not a practical, matter: a universal poet may have no appeal to a general audience. A poem's appeal may be universal only if it invokes a necessary feature of all readers, not just a likely feature of many. Universality is therefore constitutive. This is why Emerson wrote of the poet as "a beholder of ideas, and an utterer of the necessary and causal."[10]

The universality of poetry must derive from the constitution of poems and readers. One ordinarily conceives of impersonality in terms of semantic sense, but the pleasure of sensual poetic language is a richer ore of authority: poetry is most universal where it is least meaningful, in a semantic sense. Cameron observes, following Emerson, that one way to understand impersonality is "as something that appears through *bodies* . . . as a critique of the personal."[11] Bodily experience produces authority in that it derives from the constitutive base of personhood. The sounds of poems register physically, that is, impersonally, though also intimately. The sounds of phrases, clauses, and lines have a capacity to override differences. The special appeal of sonic impersonality is not that of experience: that one personally *feels* this sort of impersonality; but rather that it is unconstrained by any determinate claims that one might call ideology. The truth or falsity of a proposition has no bearing on the musicality of a line, and musicality undoes as often as it reinforces thematic sense. This is a deep paradox: music fortifies the authority of a claim by making it seem to accord with the orders of the body; but it may render semantic sense immaterial instead. As words are musically combined, they become impersonal, universal (not just general) because pleasing and satisfying to the body. An echoic structure of words, more than any semantic construction, may produce a firm basis for the universality of poetry. I will return to universality, but first I must develop its distinction from generality.

One speaks in two ways about the generality of poetry: in terms of content, reference; or of form. The first is the familiar notion that poetry engages elements of life—maturation, love, death—that seem nearly constant across space and over time. Samuel Johnson's great imitation of Juvenal, "The Vanity of Human Wishes," begins,

> Let Observation with extensive View,
> Survey Mankind, from *China* to *Peru*;
> Remark each anxious Toil, each eager Strife,
> And watch the busy Scenes of crouded Life . . .[12]

Human activities are multifarious and widely dispersed, but also comprehensible, on this account, and a grand poem manages them all. Just *that* is objectionable: that the diversity of human activity can be managed summarily. "Each anxious Toil, each eager Strife": these symmetrical phrases suggest that the labors and conflicts of the world can be held in place by a sympathetic but honest naming of single motives. Johnson's admiration of Shakespeare is the locus classicus of this pole of literary theory: "Nothing can please many, and please long, but just representations of general nature. . . . [Shakespeare's] persons act and speak by the influence of those general passions and principles by which all minds are agitated, and the whole system of life is continued in motion."[13] Johnson describes Shakespeare's generality in terms of comprehensive reference. Johnson preserves a sense of the plurality of ways of life at the same time that he asserts Shakespeare's inclusiveness. His stress is less on the singularity of human nature than on its manifold diversity. It is reasonable, though, to resist Johnson's eloquence with skeptical awareness that labor and conflict the world over are not one thing. The diversity of labor and strife may well be so great that it cannot be comprehended by survey; the range of human motivation does not reduce to "general passions and principles." The aspiration to survey an extensive area and explain diverse behavior with general terms is now understood as imperialist in itself.[14] The passage quoted from "The Vanity of Human Wishes" is only a subordinate clause; the predication of the sentence is not the issue here. One may object to other passages as universalizing propositions, but my focus here is restricted to a representation of diverse experience as supposedly one. Johnson achieves his end by extensive reference, by connecting China with Peru. A way of writing, conspicuously extensive reference, stands for a proposition that life is deeply the same around the world. The distinction between general subject matter and generalizing styles is ultimately ambiguous.

The second sense of generality is stylistic and derives from the range of reference in poetic language. Johnson's is the traditional view: a poet "does not number the streaks of the tulip."[15] The idioms of poetry, unlike those of speech, are calibrated to types and general categories, not particular instances. Exactly the generalizing locutions of Johnson and his contemporaries, however, have been embargoed by poets for over two centuries; they are rare in poetry. However, other technical means for achieving universality have been imaginatively exploited. All the figures of poetry convey generality in that they equate terms with one another, stipulating equivalence, without any end of the process foreseen. Johnson's reference begins in Asia and extends to South America. But figuration continues indefinitely; Mark Payne has argued that an aspiration to universality is implicit in figuration.[16] Modern suspicion of universalizing discourse derives from a sense that such language is duplicitous about its objectives, that it disguises particular interest as universal.[17] But poetry is actually forthright about its aspiration to universality. Poems proceed under the implicit rubric "as if" or "not the case": their fictiveness is as traditional as their universality. The opening lines of "The Vanity of Human Wishes" assert straightforwardly that human life is much the same "from China to Peru"; the operative figure entails the fiction that abstract "Observation" has a superhuman capacity of vision. No reader, then or now, mistakes "Observation" for anything but a hypothesis; the eighteenth-century view is not simply that general language accurately comprehends the diversity of experience, but that such language is intellectually potent.[18] General language may seem intellectually modest or constrained: insofar as a term stands for a class of similar items, the intellectual relation of particular to general and the direction of thought too is known and stipulated.

A plainly recognizable structure of thinking is not obviously well-suited to the intellectual exploration one rightly expects of poetry. But a poet may instead only sense and not truly know the relation of particular to general whereof he or she writes. The generality of language draws thinking along a path of conjecture. Kant speaks of aesthetic attributes that prompt "the imagination to spread over a multitude of kindred presentations that arouse more thought than can be expressed in a concept determined by words. These aesthetic attributes yield an *aesthetic idea*, which serves the mentioned rational idea as a substitute for a logical exhibition, but its proper function is to quicken [*beleben*] the mind by opening up for it a view into an immense realm of kindred presentations."[19] For Kant, the intellectuality of poetry is its primary advantage; what one truly loves are the activities of the mind, he argues. Addison instead recognizes a gap between poetic language and the experience of actual people (or what he refers to as "sense").

> The Pleasures of these Secondary Views of the Imagination, are of a wider and more universal Nature than those it has, when joined with Sight; for not only what is Great, Strange or Beautiful, but any Thing that is Disagreeable when look'd upon, pleases us in an apt Description. Here, therefore, we must enquire after a new Principle of Pleasure, which is nothing else but the Action of the Mind, which *compares* the Ideas that arise from Words, with the Ideas that arise from the Objects themselves.[20]

The pleasures of articulation exceed experience itself. Experience is diverse, as Addison realizes, but the transcendence of divisions is this art's great promise. "The Mind of Man," he says, "requires something more perfect in Matter, than what it finds there, and can never meet with any Sight in Nature which sufficiently answers its highest Ideas of Pleasantness."[21] Imaginative structures are meant as compensatory; poems proceed past the daily disappointments of ordinary experience and conform instead to ideas of value. Their forms signify the perfection of an ideal or universality. Vico makes the familiar point that metaphysical terminology is derived from terms concerning the human body and passions, but then his analysis takes an unfamiliar turn:

> Rational metaphysics teaches that man becomes all things by understanding them (*homo intelligendo fit omnia*)[;] this imaginative metaphysics shows [instead] that man becomes all things by *not* understanding them (*homo non intelligendo fit omnia*); and perhaps the latter proposition is truer than the former, for when man understands he extends his mind and takes in the things, but when he does not understand he makes the things out of himself and becomes them by transforming himself into them.[22]

The ambition of poets to write universal poetry is diffuse, often barely visible, yet vigorously effective in drawing poems to their readers; poetic figures are evidence less of understanding asserted confidently than of conjecture, or an effort to overcome bewilderment. Figurative language connects one term to another in a chain of quasi-identities: "Synecdoche developed into metaphor as particulars were elevated into universals or parts united with the other parts together with which they make up their wholes," according to Vico. The paradox is that those lines of poetry that seem, by virtue of figures, most concrete and palpable to the senses actually appeal, however implicitly, to an appetite for universal significance. The plain style, which refuses elaborate figuration, entails fewer implicit hypotheses of universal signification. It renders claims to generality explicit. But plain or troped poetic language, set to the music of verse, is all hypothetical. "For the poet, he nothing affirmeth, and therefore never lieth," according to Sidney; it is an art of hypotheses, more or less dense in one poem or another.[23] Poems are theoretical. Stanley Cavell says of some language use that "we drive words away from us, into an uncontrollable structure of transcendent service."[24] All poems are deliberately proposed for just such service, though few are chosen. Poems are usually driven away from a poet by conventions of syntax and prosody, and ultimately by literary ambition. The rules of sense-making and mnemonics that derive from grammar and prosody are disciplines of clarity, sense construction, and also leave-taking. Words, lines, sentences, and stanzas become increasingly general and autonomous as they are moved out of the body of the poet and into the conventions that first generate sense and then govern publication, retention, and interpretation. But aren't poets notoriously nonconformist with regard to the conventions of prose syntax? Yes, many are: they pull more or less strongly with and against conventions of sense-making, always in hope that the deep structures of language and especially of sound *lead*, nonetheless, to a sense that is beyond a poet's mere intention. That estranging movement is not inevitable: will propels it. The sources of subjective intensity may instead lock a poem in its particular concerns. Estrangement is a struggle.

General propositions themselves have few advocates among poets. Instead the resources of particularity have been exploited imaginatively for two centuries. Goethe said in 1825,

> It makes a great difference whether the poet seeks a universal idea among suitable particulars, or sees a universal in the particular. Allegory derives from the former method, where the particular counts only as an instance of a universal. But the nature of poetry actually corresponds to the latter method: it expresses a particular without thinking of or referring to a universal. Whoever grasps a particular in a lively fashion at the same time obtains a universal along with it without even becoming aware of it (or if aware, only in retrospect).[25]

Goethe's objection is not only to the sequence of general proposition–particular instance, but also to the intellectual constraint on particularity. The presumption here (revealed in one word: only [*nur*]) is that the substance of particulars is not fully comprehended by the universal laws that attach to them; that appearances are not systematic in this direct fashion. The word "only" expresses his conviction that poems propose relations that are more significant than the determining one between general claims and their instantiation. He prefers to leave implicit the nature of the relation between general and particular. Otherwise, his is the familiar romantic view that "living" or organic forms are more richly and complicatedly significant than conventional forms; that advance knowledge is weaker than discovered truth.

Abstractness has also been unattractive to poets more or less since the death of Johnson (1784), though the prospect that a poem might overcome the particular divisions of historical communities has steadily appealed to poets. The aged Wordsworth, looking back on his most famous poem, "Ode on Intimations of Immortality," said that to "the attentive and competent reader the whole sufficiently explains itself; but there may be no harm in adverting to particular feelings or *experiences* of my own mind on which the structure of the poem partly rests." He addressed his poem to any attentive and competent reader. His adversion to the genesis of the poem refuses to speak of his thoughts or beliefs; the basis of generality is instead in feelings or mental experiences, he carefully says. He knew in the early nineteenth century that ideas explicitly expressed were an insufficient basis for consensus. What one feels or experiences mentally—that, not thought itself, is what connects people, on this view. Yet the poem certainly posits definite propositions. Wordsworth acknowledges this, but he would not concede that he intended to advocate any particular idea. "To that dreamlike vividness and splendor which invests objects of sight in childhood, everyone, I believe, if he would look back, could bear testimony, and I need not dwell upon it here: but having in the poem regarded it as presumptive evidence of a prior state of existence, I think it right to protect oneself against a conclusion . . . that I meant to inculcate such a belief. It is far too shadowy a notion to be recommended to faith, as more than an element in our instincts of immortality."[26] The "idea" of the pre-existence of the soul is found, he said, in "the popular creeds of many nations" as well as in ancient Greek philosophy. An idea that has been believed by many people over a long period of time can be used by poets as if it were a fact rather than a claim subject to critical investigation. Ideas gain viability more from experience than from analysis.

To conceive of poetic authority as deriving from archaic sources is inevitably to introduce translated texts as models of poetic language, and then it is easy to imagine that a style becomes general by a process of subtraction, as thematic specificity is elided. Wordsworth and Johnson share a sense that the appearance of certain concepts among historically disconnected peoples is evidence of a deep structure to human experience. Antiquity and remoteness now continue to serve as signs of profundity. Stevens too understood universality to derive from profundity, a term whose antonym, shallowness, is commonly attributed to political struggle; whatever profundity is, it is not politics, on this view. "The imagination that is satisfied by politics, whatever the nature of the politics, has not the same value as the imagination that seeks to satisfy, say, the universal mind, which, in the case of a poet, would be the imagination that tries to penetrate to basic images, basic emotions, and so to compose a fundamental poetry even older than the ancient world."[27] This rift between political and metaphysical discourse sets the concept of universality aside from controversy.[28] Stevens's word "value" is instructive; Valéry and Pound use related terms. The attraction of poets to universal themes or images has everything to do with appreciation or the evaluation of poetry. Stevens recognized that poets may be valued for the (essentially political) representation of a place and time (as Allen Ginsberg, Robert Lowell, and Adrienne Rich were). A more demanding assessment is ostensibly proposed when a poet is termed profound and universal. Two kinds of poetry often seem profound: the very old and the very remote; which means that profundity—and a respite from political debate—is expected in translated poetry. Yeats, like Robert Bly, looked to translations to reveal the significance of solitude. "I have always sought to bring my mind close to the mind of Indian and Japanese poets, . . . to immerse it in the general mind where that mind is scarce separable from what we have begun to call 'the subconscious'; to liberate it from all that comes of councils and committees, from the world as it is seen from universities or from populous towns."[29] Yeats and Pound were both political poets (though neither considered political issues profound), but they realized that the authority of translation is metaphysical. A voice from far away has a chance to sound a truth too deep for the idioms of social institutions, exactly because the determining power of social language is great.

Modernist poets invested constantly in resonant details, and rarely in general statements, even though they intended to write poems they hoped would be general. Particularity was less a value in itself than a means to overcome an artistic limitation of political discourse. "*What is of value for one person only has no value*," according to Valéry. "This is the iron law of Literature."[30] Does he mean that value must be generalizable, or more modestly that the business of literature depends on shared texts? Both are true, but it matters whether poets hew to the demands of metaphysical inquiry, or attempt to manage the responses of their readers. Modernist theory disapproves of the management of readerly response, yet Pound asked not what would always be the same, but what might engage everyone in his present moment. This is a rhetorician's sense of generality: "How, then, shall the poet in this dreary day attain universality, how write what will be understood of 'the many' and lauded of 'the few'? What interests have all men in common? What forces play upon them all?"[31]

Modernists used the resources of craft—especially excision—to represent what seemed a level of perception or understanding beneath social convention, in some bedrock of nature or mind. Careful labor itself, Pound remarkably thought, might be a sound basis for broad appeal; an authentically distinguished style necessarily yields the power of generality.

> We are . . . one humanity, compounded of one mud and one aether; and every man who does his own job really well has a latent respect for every other man who does *his* own job really well; this is our lasting bond. . . . The man who really does the thing well, if he be pleased afterwards to talk about it, gets always his auditors' attention; he gets his audience the moment he says something so intimate that it proves him the expert: he does not, as a rule, sling generalities; he gives the particular case for what it is worth; the truth is individual.[32]

Expert authority derives from effective labor, an objective attained. An expert style is austere and particular, according to Pound, characterized negatively by what it excludes. One might as plausibly expect experts to discourse copiously about general propositions and particular exceptions. But the Western concept of poetic form requires the discipline of subtraction and a counterforce to subject matter. Schiller insisted that an "artist must seek to overcome . . . the limitations inherent in the particular subject matter he is treating. . . . Subject matter . . . , however sublime and all-embracing it may be, always has a limiting effect upon the spirit, and it is only from form that true aesthetic freedom can be looked for."[33] Modernist poets constructed a sense of trust in the general authority of lean, concrete language. Rhetorical and grammatical structures establish expectations concerning completeness. These poets displayed asceticism by refusing to complete these structures. Lines rather than stanzas; phrases and clauses where sentences were expected. "Immersion in what has taken individual form," Adorno said, "elevates the lyric poem to the status of something universal by making manifest something not distorted, not grasped, not yet subsumed. . . . The lyric work hopes to attain universality through unrestrained individuation."[34] Just exactly what troubles many readers—what Ashbery called "this leaving-out business"—is paradoxically intended to establish broad community.[35] Densities, surds, of image and of sound, are designed to elude social and ideological boundaries that separate readers. Distinctive, not conventional, formality is the basis of generality for modernists like Pound and Adorno.

Like time itself, translation inevitably strips poems of historical specificity and of native musicality. A translator is permitted to let the particularity of a source text—its local reference, idioms, allusions, and metric—silently fall away like outmoded manners. The enduring poem may then stand revealed, as if the features of the text requiring native sensitivity were optional, like glosses at the bottom of a page. Schelling cites Winkelmann, who compares "beauty with water drawn from the bosom of the spring, which, the less taste it has, the wholesomer it is esteemed."[36] A taste for watery translations is extensive. Chinese poetry is presented to English readers boldly stripped of temporal and spatial sources—a kind of nude. Ancient or remote poetry is read ascetically and accorded generality, something from a true source with claims on even those far away in space and time. When this style of translation prevails, as it did in the United States in the 1960s and 1970s, native poets, ever covetous of authority, write poems in a nude style, as Merwin did. Even contemporary Chinese poems, Stephen Owen explains, are now written in an austere pseudomodernist style for the translation market. "'World poetry' turns out, unsurprisingly, to be a version of Anglo-American modernism or French modernism, depending on which wave of colonial culture first washed over the intellectuals of the country in question."[37] Translation is always admittedly inadequate: the source text is understood to be deeper, more exact, more beautiful, more musical than what a translator can construct. Modernists invoked this structure as if to indicate that poetry itself is a kind of second writing of the real poem. George Steiner argues that "the concept of 'the lacking word' marks modern literature." This boundary marker from the 1870s "divides a literature essentially housed in language from one for which language has become a prison."[38]

So modernist asceticism stood for the inevitable losses entailed by literary circulation. "It were as wise," Shelley said, "to cast a violet into a crucible that you might discover the formal principle of its colour and odour, as seek to transfuse from one language to another the creations of a poet."[39] And Frost, one remembers, agreed. But there is a countertechnique too for observing and redeeming losses. Rossetti understood, and Pound after him, the semiotic connection between translation and authority. A poet may advantageously imitate not the speech of his or her moment but the displaced idioms of translatorese. The losses of translation may be marked by adventitious ornamentation, and a literary value produced where a liability had been. The concept of an urtext, prior even to the source text, is ancient and effectively authorizing. The traditional distinction between the letter and the spirit of a text entails this concept of an unreachable source, and translators invoke it to legitimate the practical liberties they take.[40] Translation is evidence of a displaced basis of agreement; local contexts, even identities, can be suspended. "Art, all art, has this characteristic," according to Tolstoy, "that it unites people."[41] Translation facilitates the construction of community across national boundaries. The traditional claim made for poetry is that it addresses all men and women across divisions of class and party. Poets negotiate the suspicion that claim arouses and try still to bear up to the grandest aspirations of the art. The particularity that poets invoke steadily yields to the generalizing pressure of interpretation. Conspicuously anachronistic locutions signify not only absences but an origin elsewhere—a fuller poem (like Ronald Johnson's *Paradise Lost*) in some other language, or time, or place. "In translation," Benjamin said, "the original rises into a higher and purer linguistic air, as it were. It cannot live there permanently, to be sure; neither can it reach that level in every aspect of the work. Yet in a singularly impressive manner, it at least points the way to this region; the predestined, hitherto inaccessible realm of reconciliation and fulfillment of languages."[42] Rossetti, Pound, and Duncan understood that labored locutions signify a greater poem elsewhere, a hidden authority; a peace that surpasseth historical division.

Translation has special significance, then, in the history of poetry and in contemporary criticism. "Every new exuberance, every new heave," Pound said, "is stimulated by translation, every allegedly great age is an age of translations."[43] The art of translation is powerfully utopian; poets turn to it when they know too well where the conventions of their own moment lead, in hope of striking out in a new direction. Hass began reading Miłosz when he was fed up with his U.S. contemporaries of the 1970s.[44] The hope of translator poets is not just for a refreshed technique but for contact with some essence of poetry, for that which endures beyond the apparent babble of diverse tongues. There is no rushing the test of time, to determine who among contemporaries has enduring appeal. But there is also a test of space: which poets manage, through translation, to cross national boundaries and establish audiences in foreign cultures? One knows which ones have been successfully imported into U.S. literary culture: Czesław Miłosz, Paul Celan preeminently, but there are many others too. These poets have found readers in English, but, more important, they have affected the writing of poetry in English. They have been absorbed by poets as well as readers. (Allen Ginsberg and Sylvia Plath are the postwar U.S. poets who have reached broad audiences elsewhere.) What features of these poets' work have been esteemed by the host cultures? Are they also the prominent features of the text in the source culture? A discrepancy between native and foreign reception may reveal the distinctive objectives of a host culture creative enough to remake another culture to suit its own needs.) To a translator, as Pound said, "distance avails not."

›››‹‹‹

Many poets have been translated for U.S. readers, but very few have actually become poets in the English language. Baudelaire, Neruda, Miłosz, and Celan are exceptional in this regard. This selection process should reveal something about the aspiration to generality. Miłosz's poems are treasured by readers of English, and he is an influence among U.S. poets. How can a poet leave behind the texture and musicality of Polish and become a poet in an unrelated language? A list of poets who have found mildly appreciative audiences for their translated work would be long and distinguished, but Miłosz has exceeded nearly all of them in his immersion in the English language. Several forces facilitated his reception: he became known in 1950s U.S. political circles as a Cold Warrior because of his early critical prose, *The Captive Mind* (1953) and *The Seizure of Power* (1955); he won the Nobel prize in 1980; finally, he had extraordinary translators, and collaborated methodically with them.

There is no question about the evaluative criterion employed to praise his poetry. One critic after another, whether Polish or American, refers to the universality of his work in both prose and poetry. The U.S. poet Edward Hirsch is dewier than Wordsworth or Goethe when he says, "In our age of profound relativism, [Miłosz] offers a search for eternal values, eternal truths. . . . I love his poetry most of all for its radiant moments of wonder and being, because of his tenderness toward the human."[45] Two terms circulate repeatedly through the reviews and essays written about his poems: "history" and "human." A Polish critic writing in a Canadian journal before the award of the Nobel Prize, Bogdan Czaykowski, makes clear that what "human" means is "the vulnerability of the individual in the face of the combined forces of history, geography and ideology."[46] The relevant historical subject is that of central and Western Europe since 1939: the Nazi occupation, the transport of European Jews to the death camps, and the Stalinization of central Europe. Robert Pinsky specifies Miłosz's importance to younger U.S. poets in this way.

> Before he was a world figure, Miłosz was a vital figure for American poets. Why? One answer goes like this: poets have found in this body of work a human response to history, and history dealt with neither as a picture-book for ideology (in the old style of determinism) nor as a proving-ground for ironic skepticisms (in the current style of determinism). Rather, the poems of Miłosz seem to offer an intellectual and emotional response to historical reality that is grounded somehow in the precious center of life; history, not as the past nor as ingenious academic theories about the past, but as the reality that inheres in the shape of a plant.[47]

Miłosz participated in the events that now are seen to have constituted the recent history of Europe. His knowledge of these events seems direct, unmediated. That is the basis of his importance to U.S. poets who can know this history only through textual representations and the ideological filters that give them form. However, it is not mere historical experience that has counted for critics; the particular point—and it is political as well as poetic—is rather that Miłosz has not been brought low by his experience of Nazi occupation and Stalinist state formation. As Richard Rorty says of inspirational literary works, Miłosz's poems do "make people think that there is more to this life than they ever imagined."[48] Some important critics have expressly appreciated his affirmation of values that are not essentially critical or skeptical. Terrence des Pres, for instance, wrote,

> I know of no poet more driven to celebration, to sing of the earth in its plainness and glory, and therefore no poet more tormented . . . by the terrible detour through history which must be taken if, in pursuit of joyous song, the authority of poetic affirmation is not to remain untested or open to the charge of ignorance. . . . To equate life with happiness *and mean it* is an astonishing victory in our brute century.[49]

Miłosz's poems demonstrate the vigor and validity of affirmative song in the face of the worst the century had to pit against faith in a future. These poems have earned credit not for Miłosz alone but for an approach to the making of celebratory art.

Miłosz is a master of exemplary terms and figures, which mastery has helped establish his wide readership. Poems are always meant to be exemplary in the sense of exceptional: they depart from ordinary discourse, most conspicuously in musical structure, but there are other departure points too (and musical structure is always lost in translation). Although poems are frequently presented as one part of a series of some sort—prosodic form implies a series, for example, of sonnets, villanelles, quatrains, or even pentameter lines—great ones nonetheless are one of a kind. An exemplary poem, in this sense, draws boundaries. A poet's objective is to make something that would otherwise not be in the world at all. Hardy's career ambition was to add a couple of poems to Palgrave's anthology. This sense of the exceptionality of individual poems leads one to suspect that the relative measure of poems, after a point, is misdirected; each means to be beyond compare. Kant's view was that beautiful objects are inadequately assessed as instances of concepts; a beautiful object does not, insofar as it is beautiful, match a concept. Aesthetic judgment must circumvent concepts.

Then there is the contrary sense of "exemplary"—a capacity to serve as an instance of a general phenomenon, or representative of a class—that bears especially on Miłosz. When are poems adequately described as instances of classes? Is his paradoxical "Rivers Grow Small" (1963) an example of his poetry generally, or of the wisdom of old men? Or is either a reductive account of one of his best poems? This logic of exemplarity, or representativeness, implies that one wishes to know the nature of Miłosz's poetry, or of something else more inclusive than one poem on a page; but the implication may well be entirely mistaken. What is the general class, a critic asks, to which a particular poem belongs? But the question is a sharp curb to literary curiosity, even to pleasure. One may prefer, out of satisfaction with "Rivers

Grow Small," not to know that Miłosz wrote anything comparable. Resemblances between one poem and another may obscure the distinctive features of each instance of the general class. One may wisely prefer to take such a poem entirely by itself. Some poets, looking for that reception, block all views on their workshops. Shortly before his death in 1967, Yvor Winters set flame to his manuscript drafts and the correspondence he had received—with the exception of his letters from Hart Crane.[50] And Eliot effectively obstructed access to his manuscripts and correspondence for decades.

Here is Miłosz's translation of his own poem.

Rivers grow small. Cities grow small. And splendid gardens
show what we did not see there before: crippled leaves and dust.
When for the first time I swam across the lake
it seemed immense, had I gone there these days
it would have been a shaving bowl
between post-glacial rocks and junipers.
The forest near the village of Halina once was for me primeval,
smelling of the last but recently killed bear,
though a ploughed field was visible through the pines.
What was individual becomes a variety of a general pattern.
Consciousness even in my sleep changes primary colors.
The features of my face melt like a wax doll in the fire.
And who can consent to see in the mirror the mere face of man?[51]

Miłosz tells a reassuringly familiar story: what seemed grand to one when young is revealed as small when re-encountered in maturity. Writers identify their topics in greater or lesser proximity to recognized patterns of thinking and speaking: Miłosz works close to these patterns; his readers know at once that he is addressing what oft was thought, though just what he may say about a topic is unconstrained by common discourse. Why do the grand experiences of youth look small in retrospect? Not because we were small then and everything seemed grand (that's the common answer), but because we had no sense of how to name particular experiences, or to see through the experiences of others. "Post-glacial" and "junipers" are names of general categories borrowed from the imaginings of others. The categories one accrues in time for measuring and interpreting experience bring a sublimely large world down to size. The great benefits of categories bear costs to the spirit too. The young overlook mortality—fallen leaves and dust; they can afford to do so. In a state of innocence, experience seems undifferentiated, all of a piece, more or less sunny; the knowledge of youth is quite general in that sense. Names provide qualifying particularity to one's knowledge; one would not ordinarily say that experience grows more general as one learns a culture's distinctions, though that is the drift of things that engages the poet. A paradox arises from the fact that names are sites of recurrence; particularities become general as they recur. Names even imply narratives, and a terminus, as all distinctions do. By the time a farm is worked, the bears of the area are only a memory. Particular instances of a general phenomenon expire, but general phenomena continue. In that sense the path to maturity leads to more general knowledge. However comforting that is in the case of grass and birds, it gives little solace to a man sinking into generic folds of skin.

Hans-Georg Gadamer noted that poems achieve generality by appealing to readers for recognition. "Where something is recognized," he observed, "it has liberated itself from the uniqueness and contingency of the circumstances in which it was encountered. It is a matter neither of there and then, nor of here and now, but it is encountered as the very self-same. Thereby it begins to rise to its permanent essence."[52] By the time one recognizes a phenomenon as an instance, one major poetic resource has been depleted: uncertainty. Stevens thought that poems are comprised of examples, but poets are uncertain what their examples are examples *of*. Poems take form in the process of just this inquiry: something apparently extraordinary must be interpreted. What, a poet asks, might this woman, man, bird, sunrise, or death exemplify? Poems press toward answers with faith in exemplarity. Yet when a poem answers that question, its end has come. A stable, plausible relation between example and generality, or law, is what one wants in an explanation, but a sign of profound trouble to poets, who can certainly know too much. A poem confident of the exemplifying efficacy of its terms, needs some other warrant—other than its being an exploration—of its exceptionality. A popular audience may gladly recognize the relation of particularity to generality in a poem; but a critical one, mindful of the need for a great poem to establish its authority as exceptional, distinct from other discourse, must suspect neat fits of all kinds in an art pledged to looking for trouble.

Consider Miłosz's much admired "Bypassing Rue Descartes" (1980), translated by Robert Hass and Renata Gorczynski:

> Bypassing rue Descartes
> I descended toward the Seine, shy, a traveler,
> A young barbarian just come to the capital of the world.
>
> We were many, from Jassy and Koloshvar, Wilno and Bucharest,
> Saigon and Marrakesh,
> Ashamed to remember the customs of our homes,
> About which nobody here should ever be told:
> The clapping for servants, barefooted girls hurry in,
> Dividing food with incantations,
> Choral prayers recited by master and household together.
>
> I had left the cloudy provinces behind,
> I entered the universal, dazzled and desiring.
>
> Soon enough, many from Jassy and Koloshvar, or Saigon or
> Marrakesh
> Would be killed because they wanted to abolish the customs
> of their homes.
>
> Soon enough, their peers were seizing power
> In order to kill in the name of the universal, beautiful ideas.
>
> Meanwhile the city behaved in accordance with its nature,
> Rustling with throaty laughter in the dark,
> Baking long breads and pouring wine into clay pitchers,
> Buying fish, lemons and garlic at street markets,
> Indifferent as it was to honor and shame and greatness and
> glory,
> Because that had been done already and had transformed itself

Into monuments representing nobody knows whom,
Into arias hardly audible and into turns of speech.

Again I lean on the rough granite of the embankment,
As if I had returned from travels through the underworlds
And suddenly saw in the light the reeling wheel of the seasons
Where empires have fallen and those once living are now dead.

There is no capital of the world, neither here nor anywhere else,
And the abolished customs are restored to their small fame
And now I know that the time of human generations is not like
the time of the earth.

As to my heavy sins, I remember one most vividly:
How, one day, walking on a forest path along a stream,
I pushed a rock down onto a water snake coiled in the grass.

And what I have met with in life was the just punishment
Which reaches, sooner or later, the breaker of a taboo.[53]

This is a Cold War parable about the failure of intellectual Marxism to establish a just command over third-world cultures. Miłosz says explicitly that democratic Paris cannot exemplify the aspirations of these cultures: "There is no capital of the world, neither here nor anywhere else" (28). The Enlightenment ideal of a secular center of "the universal, beautiful ideas" (15) is an illusion of the left. His own language, here English for his Polish, acknowledges distance from daily experience of the city: baguettes and pichets are translated laboriously as long breads and wine in clay pitchers (18), as though a French text of life were being interpreted with a dictionary. The truth is that local knowledge, based on religion, custom, and hierarchy, endures better than left universalism (29). Knowledge is particular, not universal. There is, however, a deeper paradox in the poem. Miłosz imagines himself to have been a typical third-world writer-intellectual. He seems unaware of the gap between his own assertion of typicality and his claim about the authority of local knowledge. He has learned that Paris cannot justly absorb third-world cultures, but not that Moroccan, Vietnamese, Rumanian, Hungarian, and

Lithuanian writer-intellectuals do not constitute a single class. Much of the poem's language, beginning with the title, invokes well-established habits of interpretation. The rue Descartes, which bounds the Sorbonne, stands for postwar secular intellectual culture; that is what is being bypassed.[54] Miłosz's language, here as elsewhere, is fully committed to representation within mainstream codes.

Here is an anticommunist poem, but no defence of capitalism. From Miłosz's viewpoint, the concept of secular universal values is not wrong in itself; the problem is with the effects of the concept. Universalism induces shame because local custom is hierarchical, exploitative, and enforced by mystification (5–9). This is the originating problem with universal ideals: they lead to denial of the status quo, and then to an effort not just to modify the status quo, preserving what is valuable, altering gradually what is not, but to obliteration of that which should not exist, in view of universal enlightenment. Then follows reckless political ambition and bloodshed. Miłosz's esteem for local knowledge or custom is not motivated by principle, but rather by prudence. Secular ideals lose force over time. What persists are the daily efforts of people to feed themselves and to observe the customs of their ancestors. When at the end of the poem he refers to his punishment for breaking a taboo as just, he stresses the unreasonableness of customary values. If there is any rational sense in which his punishment is just, he does not see or state it. He rather asserts an acquiescent faith in custom's justness, as one recites dogmas from a catechism, or choral prayers before a meal. How is it that such a retro ideological position could produce political poetry that finds a wide readership? Miłosz's appeal to patriotic U.S. advocates of capitalism should be minimal, and his religious position in this poem is pagan. But his political disaffection, his skepticism about the enduring value of any political ideal—this may be the firm ground on which he finds his audiences. He is the West's most popular libertarian poet.

Donald Davie has praised at length Miłosz's courage in writing didactic poetry. "A reader would not go far wrong," according to Davie, "who thought of the longer poems in *Bells in Winter*, to begin with, as so many essays in verse."[55] Ideas govern Miłosz's poems, as they rightly do an essay. Davie argues too that Miłosz has lost readers by refusing to write strictly as a lyric poet, but I think that the contrary is the case, in a way that affects one's understanding of poetry's generality.[56] The very clarity of Miłosz's didactic objectives has rather helped him to build a larger audience than Davie seems to recognize. Miłosz's objectives are displayed most plainly in the structure of his poems, though one senses them too at the level even of simple pronouns such as "we," as I have noted. Seamus Heaney admires the vigor of rhetorical structure in Miłosz's poems. Miłosz speaks with conviction, "complete certitude about the shape of things."[57] This directness of utterance or assertion stands in marked contrast, Heaney notes, to the "conditional, the indeterminate mood" of so much U.S. poetry.[58] The notion that poetry is an exploratory art is remote from Miłosz's poems and of little concern to their admirers. "The speaker in the poem ['Incantation']," Heaney observes, "seemed to be irrefutably one with the voice of the poet; he seemed, moreover, to know exactly what he wanted to say before he began to say it, and indeed the poem aspired to deliver what we had once long ago been assured it was not any poem's business to deliver: a message."[59] Although English-readers have no approach to the musical structure of the poem in Polish, the bold rhetorical structure of "Bypassing Rue Descartes" survives translation: it rests on a number of paired contraries, at various levels of construction. The poem is framed by two walks to the water: one to a city river (2), one to a country stream (32–33). There is a matching frame of descent to the riverbank, where the underclass of Paris stays (2), and ascent to the same spot from imagined underworlds (24–25). He is "come to the capital of the world" in the third line, and twenty-five lines later "There is no capital of the world." The most consequential of these pairs is the clear and distinct ideas of Descartes and the shameful customs of the "cloudy provinces." The intellectuals of Miłosz's generation would be killed because, in the name of the former, they wished to abolish the latter (12–13). These intellectuals would also kill others in the name of the former (14–15). These are the outlines of the poem's rhetorical structure, which is not quite synonymous with its ideational structure, though the two are tightly related. The ideas of the poem remain implicit despite the explicit rhetorical structure. There is an ideational gap between seeking enlightenment and killing one's political adversaries, though Miłosz asserts the former as the cause of the latter. The rhetorical or affective structure of the poem holds this gap open to view, but no effort is taken to articulate the ideas that explain how enlightenment leads to death. The poem, like an essay, has a point to make, but that point is not made as an essayist might, by explaining ideas.

›››‹‹‹

Like Miłosz, Celan has markedly influenced English-language poetry. The poet Robert Kelly has said that Celan's "greatness reaches into English and American poetry, leaving its mark on our poetry; it's hard to think of any contemporary foreign poet who has cast such a spell on our sense of what a poem is."[60] Kelly argues that Celan's style itself demonstrates general appeal: "It was the peculiar genius of Paul Celan to be able to strip language of its normal socioeconomic occasions without cutting the lines that lead language to the heart."[61] Yet Celan's poems are closely tied to recent political history. At every moment in his English-language reception he has been identified directly with the Shoah. That reception began in 1955 in the political press, rather than in poetry magazines, with a translation of "Todesfuge" by Clement Greenberg. The note on the translation identifies Celan (incorrectly) as "a survivor of the concentration camps."[62] He was taken as a spokesperson for a particular group and their historical experience. He and Nelly Sachs were said by a *TLS* reviewer in 1971 to be the culmination of a line of German-Jewish intellectual culture that lives only in these survivors of the Shoah.[63] But within the claim to representative authority was the further notion that that which he represented defined a much greater experience. The first review of his work in the *TLS* spoke of his words as "festering images of Auschwitz which are relevant not only to Germany and not only to an era that ended in 1945."[64] The Shoah is understood to be the one indisputably general historical experience of the twentieth century. This is why the term "universal" plays so prominent a role in the reception of a contemporary poet, as the strongest critics understood. J. M. Coetzee said of "Todesfuge" that "its impact is immediate and universal."[65] Similarly George Steiner, who shaped the English-language reception of Celan, wrote that "the holocaust motif returns [in Celan's later work], strongly, but it is now [in *Fadensonnen*, 1968] so cryptic, so private in its universality as to be almost undecipherable."[66] Coetzee and Steiner, as writers, understand that, in terms of literary reputation, Celan engaged the most high-stakes subject of the twentieth century.

Celan is rightly considered an orphic modernist who wrote in a tradition of obscure and vatic concision; this was Pound's tradition too. There are two ways to justify Celan's obscurity, allusiveness, and extreme concision. One is to note that he responded to the disruptive features of modern experience that make coherent, assured art seem generally implausible. Or, as an anonymous *TLS* reviewer put it in 1971, Celan's obscure language accurately reflects "the confusion, terror, and sense of mystery that the modern world inspires in so many of its more sensitive inhabitants."[67] This justification of difficulty has been proposed countless times for modernist work like Pound's, but it has proved insufficient to override objections to obscurity. The claim that a general modern malaise warrants linguistic difficulty has met abiding resistance. The second justification of Celan's obscurity is really a variety of this contested claim: that he is responding to the disruption of Western historical culture that was wrought by the Shoah. He and Primo Levi, George Steiner wrote, "came nearest to bringing human language to bear on that which no tongue ought ever to have known or articulated."[68] It requires only a short step to say then that the Shoah *required* obscurity, as Rika Lesser does: "Celan's language—peculiar, idiosyncratic, transformational, at times almost incomprehensible—seems the only one capable of absorbing and expressing a world changed by the Holocaust."[69] From this point of view, the difficulty of Celan's poetry is not so much justifiable, as it is desirable. There are anthologies of lucid and anecdotal Holocaust poems, but the one poet believed to have written true poems of the Shoah is intensely difficult to understand. The ruptures in reading Celan fortify the belief that the Shoah is that which cannot be adequately explained or described.

Although Celan's poems are experimental in that they characteristically explore possibilities of sense-making, the poems that mean most to wide audiences are rhetorical productions. Most readers want clear markers of attitude, sharp distinctions between one thing and another, firm management. "Todesfuge" was his first published poem, and for that he is most honored (as Langston Hughes is for "The Negro Speaks of Rivers")—a travesty of judgment in both cases. "Psalm" is his next most analyzed poem, John Felstiner observes; these are satirical works, in the sense that Blake was a satirist. "Psalm," by far the strongest of these three famous poems, inverts the structures of Judaic and Christian prayer, to make art out of the failure of religion.

Niemand knetet uns wieder aus Erde und Lehm,
niemand bespricht unsern Staub.
Niemand.

Gelobt seist du, Niemand.
Dir zulieb wollen wir blühn.
Dir
Entgegen.

Ein Nichts
waren wir, sind wir, werden
wir bleiben, blühend:
die Nichts—, die
Niemandsrose.

Mit
dem Griffel seelenhell,
dem Staubfaden himmelswüst,
der Krone rot
vom Purpurwort, das wir sangen

über, o über
dem Dorn.

PSALM

No one kneads us again out of earth and clay,
no one incants our dust.
No one.

Blessed art thou, No One.
In thy sight would
we bloom.
In thy
spite.

A Nothing
we were, are now, and ever
shall be, blooming:
the Nothing—, the
No-One's-Rose.

With
our pistil soul-bright,
our stamen heaven-waste,
our corona red
from the purpleword we sang
over, O over
the thorn.[70]

(Translated by John Felstiner)

The poem begins in a thoroughly postwar God-forsaken state. The complaint is not that God did not protect His people, but that no one has recreated us after the Shoah (*wieder*). We can understand the first-person plural broadly as Celan's contemporaries (or narrowly, as the *nicht ganz Vernichteten*, or surviving Jews). By January 1961, when the poem was written, a great deal of earth and clay had been moved to reconstruct the physical plant of Germany.[71] Celan's point is rather that the fifteen years after the camps opened to scrutiny brought no revival of the spirit. The postwar covenant is with Blake's Nobodaddy and

Homer's cunning *Outis*. The punning second and third strophes are written from within the admired cleverness of postwar capitalism. The obviously attractive feature of the poem is the tough vigor of its protest at being forsaken. This is what one loves in Wyatt too: the courage to make acid art in the face of power. The last strophe is extraordinary in asserting after all an erotic readiness to make a materialist future out of a failure of the spirit. The past tense of line 17 (or line 18 in Felstiner's translation) has a special significance. Judeo-Christian religion is based on the transformation of adversity into advantage, psalms out of suffering. Until that line the poem is nearly entirely in the present tense. Celan stresses the fact that in the past we *sang* over the thorn: like the ready rose, that is, we asked for it.

"Unten" is a rarely discussed but nonetheless distinguished poem of a subtler, more conflicted kind—far from the lucid rhetorical structures that readers want from Miłosz and Celan.

Heimgeführt ins Vergessen
das Gast-Gespräch unsrer
langsamen Augen.

Heimgeführt Silbe um Silbe, verteilt
auf die tagblinden Würfel, nach denen
die spielende Hand greift, gross,
im Erwachen.

Und das Zuviel meiner Rede:
Angelagert dem kleinen
Kristall in der Tracht deines Schweigens.

BELOW

Led home into oblivion
the sociable talk of
our slow eyes.

Led home, syllable after syllable, shared
out among the dayblind dice, for which
the playing hand reaches out, large,
awakening.

And the too much of my speaking:
Heaped up round the little
Crystal dressed in the style of your silence.[72]
(Translated by Michael Hamburger)

The allure of a return and the best of all returns—*heimgeführt*, one of only two repeated words in the poem. Poems are essentially, Celan said in "The Meridian," a kind of homecoming.[73] "Once there was a way to get back homeward, / Once there was a way to get back home," John Lennon wrote. One wants to elude the present, and especially other people, when they are too present; one wants to go *under* all that to what is not apparent. Think too of the symbolist escape wish (Mallarmé's "Les Fenêtres," for instance). The pertinent paradox is that one normally remembers home well; Michael Hamburger takes an instructive liberty in referring to oblivion (1), because the German term is a substantive for the everyday verb, to forget. (*Vergessenheit* is the common term for oblivion.) *Das Vergessen* might mean the forgetting, or the forgotten, or oblivion, but the simple verbal form—a common basis for reproach—is inevitably present. *Led* home to oblivion: that makes a plausible sense. But led home to that which one forgets, or is forgotten: this is more complicated. The verb *führen*, to lead, is transitive and entails a distinction between a leader and a follower. The first word of the poem makes one want to know who is doing what to whom, particularly because one may be reproached for forgetting; but grammaticality goes only so far in this poem. Lines 1 and 2, for instance, are not connected by any punctuation; one nonetheless conjectures an appositional relationship between *Vergessen* and *Gast-Gespräch*. Presumably Celan means to refer to the superficiality of social discourse, its weak hold on past experience. There are first-person (singular and plural) and second-person (singular, familiar) grammatical positions here, but none for a third-person—a "they." One cannot attribute forgetting to a third person. Insofar as forgetting requires an agent, the first or second person must serve. One may understand forgetting as something regrettable that people in social relations commonly do, but there is no indication that judgment of others is an objective of the poem or the poet: only the I, we, and thou matter here; forgetting is of consequence insofar as they forget or are forgotten. The ambiguity of the grammar reveals a difficulty not overcome in determining and expressing who is forgetting and who is being forgotten (i.e., who is open to reproach), as though that were just hard to say in both senses.

Syllables themselves, even Celan's, are increments, not of enlightenment, but of blindness: each dot on a die, a dead eye. (The transition to gambling seems to come from a resemblance between the pyramid of three dots to signify blindness and the dots on dice.) "Only truthful hands write true poems," Celan wrote.[74] A gambling (or writing) hand grasps greedily at blindness to the day's light. The association of largeness, excess, and greed takes emphasis in line 6, because of the consonance of "greift, gross," and then "Zuviel" is associated with the speaker's own language (8). The phrase "meiner Rede" develops the disapproval of colloquial speech (from line 2); *reden* is a verb for casual conversation, but the noun *die Rede* refers instead to a talk given to an audience. The poem has turned against light and talk, light talk and public utterance; it has built to a colon (8) preceding an imagistic expression of the kernel conflict. The speaker's talk is heaped up against its contrary, a singular, familiar crystal of silence. However, it is not only that Celan, like other modernists, feels a metaphysical attraction to silence, and an aversion to public speaking. The poem of his time, Celan said in "The Meridian," "clearly shows a strong tendency toward silence."[75] *Angelagert* is especially loaded. First, it echoes the phrase "gelagertes Weiss" (referring to piles of snow) from the preceding poem "Heimkehr" (Homecoming) that Celan paired with "Unten" in *Sprachgitter* (1959):

> Weithin gelagertes Weiss.
> Drüberhin, endlos,
> die Schlittenspur des Verlornen.
>
> Continuing distinct white.
> Over there, without end,
> the sleigh-track of the lost.[76]

And the root of these terms, *lager*, is the notorious name of the camps: *Konzentrationslager*. "Kristall in der Tracht deines Schweigens." *Tracht* signifies not just "style," as Hamburger has it, but the traditional Germanic clothing worn especially proudly in the southern countryside. This is a style of resistance: it expresses a retrospective, patriotic affirmation of a native economy and way of life very different from those of postwar urban Germany or France. "Kristall in der Tracht"; *Überfall in der Nacht*; *Kristallnacht*. That hypothetical rhyme is buried in the heaps of snow. The identity of the lost one, now Germanified, absorbed in the words themselves. Celan makes no explicit reference to the Shoah, but in rhymes and etymons one hears the standard that damns sociable discourse and fluency together. One follows easily enough how sociality may require the forgetting of old scores: one lightens up in order to move on. But why might Celan think of this sociality as his home? That is the distinctive thematic feature of the poem. He avows his own estrangement from his origin: he is at home as a guest, not as a native. His inclination is toward the syllables, talk, not silence. The second person, who seems to stare out of the stunning last line, radiates Germanic self-possession. "Unten," like so many of Celan's poems, is a veiled self-reproach. He blames himself for fluency, absorption in the language of the silencers.

The Shoah is typically not subject matter for Celan; he draws no confidence from the missionary objective of testimony. It is instead a point of orientation, as home is; what occurred continues to realign what is said. The Shoah is the east that has shifted. Which way lies home? Through light or darkness, memory or forgetting, speech or silence? Toward or away from Germanic culture? *Unten*, below, is the direction of the deep and dark forces, since long before the *Antigone*; its contrary is *oben*, above, as in *oberflächlich*, superficial. After the shift, though, these coordinates will not hold. "Unten" addresses these questions, but Celan's work generally sets the metaphysical concerns of his generation—specifically, with language—in configurations oriented by the Shoah, although he does not talk about the Shoah. This is an intellectual, even a political, orientation, but it is above all ethical. There is so little consensus among contemporaries that disputes are pulled inevitably toward extremes or limit-cases. The Shoah is that: surely everyone can agree that what was made to happen was immoral, a violation beyond controversy.[77] This much about the Shoah is comforting, though it is grim to say so: we have at least one ethical basis on which to cobble ad hoc agreements. This is a sort of negative universality: Nazi atrocity cannot be accepted as an expression of human nature. Moreover it is commonly presumed that what occurred was so wrong that language cannot adequately represent the violation.[78] Without reference to God or love (terms of contention), there is still warrant for ineffability, or the figure of *impossibilia*, a trope of profundity.

What might English-language readers or poets consider especially rare in Celan's poems? In terms of style, the poems move with modernist intensity and privacy. Similarities with Pound's late cantos are clear. But Celan's access to abstract diction is unlike that of any modernist poet in English. Pound told the young Robert Creeley to "go in fear of abstractions." His Imagist advocacy turned readers and poets away from any form of allegory: "dim lands of peace" struck him as inadmissible because it links an abstraction with something concrete. Poetry in English lost a wide range of language use through the ascendancy of modernist doctrine, though of course there were gains too. The German language differs from English in regard to abstraction: German adjectives and verbs convert easily and systematically into abstractions, as they do not in English. The forgetting, the awakening, the too much, the lost—these expressions are naturalized into English speech only through labor; they are usable but ponderous in English, and in poetry after modernism they seem hardly usable. There is candor in abstraction when one lives less among people and things than among memories, ideas, and imaginings; and an exactness too. I forget, we forget, you are forgotten: this series, in which forgetting is predicated of each relevant grammatical subject position, has a bearing on Celan's poem. It may be accurately summed up in the un-English phrase "the forgetting" (*das Vergessen*). Forgetting affects all subjects. These claims are easily and economically mobilized in this German poem, but only awkwardly reconstructed in English prose. It is no help to hold with Pound that "the natural object is always the adequate symbol." Natural speech and analytical thought often reasonably diverge.

Celan's poems, like Pound's, are syntactically fractured and intricately allusive, which is revealing: those stylistic features that seem to have obstructed the reception of modernist poets have facilitated Celan's reception; he has found wide, appreciative audiences in German and English. There is no reason to think that he might have done better to have written in a less absolutist style. Modernist conventions were apparently just right for him and for his audiences. Why is that so for Celan, and not for Pound? The answer is that the Shoah is commonly understood to have disrupted linguistic orders; to just what extent, is controversial. Susan Gubar speaks of "the trauma of the Shoah as a linguistic disaster," largely because of the extinction of Yiddish.[79] Celan's poems engage the Shoah as a philological event; the German language itself has been radically altered by twelve years of political history. Its rules of meaning-making and terms of reference have been seriously, though not utterly, discredited.

The pressure on intellectuals to generalize on the basis of the Shoah is very great, and often misleading with regard to language. Susan Gubar depicts the state of literary opinion fairly when she writes, "According to men and women of letters . . . the Shoah discredited authoritarianism as well as authoritative deployments of language, whether public or private, nationalistic or individualistic, sacred or secular."[80] Adorno's dictate is thereby honored: poetry is certainly discredited insofar as authoritative literary language is indistinguishable from authoritarianism. The Nazi abuse of power and language does not legitimately discredit the language of Kant, Hölderlin, Wittgenstein, and Celan, let alone all authoritative language. No one should welcome a language in which all claims are hedged. But it is true that language skepticism has constrained poetic practice. The utopian formal aspirations of the modernists—their efforts to construct art that hewed especially closely to the structures of perception—have given way to a satiric approach to syntactic and generic conventions. And this now seems deeply right to diverse readers of poetry. Celan devoted his life to the creation of compelling, memorable art in the German language; he recognized the corruptions of German but nonetheless took it as his medium. J. M. Coetzee has observed that "Todesfuge" implies that "the German language . . . , corrupted to the bone during the Nazi era by euphemism and a kind of leering doublespeak, is capable of telling the truth about Germany's immediate past."[81] As George Steiner has said, Celan knew himself "to be of the company of Hölderlin and Rilke—that is to say, one who would be bringing further radiance and life force to the tongue in which his parents and his community (that of East European Judaism) had been condemned to hideous death."[82] And like Conrad and Nabokov, he had other options. It should be recognized, though, that Celan's German is rarely colloquial beyond a single phrase or clause.[83] As Milton wrote an English no one spoke, Celan wrote in bookish and idiosyncratic German. The words come one by one from lexicons to the poems. He seems to have held to the modernist notion that a poet purifies the language of the tribe. He lived in France and wrote in an eccentric German; that is the life he made for himself.

›››‹‹‹

The English-language reception of Miłosz and Celan focuses directly on historicity and universality; these are the very terms critics repeatedly invoke. English-language readers want a particular epochal historicity from poetry so ardently that they seek it out in foreign languages. Another way to interpret this reception is to say that it reveals the values that U.S. literary culture wishes to be known to treasure. Pascale Casanova analyzes the cultural authority gained by nations whose poets are imported into metropolitan literary cultures, and also the imperial ambition that is legitimated when nations convincingly establish themselves as curators of the world's poetries. The evolution of U.S. cultural authority since 1945 shows that it is unnecessary, even undesirable, for an imperial power to promote its own poets: an empire instead presents itself advantageously as a vigilant guardian of its colonies' accomplishments; the traditional model of translation as appropriation—"one conquered, when one translated," Nietzsche said—is too blunt.[84] U.S. imperial authority is all the stronger if U.S. poets do not contend with Polish, Russian, and Caribbean poets. The universality of the empire seems validated by the fact that national literary prestige is not the direct object of U.S. culture. "The knowledge of our civilization," Pound said at the outset of the twentieth century, "embraces the world, we have mastered the elements."[85] The United States, the United Kingdom, even Germany in the nineteenth century all emulated the Roman model. *We care for you* is the modern imperial message. "Our nation seems to be destined," Schleiermacher said in 1813,

> because of its respect for things foreign, and because of its disposition toward mediation, to carry all the treasures of foreign art and scholarship, together with its own, in its language, to unite them into a great historical whole, as it were, which would be kept safe in the center and heart of Europe; so that now, with the help of our language, everyone can enjoy, as purely and perfectly as it is possible for the foreigner, that which the most varied ages have brought forth. This seems indeed the true historical goal of translation on a large scale, as it is now indigenous to us.[86]

Heidegger attributed the hollowness of modern culture to exactly this custodial spirit. "*Roman thought takes over the Greek words,*" he said, "*without a corresponding, equally authentic experience of what they say, without the Greek word.* The rootlessness of Western thought begins with this translation."[87] A modern imperial state has no incentive to promote translations of its own poets and novelists, but a good reason to promote the translations they themselves undertake. Scholars and translators demonstrate apparent disinterestedness, a concern more generous than narrow national interest.

Casanova argues cogently that literary culture is structured in accord with several laws: two forces—one national, one international—have produced a world literary space at the conceptual level. First, all authors begin as national writers responding to the lived experience of their particular time and place; most literary interpretation positions writers in reconstructions of these contexts. Second, a small number of authors (and a tiny number of poets) are assessed by critics as viable candidates for international currency; some critics and translators are able to persuade many readers that those select authors deserve the prestige and authority granted to world (or universal) writers. National literary cultures that produce such writers gain prestige and authority by this selection. The process is constant: authors are locked in competition for greater prestige in a bourse of legitimacy and authority. Even insistently national poets are candidates as well for the status of world poet. Whitman recommends himself:

> These are really the thoughts of all men in all ages and lands, they
> are not original with me,
> If they are not yours as much as mine they are nothing, or next to
> nothing,
> If they are not the riddle and the untying of the riddle they are
> nothing,
> If they are not just as close as they are distant they are nothing.[88]

Among poets, an ardent patriot may be nonetheless a citizen of the world.

Although Casanova refers to "the laws of world literary space," she regards the literary-critical assessment of poetry as irrational and duplicitous. Critics, on her view, have no considerable reasons for their judgments; they are confidence men who hoodwink their readers into belief. The notion of universality, she claims, "is one of the most diabolical inventions of the center, for in denying the antagonistic and hierarchical structure of the world, and proclaiming the equality of all the citizens of the republic of letters, the monopolists of universality command others to submit to their law. Universality is what they—and they alone—declare to be acceptable and accessible to all."[89] Translators are "the true architects of the universal," on her account, even though they circumvent public literary-critical debate and produce not reasons but texts.[90] She claims that the circulation of authority rests on belief, credit, not on knowledge or reasons.[91] The legitimacy granted by the selection process she analyzes is due not to principles but to proficiency at the game of publicity.[92] This skeptical alternative to explicit literary-critical evaluation offers no hope of a cognitive gain: readers acquaint themselves with one literary culture after another in order to accumulate local knowledge of unending difference. "I buy . . . an ugly NEW WORLD WRITING to see what the poets / in Ghana are doing these days."[93]

What is the function of evaluative principles in the assessment of poetry? The idea of thematically general poetry entails a notion that poems are well judged for their fit with certain general principles, as though poems were instances. This unattractive presumption subordinates poems to known principles and thereby discounts them as sources of knowledge. The assessment of poems and poets is commonly thought, especially in academic literary culture, to be determined by personal, local inclinations, and only misleadingly sublimated into a contest of ideas (Casanova's skepticism is widely shared). Yet literary opinion is not anarchic; nor does social class account for prominent disagreements. Readers of poetry obviously tend toward agreement about the value of particular poems and poets, even though the basis of agreement is controversial; agreement is not comprehensive, but it clusters around many points of mutuality. Critical controversy about universality understandably focuses on the qualities of particular poems, as though certain qualities were conducive to inevitable appreciation. However, the strongest advocate of universality as a criterion of aesthetic judgment held rather that no such qualities inhere in poems; rather, the cognitive faculties of human beings are universal, and judgments refer to those faculties, not to features of poems. Even so, Kant does not propose claims about cognition that might be disproved by empirical psychology. His claim is that when one recognizes a poem as beautiful, one asserts that others *should* (not *will*) by necessity of their cognitive capacities share in that recognition. If others do not in fact share such an assessment or recognition, it does not follow that the judgment is mistaken. It may be instead that some contingent cause prevents others from sharing a recognition they should, under ideal circumstances, share.

The advantage of explicitly principled judgments over personal preferences is not that principles extend agreement. On the contrary, Edmund Burke observed, "there is rather less difference upon matters of Taste among mankind, than upon most of those which depend upon the naked reason; . . . men are far better agreed on the excellence of a description in Virgil, than on the truth or falsehood of a theory of Aristotle."[94] Evaluative judgments are not expected to promote conformity in a democratic literary culture; they facilitate inquiry and controversy by rendering visible what might otherwise remain obscure—that is, *why* one values poems. Kant speaks of aesthetic judgment as the adducing of a concept that might account for a "cognitively unmastered" particular object. "Judgment in general," he says, "is the faculty of thinking the particular as contained under the universal." But for aesthetic judgment, "only the particular [is] given for which the universal has to be formed, the judgment is merely *reflexive*."[95] Aesthetic judgment constantly confronts unfamiliar or wild objects, and advances understanding by hypothesizing a concept to facilitate cognition.[96] An explicit reference to an evaluative criterion enables one to conjecture what a particular poem implicitly asks of readers, and to precipitate terms of dissent. Kant notes that if aesthetic judgments "had no principle at all, like judgments of the mere taste of sense, then the thought that they have a necessity would not occur to us at all."[97] Practical literary critics presume that poems can be fruitfully analyzed in terms of principles, and that there is a point to disputing judgments of taste. The challenge critics feel is not to prove the existence of a single relation between judgments and principles, but rather to define such a relation in a particular case, since cases obviously vary. Judgments are explicatory and hypothetical; they unfold the implications of poems and readers.

›››‹‹‹

The aspiration to generality is a necessary part of literary system. Harold Bloom has asserted, against the current, that "the final aim of literary study" is "the search for a kind of value that transcends the particular prejudices and needs of societies at fixed points in time."[98] Texts compete for authority, as critics as diverse as Bloom and Casanova show. Texts, authors, and literatures that succeed in the contest do not so much displace others as they rise above their competitors. The winners are said to appeal to more readers in time and space: they are called the universal poets. Emerson refers to the joy, wonder, and awe felt when Chaucer, Marvell, or Dryden seem to speak as contemporaries.[99] What such poets actually achieve is a level of general address. They do so, it appears, by various means of general reference, in part by engaging quite specific historical subjects, such as the Shoah and the Stalinization of Europe—and also by finding a music in words. The claim that a poem has universal appeal means only that generality of address has been achieved, that a contest has been won. Specific reference is certainly not an obstacle to general address: the contrary is the case. The orientation of Miłosz on the division of Europe and that of Celan on the consequences of the Shoah show that specificity is often a firm basis of general address. There is nonetheless a sense in which poetic language does genuinely aspire to universality: the musical and figurative structures of poetic language open to an indefinitely expanding range of signification.

Conclusion

In "The Meridian" Celan speaks of the absolute poem, even though, he acknowledges, it cannot exist. I have referred throughout to "poetry" or "lyric poetry," though my experience is of single poems from several historical periods. A critic responds to the diversity of the art and expects from each poem a surprise, but nonetheless generalizes and idealizes poetry in order to clarify criteria by which to admire or choose among poems on offer. One may live by faith, law, art, utility, or momentary inclination, or now and then all these. If in some sense by art, though, which art? Kant requires that one be able to recommend one's choice to another, as one regularly does in conversation. And teachers of poetry recommend preferences: why read and discuss one rather than another poem? Students expect to hear at least one answer before they choose for themselves. Evaluation is a constant feature of practical literary life, and it leads inevitably and rightly to abstraction. One's object is admittedly a kind of self-aware connoisseurship, the kind of knowing that comes of wide acquaintance. One wants to know the scope of the art—what it encompasses—in order to name its elements, as one can acquaintances. But still more one wants to understand the reasons to keep such company.

My argument is that lyric poetry is by definition musical, and that its sounds evoke a sense of justness. They summon into being patterns of thought and feeling that are unsatisfactorily accounted for in disciplined prose—hence "a sense of." This art often reveals forms of thinking and feeling of which one had little idea, and of which one eventually achieves only an indefinite idea. One does not even hear at once all the music of poetry, and only a portion of what one hears can one identify. Critics search out the orders and name them arcanely, or characterize them by approximation. Named or not, musical elements are combinatory: echoes link words and phrases in ways that do not depend on concepts or propositions. Victor Zuckerkandl says that a melody is a series of tones that, like a sentence, hold together.[1] But syntax is only an analogy; it suggests the way that musicality seems to make lawful sense, though one cannot name all the laws. Before one identifies such orders of tones, one may accurately speak of signification, or imagination, but not of lyric achievement.

Poetry and music collaborate deeply and darkly. Sounds warrant what poets say by giving words palpable form: one hears the orders, senses achievement, and extends credence. Musicality underwrites the authority of a proposition (Pope's "Whatever is, is right"), or of an observation (Eliot's "I had not thought death had undone so many"), but the collaboration of sound and sense goes further. This authority concerns as well the idiom of a passage: musicality warrants not only the validity of a claim but also the authority of a range of language use. When one can locate that range in relation to a speech community (and this is often not the case), the cultural authority of that community is generally enhanced because art has been made of its medium; Dante is credited with enhancing Tuscany in this way. This accreditation process is always affirmative: the authority of a proposition or observation, of a community or sensibility, is enhanced, never qualified, by the achievement of musical form. One can say, more diffusely, that the authority of poetic language, as distinct from the established professional discourses of history, philosophy, and social policy, is enhanced by each achievement of musical form, even when no clear or significant paraphrasable sense is involved. In "Frost at Midnight" Coleridge refers to the tolling bells of a churchtower as "the poor man's only music." The chimes, he says, fall "on mine ear / Most like articulate sounds of things to come!" (29, 32–33). He means to represent these sounds in a manner suitable to the adversity of the poor; it is a song full of hope. One often reads poems in a state of desire or want; musical form anticipates resolution. The justness of musical form refers to a sonic fit of syllables, one with the next, but signifies too a pleasure one experiences, as Coleridge did, in the form of a premonition. Something's coming.

What is the future that lyrics foretell? Simon Jarvis recently put the case that poetic musicality is cognitive, inherent to the intellectual experience of a poem. Hegel speaks of a "musical thinking that does not get as far as the Notion, . . . does not make its appearance in conceptual form."[2] The significance of musicality is temporal: it develops toward an unattained goal, that of conceptual expression. Hegel speaks of the movement of music toward a *beyond*. Jean-Luc Nancy describes listening to music as dwelling in a "nascent state," "ahead of signification."[3] Jarvis asks whether "there is something constitutively illusory about what it is that music attempts to express."[4] Does one indeed approach a significant *beyond*? The danger Jarvis recognizes is complacency: too readily converting "we do not know" into "we cannot know"; an assertion of cognitive limits easily produces resignation and consolation.[5] Insofar as musicality implies the approach of a concept that fits, neatly and fully, the feelings aroused by the sounds: no reason to think that such concepts arrive. However, one has reason to appreciate, as Kant would, language that refuses conceptual formulation. Its value lies in a difference from recognizable conceptual formulation. A lyric poem sounds a distinctive range of life in language. That this range extends beyond determinate concepts is certain, but that is an intellectual advantage, rather than a liability, in an intellectual economy dominated by professional discourses: music and poetry obstruct the circulation of ideas by means of paraphrase, as though language were entirely semantic, and meaning entirely linguistic.[6] Paraphrasable truths are thought to travel well. Musical effects endorse the local: a determinate set of words (not others just like them), in a distinct sequence, at a particular point in a poem seem just. The achievement of musicality paradoxically summons an authority beyond words on behalf of only these words, in this order, at this point.

The musicality of poetry is the fulfillment of what is meant by beautiful language. Many combinations of words give immediate pleasure. And just this pleasure is suspect to much contemporary criticism and aesthetic theory. A strenuous sense of realism often leads critics to mistrust pleasure that is not instrumental to improvement of the social and economic situation of the oppressed. Arthur Danto comes to the conclusion that beauty "is a necessary condition for life as we would want to live it," but that it is merely an option for art.[7] He evidently concurs with Philip Guston's proud and parsimonious belief that "the world as it is does not deserve beauty"; hence Danto's awkwardly conditional formulation.[8] On this view, lyric poetry would be for *after* the revolution. However, beauty, pleasure, and musicality may in the interim facilitate artistic projects to advance understanding, as a coating eases the swallowing of a pill, but they are, on this view, unworthy ends in themselves until social changes have removed more pressing concerns. The intellectual shortcoming of this social realism is that it provides only a shallow, rhetorical account of the evident power of poetry. Critique and representation are inessential to lyric; musicality summons praise.

Affirmation is essential to lyric poetry, but deeply controversial in intellectual discourse. Consider these two quatrains from the proem to Hart Crane's *The Bridge* (1930), the greatest modernist praise poem:

O harp and altar, of the fury fused,
(How could mere toil align thy choiring strings!)
Terrific threshold of the prophet's pledge,
Prayer of pariah, and the lover's cry,—

. . . .

O Sleepless as the river under thee,
Vaulting the sea, the prairies' dreaming sod,
Unto us lowliest sometime sweep, descend
And of the curveship lend a myth to God.[9]

How extraordinary that Crane invokes the ancient notion that music, in particular that of the harp, expresses the order of the heavens. By Crane's time, this idea could be entertained only with awareness of the historical divide between readers of this modernist poem and those who first listened to Pythagoras explain the three orders of music: the cosmic or heavenly music, the human music of the ordered spirit, and the technical music made by voices and lyres.[10] Crane's interest is in the first of these orders, the one commonly thought most remote from modern thought. His parenthetical question—"How could mere toil align thy choiring strings"?—is punctuated as a declaration. This is just the point that bears directly on his own composition. His mere toil is evident in the prosodic regularity of his quatrains. He proposes, though, that such toil at some point can generate a higher, divine order, that mere prosody can produce harp-like music, and then that music can "lend a myth" to God. Crane imagines a transformative threshold, where mundane labor transcends itself by an act of representation, not by divine fiat. The Brooklyn Bridge is like David's harp; and Crane's quatrains, like David's songs. All three: instruments of willed representations of divine authority.

The concept of a threshold has practical critical utility. It is not the case that poems are rightly assessed only in terms of sonic structure, that a more echoic poem is thereby better than a less echoic one. I am not proposing general principles for the relative assessment of various musicalities. However, not every text that is intended to be a lyric poem in fact is one. Rarely is every text in a book of ostensible lyrics an achieved lyric: some poems successfully attain musicality, and most do not. When a poem achieves some measure of sonic structure, it gains authority as a genuine poem. Critics try to discriminate lyrics from sketches for poems that do not come off. A musical utterance is not held to the same tests that deflate prosaic aspirations. Some poems are rich and conspicuous in their sonic order; others are much less so. The concept of a threshold is just right: at a certain point, a poem gains warrant to speak differently, in a second discourse, not prose.

Back to the futures proposed by musical language: intellectual poems, as well as musical ones, foretell futures. To assess a poem intellectually, one often distinguishes between a compelling representation of a recognizable line of thinking (Bronk is my example; Pope is Helen Vendler's) and an evocation of the edge of what one comprehends. Rilke, Pound, and Celan, apprehending more than they could comprehend, wrote beyond intelligibility, and are highly esteemed for their efforts. They could not clearly name the concepts that perfectly matched the perceptions and reflections that they rendered memorable. Pound dealt with this issue theoretically in his collaboration with Fenollosa on the essay on the Chinese written character. In any number of cantos he was able to draw together and render musical multiple features of thought, feeling, and perception, but he could not name the concept that unified these features. Having summoned cherry, flamingo, and iron rust, he could not say "redness." Yet most cantos imply the existence of an intellectual coherence (a concept or ideogram) that will, one by one, render the poems lucid. Why is a prospect of fuller understanding so attractive? Form implies a state of perfection that lies in an achieved future of Hope Realized. Poetry, because of its formality, is always implicitly prospective. In a conceivable future the language of poetry is full of being. In nearly every line of Hopkins, Dickinson, Pound, or Celan, one hears of a distinctive life in language. Their poems illuminate the range of language beyond socially realized discourses. Only once did Pound, dominated by ideology, name a governing concept: usury in Canto 45, the one lucid poem in the sequence.

Orphic poetry produces value by estranging social discourse, whereas the civil approach to poetry produces value indirectly by exhibiting artistic achievement as evidence of the authority of an identifiable social group. One might think that religious art would generate value from doctrine, but this is not the case. The value orphic poetry produces comes from its display of unfamiliar ways to live in language. Laura (Riding) Jackson claims that poetry necessarily circulates such promissory notes, and that they are falsely tendered. She asks whether the taste for poetry does not itself impede intellectual and spiritual progress: does poetry, "existing, prevent the realization of it ['the full of truth'] by ever futurizing it . . . ?"[11] But not all poets do, as she believes, insist on future fulfillment. Civil poets do not expect to summon sticks, stones, and beasts to a new order. Their language fulfills the idioms shared by contemporary citizens in social, political, economic, and legal circumstances; their poems imply not only legitimacy but even hope for the survival of existing social institutions. These poets encourage one to appreciate honest engagement with the medium in which we actually live. Rather than art from the edge, one may prefer poems that engage life at some distance from boundary conditions. The objective, as Arnold said, is to see life steadily and whole. Or is it to change life?

That is a costly choice, for critics as for poets: one wants to hold both options open. The language of our time might be transformed into something consistent with but greater than its established civic uses. Mallarmé had an elaborate vision of this reconciliation:

> The disinterested poet, eschewing all virtuosity and bravado, must project his vision of the world and use the languages of the school, home, and market place which seem most fitting to that purpose. Then poetry will be lifted to some frightening, wavering, ecstatic pitch—like an orchestral wing spread wide in flight, but with its talons still rooted deep within your earth. Wherever you find it, you must deny the ineffable; for somehow it will speak.[12]

This assimilative poet—could he have had Whitman in mind?—resists partisanship, because the promiscuous combination of diverse idioms extends poetry's reach. Yet this poet is in no sense neutral: he or she is not a realistic analyst but a proponent of a distinct "vision of the world." The disinterestedness Mallarmé proposes seems to concern freedom from group affiliation. A plain, not a vatic, style, according to him, has this capacity to absorb differences of linguistic practice, to range productively over social boundaries. "Donner un sens plus pur aux mots de la tribu": a tribe is one. He advocates not piety, or even stillness, before "the ineffable." Instead he imagines a progressive articulation of just that which seems awesomely silent. The progress of the spirit works through language against mute experience, thought, feeling.

While one waits for a Dante, Whitman, or Eliot to draw together these orphic and civil lines of poetic practice, there are only timely adjustments between them. Lyric derives its greatest authority from orphic poetics; the poets who hew closely to the norms of contemporary speech have a more modest but still considerable authority on which to ground their art (modest, because subject to practical political judgment). Both lines of poetic art are not only desirable, they are necessary. Orphic values help one distinguish especially ambitious work from academic or industrial product, and music is the chief criterion; conversely, the achievements of poets who write well in the idioms we actually speak make evident some of the fakery of poor orphic verse. No one is helped by mere pretension or mystification. Hass, Pinsky, and Glück keep readers honest about the value of skeptical intelligence. Controversy between these two lines of poetic practice is productive. When the civic mode grows complacent or provincial—and it does—memory of the work of Rilke, Pound, and Celan makes evident a need for change. Poets are then expected to *know more* about life and art, to convey not only what is not otherwise being said, but even what is not known. Orpheus's power is his music; poetry's music is a sign of this not-known that poets somehow know. Stevens recognized that the indefiniteness of music indicates more general limits on knowledge: "You have somehow to know the sound that is the exact sound; and you do in fact know, without knowing how. Your knowledge is irrational. In that sense life is mysterious; and if it is mysterious at all, I suppose that it is cosmically mysterious. I hope that we agree that it is at least mysterious. What is true of sounds is true of everything."[13]

Poets are drawn to sublimity by ambition, a chance to produce intensely affecting, memorable art. "For a *writer's* purposes," according to Schiller, "the only thing useful about even expressions of the most sublime virtue is the *power* they possess. He does not bother in the slightest about the orientation of the power."[14]

Sublimity is a category of rhetoric, or design on another, but its attachment to an ethical goal, as Schiller said, is faint. The sublime, as Burke says, "is productive of the strongest emotion which the mind is capable of feeling."[15] That is what matters: force. Just when art seems to be rising toward spirit, it is conniving for one effect: to be felt. The celebratory mode of praise is not the same as the sublime, though the celebratory is one mode of the sublime. Burke's vision of the sublime is actually kind of nasty, cowardly. The mind swells only so long as it observes the terrible from a safe remove. One wants an illusion of terror, not the real, demeaning thing itself. "Actual and serious fear," Schiller notes, "overcomes all freedom of mind."[16] And the truth is that grand artistic ambition is at odds with the practical reasoning that allows people to live peacefully with one another in communities. "Civility" is always a term of limit, even when not preceded by "mere": communities are constituted by restraints. Robert Pinsky's "From the Childhood of Jesus" reveals some of the icy egotism of sublime art.

> One Saturday morning he went to the river to play.
> He modeled twelve sparrows out of the river clay.
>
> And scooped a clear pond, with a dam of twigs and mud.
> Around the pond he set the birds he had made,
>
> Evenly as the hours. Jesus was five. He smiled,
> As a child would who had made a little world
>
> Of clear still water and clay beside a river.
> But a certain Jew came by, a friend of his father,
>
> And he scolded the child and ran at once to Joseph,
> Saying, "Come see how your child has profaned the Sabbath,
>
> Making images at the river on the Day of Rest."
> So Joseph came to the place and took his wrist
>
> And told him, "Child, you have offended the Word."
> Then Jesus freed the hand that Joseph held
>
> And clapped his hands and shouted to the birds
> To go away. They raised their beaks at his words

And breathed and stirred their feathers and flew away.
The people were frightened. Meanwhile, another boy,

The son of Annas the scribe, had idly taken
A branch of driftwood and leaning against it had broken

The dam and muddied the little pond and scattered
The twigs and stones. Then Jesus was angry and shouted,

"Unrighteous, impious, ignorant, what did the water
Do to harm you? Now you are going to wither

The way a tree does, you shall bear no fruit
And no leaves, you shall wither down to the root."

At once, the boy was all withered. His parents moaned,
The Jews gasped, Jesus began to leave, then turned

And prophesied, his child's face wet with tears:
"Twelve times twelve times twelve thousands of years

Before these heavens and this earth were made,
The Creator set a jewel in the throne of God

With Hell on the left and Heaven on the right,
The Sanctuary in front, and behind, an endless night

Endlessly fleeing a Torah written in flame.
And on that jewel in the throne, God wrote my name."

Then Jesus left and went into Joseph's house.
The family of the withered one also left the place,

Carrying him home. The Sabbath was nearly over.
By dusk, the Jews were all gone from the river.

Small creatures came from the undergrowth to drink
And foraged in the shadows along the bank.

Alone in his cot in Joseph's house, the Son
Of Man was crying himself to sleep. The moon

Rose higher, the Jews put out their lights and slept,
And all was calm and as it had been, except

In the agitated household of the scribe Annas,
And high in the dark, where unknown even to Jesus

The twelve new sparrows flew aimlessly through the night,
Not blinking or resting, as if never to alight.[17]

This parable of Jesus' terrifying creative and destructive power begins benignly, recirculating a couple of Yeats's terms from "The Lake Isle of Innisfree," but ends with the blank terror that follows an irreversible catastrophe. Jesus wields his might without concern for the distinctions that mortals invoke to hold in place a habitable world. The intent or agency of Annas's son counts for nothing: whether he meant to destroy Jesus' little dam or was lazily observing someone else's troubles is ambiguous. The misery of Annas's family, the ruination of a child's body—these too count for nothing. When the parents moan for their wasted child, Jesus coldly "began to leave" (27–28). Joseph's comprehension of the basic terms of Christian theology and worship (of the Word and the Sabbath) is paradoxically off the mark; he is merely a mortal father who does not understand all that Jesus brings. Jesus is indifferent to family love and mortal hope. His attention is absorbed in a symbolic order: twelve sparrows; his own origin twelve times twelve times twelve thousand years before what mortals call Creation. One hears this disconnect as this straightforward narrative proceeds without impediment through twenty-five heroic couplets, almost as if these prosodic structures were not there. What is terrifying is not that we have this story too of Jesus (from the *Apocrypha*), but that creative power and humane judgment are so utterly at odds. Jesus knows his own power (30–36) and cares nothing for other matters. Like Orpheus, he overthrows natural and human orders. Pinsky's prince of peace weeps, as a poet might, for his images and his threatened prerogatives, not for a withered child or a crushed family.

›››‹‹‹

Pinsky's poem questions the ethics of transformative art, but a deeper skepticism than his altogether doubts that art has a transformative capacity. The boldest recent account of this view is that of Laura (Riding) Jackson. She began as an ardent believer in the art. Until the late 1930s, she held to a "creed" of poetry that affirms "an ideal condition of the human personality characterized by complete awareness, complete articulateness, completely intelligent liberation of spirit from the gross physical preoccupations incidental to human existence, and that . . . condition is realizable in poems as nowhere else."[18] She came to the realization, however, that not only her own poems but all poems could not possibly achieve the ends that drove her to write poems in the first place; she renounced the art in 1938 and continued for many years thereafter to write prose about the failure of poetry. This poetic creed—to which she counted all poets as adherents—came to seem to her false exactly because she thought of form and music, as readers commonly do, as separate from sense. The value of poetic statement, by her account, rests on thematic significance alone. The musicality she hears in poetic language is entirely artificial in that it derives from craft, not from the intellectual project of a particular poem. Poetic form of all sorts, but especially sonic form, is an imposition on what she thinks of as the "original" and "natural" thought that generates a particular poem.[19] The equivalence of poetry and truth that she sought "was ever sucked into the whorl of poetic artifice, with its overpowering necessities of patterned rhythm and harmonic sound-play, which work distortions upon the natural proprieties of tone and word."[20] A poet's preoccupation with sound is "predetermined" and exists "apart from the preoccupation with sense and sense-development."[21] She could not trust form as a source of change in an intellectual project, even though many of her contemporaries, such as Crane, Louis Zukofsky, and Yvor Winters, effectively argued that form reveals sense. They gladly followed the lead of vowel tones, consonance, rhymes, and rhythms in the prospect of a discovery of thought and feeling. The music transforms one thought into another, usually unforeseen, and sometimes indeterminate too. The power of poetry to change hearts and minds rests on trust: that form alters all.

Notes

INTRODUCTION

1. Wallace Stevens, *Opus Posthumous*, ed. Samuel French Morse (New York: Knopf, 1957), 166.

2. See James L. Kugel, ed., *Poetry and Prophecy* (Ithaca: Cornell University Press, 1990).

3. William Wordsworth, preface to *Lyrical Ballads*, in *Critical Theory since Plato*, ed. Hazard Adams and Leroy Searle, 3rd ed. (Boston: Thomson Wadsworth, 2005), 487.

4. Walter Benn Michaels, *The Shape of the Signifier* (Princeton: Princeton University Press, 2004), 1–10.

5. Stevens, *Opus Posthumous*, 171.

6. John Crowe Ransom, *The World's Body* (New York: Charles Scribner's, 1938), 118.

7. Samuel Taylor Coleridge, *Biographia Literaria*, ed. James Engell and Walter Jackson Bate (Princeton: Princeton University Press, 1983), 2:6.

8. "Of Cato the Younger," *The Complete Essays of Montaigne*, ed. Donald M. Frame (Stanford: Stanford University Press, 1958), 171.

9. [Longinus], "On the Sublime" [chapter 1], in *Critical Theory since Plato*, ed. Hazard Adams, rev. ed. (Fort Worth, TX: Harcourt Brace Jovanovich, 1992), 76.

10. Gerald Bruns, *The Materials of Poetry* (Athens: University of Georgia Press, 2005), 5.

11. Ibid., 4.

12. Noam Chomsky, e.g., develops this notion from August Schlegel in *Cartesian Linguistics* (New York: Harper and Row, 1966), 17–18.

13. Martin Heidegger, *Poetry, Language, Thought*, trans. Albert Hofstadter (New York: Harper and Row, 1971), 71.

14. Steven Knapp, *Literary Interest* (Cambridge, MA: Harvard University Press, 1993), 1.

15. We have had ambitious poet-critics in the last thirty years: Adrienne Rich, Gary Snyder, Wendell Berry, Robert Bly. Like Pound and Eliot before them, they all directly addressed large-scale social and political issues facing the nation. However, the modernists had a sense of a fresh, distinctive, and conceptual role for poetry in cultural change. Their successors have modestly claimed much less for their own art. Recent poet-critics write less confidently about art and society; poets have grown more modest as explainers.

CHAPTER 1

1. Robert Pinsky has surveyed U.S. opinion concerning poems, if not poetry itself, and produced a video archive of readings of favorite poems by citizens from diverse regions and occupational groups. The selections are collected in two anthologies: *America's Favorite Poems*, ed. Robert Pinsky and Maggie Dietz (New York: Norton, 2000); *Poems to Read*, ed. Robert Pinsky and Maggie Dietz (New York: Norton, 2002).

2. Steven Knapp, *Literary Interest* (Cambridge, MA: Harvard University Press, 1993), 106.

3. Hannah Arendt, *Between Past and Future* (1961; New York: Penguin, 1968), 121–22.

4. Roman Jakobson, *My Futurist Years*, ed. Bengt Jangfeldt, trans. Stephen Rudy (New York: Marsilio, 1997), 174–75. A poem by Michael Fried, "The Essence of Poetry," in *The Next Bend in the River* (Chicago: University of Chicago Press, 2004), brought this passage to my attention.

5. Goethe, *The Autobiography*, trans. John Oxenford (Chicago: University of Chicago Press, 1974), 1:235.

6. Adam Zagajewski, *A Defense of Ardor*, trans. Clare Cavanaugh (New York: Farrar, Straus, Giroux, 2004), 65.

7. Friedrich Schiller, *Essays*, ed. Walter Hinderer and Daniel O. Dahlstrom (New York: Continuum, 1993), 150–51.

8. Theodor W. Adorno, *Notes to Literature*, ed. Rolf Tiedemann,

trans. Shierry Weber Nicholsen (New York: Columbia University Press, 1992), 1:37.

9. John Crowe Ransom, *The World's Body* (New York: Charles Scribner's, 1938), 247–48.

10. Ibid., 131.

11. Daniel Tiffany, "Kitsching *The Cantos*," *Modernism/Modernity* 12:2 (April 2005), 332–33.

12. Yves Bonnefoy, *The Act and the Place of Poetry*, ed. John T. Naughton (Chicago: University of Chicago Press, 1989), 139.

13. Wallace Stevens, "Adagia," in *Opus Posthumous*, ed. Samuel French Morse (New York: Knopf, 1957), 173.

14. Walt Whitman, "Out of the Cradle Endlessly Rocking," lines 148 and 156; in *Leaves of Grass*, ed. Sculley Bradley and Harold W. Blodgett (New York: Norton, 1973), 252.

15. Maurice Blanchot argues that Orpheus turns in impatience to look after Eurydice. Blanchot, "Orpheus' Gaze," in *The Space of Literature*, trans. Ann Smock (Lincoln: University of Nebraska Press, 1989), 173.

16. Seamus Heaney, "Orpheus and Eurydice," in *After Ovid*, ed. Michael Hofmann and James Lasdun (London: Faber, 1994), 225.

17. Seamus Heaney, "Death of Orpheus," in *After Ovid*, ed. Hofmann and Lasdun, 226.

18. "The Death of Orpheus," in *Ovid Metamorphoses*, trans. Charles Martin (New York: Norton, 2004), 370.

19. Fanny Howe, *The Wedding Dress* (Berkeley: University of California Press, 2003), 6.

20. Ibid., 17.

21. W. R. Johnson, *The Idea of Lyric* (Berkeley: University of California Press, 1982), 61.

22. Ibid., 59.

23. Robert Creeley, *Contexts of Poetry*, ed. Donald Allen (Bolinas: Four Seasons, 1973), 127.

24. T. S. Eliot, "East Coker," in *The Complete Poems and Plays* (New York: Harcourt, Brace and World, 1952), 129; confirmed by Theodore Roethke in his "North American Sequence," in *Collected Poems* (Garden City, NY: Doubleday, 1965), 189.

25. Stevens, *Opus Posthumous*, 228.

26. Bonnefoy, *The Act and the Place of Poetry*, 104.

27. Michael Murrin, *The Veil of Allegory* (Chicago: University of Chicago Press, 1969), 11.

28. For a brilliant discussion of the connections between oracles and poetic language, see Brett Bourbon, *Finding a Replacement for the Soul* (Cambridge, MA: Harvard University Press, 2004), chap. 5.

29. Ibid., 31; cf. 47.

30. Stevens, *Opus Posthumous*, 169.

31. Goethe, *Autobiography*, 2:106.

32. Immanuel Kant, *Critique of Judgment*, trans. Werner S. Pluhar (Indianapolis: Hackett, 1987), 69 [§ 13].

33. Plutarch, *Life of Solon*, 8:1–4.

34. Seamus Heaney, *The Government of the Tongue* (New York: Farrar, Straus and Giroux, 1988), 92–93.

35. Timothy Clark, *The Theory of Inspiration* (Manchester: Manchester University Press, 1997), 1–2.

36. John Milton, *Complete Poems and Major Prose*, ed. Merritt Y. Hughes (New York: Odyssey, 1957); *Paradise Lost* 9.23–24.

37. William Kerrigan, *The Prophetic Milton* (Charlottesville: University Press of Virginia, 1974), 28, 30.

38. Ibid., 42.

39. William Matthews, *The Poetry Blues* (Ann Arbor: University of Michigan Press, 2001), 38.

40. Allen Grossman, *The Sighted Singer* (Baltimore: Johns Hopkins University Press, 1992), 147–48. I should add here that my analysis of poetic authority has benefited from the excellent treatment of this topic by John Guillory, *Poetic Authority* (New York: Columbia University Press, 1983).

41. Plato, *Ion*, trans. Benjamin Jowett, in *Critical Theory since Plato*, ed. Hazard Adams, rev. ed. (Fort Worth, TX: Harcourt Brace Jovanovich, 1992), 14.

42. Kerrigan, *The Prophetic Milton*, chap. 1 passim, but esp. pp. 56, 61.

43. Ibid., 72–73.

44. Ibid., 82.

45. Richard Helgerson, *Self-Crowned Laureates* (Berkeley: University of California Press, 1983), 233–34.

46. Ibid., 117.

47. Ibid., 219.

48. Ibid., 2.

49. Ibid., 182.

50. Ibid., 282.

51. Ezra Pound, *The Literary Essays*, ed. T. S. Eliot (New York: New Directions, 1954), 285.

52. Ibid., 431.

53. See, however, Jennifer Bervin's recent *Nets* (Brooklyn: Ugly Duckling, 2004), a cut-out version of Shakespeare's sonnets.

54. Grossman, *Sighted Singer*, 165.

55. Susan Stewart, *The Fate of the Senses* (Chicago: University of Chicago Press, 2002), 198.

56. Ibid., 116.

57. Ronald Johnson, *Radi os* (1977; Chicago: Flood, 2005), 16–17. The two pages quoted here face one another. The numbers I have inserted in brackets correspond to the source lines in John Milton, *Paradise Lost*, in *Milton's Poetical Works* (New York: Thomas Y. Crowell, 1892), the edition consulted by Johnson.

58. Gregory Nagy, "Ancient Greek Poetry, Prophecy, and Concepts of Theory," in *Poetry and Prophecy*, ed. James L. Kugel (Ithaca: Cornell University Press, 1990), 63.

59. My colleague David Wellbery, in conversation, proposed the apt figure of camouflage for this sort of literary construction.

60. Gerard Manley Hopkins, *Poems and Prose*, ed. W. H. Gardner (London: Penguin, 1953), 27.

61. Peter O'Leary, "Gilding the Buddha: My Apprenticeship with Ronald Johnson," *Sagetrieb*, forthcoming.

62. Ronald Johnson, *Ark* (Albuquerque: Living Batch, 1996), 89.

63. David Quint, *Origin and Originality in Renaissance Literature* (New Haven: Yale University Press, 1983), chap. 1.

64. Ronald Johnson to Peter O'Leary, October 22, 1992; quoted in O'Leary, "Gilding the Buddha."

65. Quint, *Origin and Originality*, 40.

66. Ibid., 76–77.

67. Virgil, *The Georgics*, trans. L. P. Wilkinson (London: Penguin, 1982), 137–38.

CHAPTER 2

1. *The Collected Works of Ralph Waldo Emerson*, ed. Robert E. Spiller et al. (Cambridge, MA: Harvard University Press, 1971–2003), 2:159.

2. Ezra Pound, "How to Read," *The Literary Essays,* ed. T. S. Eliot (New York: New Directions, 1954), 20.

3. Plato, *The Republic,* ed. G. R. F. Ferrari, trans. Tom Griffith (Cambridge: Cambridge University Press, 2000), 387d–388a.

4. James Merrill, *Collected Poems,* ed. J. D. McClatchy and Stephen Yenser (New York: Knopf, 2002), 185.

5. *Shelley's Poetry and Prose,* ed. Donald H. Reiman and Sharon B. Powers (New York: Norton, 1977), 226.

6. John Milton, *Complete Poems and Major Prose,* ed., Merritt Y. Hughes (New York: Odyssey, 1957); *Paradise Lost,* 9.24.

7. *Shelley's Poetry and Prose,* 504.

8. Wordsworth, "Resolution and Independence," *The Norton Anthology of Poetry,* ed. Margaret Ferguson et al., 5th ed. (New York: Norton, 2005), 792.

9. Bacchylides, *Complete Poems,* trans. Robert Fagles (New Haven: Yale University Press, 1998), 27.

10. Andrew Ford, *The Origins of Criticism* (Princeton: Princeton University Press, 2002), 109.

11. My interpretation depends directly on Robert Fagles's interpellated conjectures concerning the circulation of fame among the dead. Richard C. Jebb notes that the opening three lines refer to the circulation of fame "even to the nether world," but he does not conjecture beyond that. (Richard C. Jebb, ed., *Bacchylides: The Poems and Fragments* [Cambridge: Cambridge University Press, 1905], 313.) David R. Slavitt's translation marks a lacuna in the opening lines, but does not conjecture where Fagles does. David R. Slavitt, ed. and trans., *Epinician Odes and Dithyrambs of Bacchylides* (Philadelphia: University of Pennsylvania Press, 1998), 44.

12. Emile Benveniste, *Indo-European Language and Society*, trans. E. Palmer (London: Faber, 1973), 348; cited by Leslie Kurke, "The Economy of *Kudos*," in *Cultural Poetics in Archaic Greece*, ed. Carol Dougherty and Leslie Kurke (New York: Oxford University Press, 1998), 132.

13. Kurke, *The Traffic in Praise* (Ithaca: Cornell University Press, 1991), 86.

14. Ibid., 99–101.

15. Ibid., 208.

16. *Pindar's Victory Songs*, trans. Frank J. Nisetich (Baltimore: Johns Hopkins University Press, 1980), 165.

17. Kurke, *Traffic*, 99.

18. Ibid., 103.

19. Ibid., 43, 66–67.

20. Ibid., 137–38.

21. Bacchylides, *Complete Poems*, 28–29.

22. See Harold Bloom, *The Western Canon* (New York: Riverhead, 1994), 31, where he wittily, but superficially, says, "Pindar . . . invested his art in the celebratory exercise of exchanging odes for grand prices, thus praising the wealthy for their generous support of his generous exaltation of their divine lineage."

23. Stanley Cavell, *Philosophy the Day after Tomorrow* (Cambridge, MA: Harvard University Press, 2005), 3.

24. Christopher Smart, *A Translation of the Psalms of David* (London, 1765), 88.

25. Hopkins, "No Worst, There Is None," in *Poems and Prose*, ed. Gardner, 61.

26. Donald Davie, "Sing Unto the Lord a New Song," in *To Scorch or Freeze* (Chicago: University of Chicago Press, 1988), 6.

27. Stephen Mitchell, trans., *A Book of Psalms* (New York: HarperCollins, 1993), 40–41.

28. The citation of Rilke comes from *Letters to a Young Poet*, chap. 4, July 16, 1903.

29. Anchor Bible, Psalm 92, 8–12.

30. *Pindar's Victory Songs*, 304.

31. Mark Payne, "On Being Vatic: Pindar, Pragmatism and Historicism," *American Journal of Philology* 127:2 (October 2006), 159–84.

32. *Pindar's Victory Songs*, 163.

33. Ibid., 131–32.

34. Ibid., 205.

35. Ibid., 105.

36. Ibid., 173.

37. Richard Rorty has addressed this matter boldly: "In both popular and elite culture, most descriptions of what America will be like in the twenty-first century are written in tones either of self-mockery or of self-disgust" (*Achieving Our Country* [Cambridge, MA: Harvard University Press, 1998], 4).

38. Robert Lowell, *History* (New York: Farrar, Straus and Giroux, 1973), 175; Robert Pinsky, *Jersey Rain* (New York: Farrar, Straus and Giroux, 2000), 43–44.

39. Thylias Moss, *Last Chance for the Tarzan Holler* (New York: Persea, 1998), 38.

40. Hans Ulrich Gumbrecht, *In Praise of Athletic Beauty* (Cambridge, MA: Harvard University Press, 2006), 35–36.

41. *Collected Works of Ralph Waldo Emerson*, ed. Spiller et al., 1:123.

42. Margaret Walker, *This Is My Century* (Athens: University of Georgia Press, 1989), 76.

43. Adam Zagajewski, *A Defense of Ardor*, trans. Clare Cavanagh (New York: Farrar, Straus and Giroux, 2004), 129.

44. Ibid., 152.

45. Ibid., 148–49.

46. Ibid., 31.

CHAPTER 3

1. Roland Barthes, "The Death of the Author," in *The Rustle of Language*, trans. Richard Howard (Berkeley: University of California Press, 1989), 49.

2. Ezra Pound, *The Literary Essays*, ed. T. S. Eliot (New York: New Directions, 1954), 30.

3. J. L. Austin, *How to Do Things with Words* (Cambridge, MA: Harvard University Press, 1962), 22.

4. Jean-Jacques Rousseau, "Essay on the Origin of Languages," in *On the Origin of Language*, trans. John H. Moran and Alexander Gode (Chicago: University of Chicago Press, 1966), 27.

5. M. M. Bakhtin, *Speech Genres and Other Late Essays*, ed. Caryl Emerson and Michael Holquist, trans. Vern W. McGee (Austin: University of Texas Press, 1986), 69.

6. Marjorie Perloff, *Radical Artifice* (Chicago: University of Chicago Press, 1991), 20.

7. Jan Mukařovský, "Standard Language and Poetic Language," in *A Prague School Reader*, ed. and trans. Paul L. Garvin (Washington, D.C.: Georgetown University Press, 1964), 18.

8. Ezra Pound, *Selected Prose*, ed. William Cookson (New York: New Directions, 1973), 41–42. Marjorie Perloff argues that Eliot was a spokesman of modernist practice generally, but the range of views on the role of speech in poetry was wide among modernist poets. For a comparison of the diction of Stevens and Williams, see Hugh Kenner, *A Homemade World* (1975; Baltimore: Johns Hopkins University Press,

1989), 50–90. Marianne Moore and Hart Crane (as Perloff acknowledges) do not fit the speech model well, either.

The definitive treatment of this topic is Derek Attridge's *Peculiar Language* (Ithaca: Cornell University Press, 1988). He notes that the tradition of a peculiar language for poetry extends back to Aristotle, but so does the idea of the naturalness of poetic language. Both elements are there near the source of Western poetic thought (3).

9. C. D. Wright, *Cooling Time* (Port Townsend, WA: Copper Canyon, 2005), 62.

10. Paul Valéry, *The Art of Poetry*, trans. Denise Folliot (New York: Random House, 1958), 171.

11. Yves Bonnefoy, *The Act and the Place of Poetry*, ed. John T. Naughton (Chicago: University of Chicago Press, 1989), 103.

12. Theodor W. Adorno, *Notes to Literature*, ed. Rolf Tiedemann, trans. Shierry Weber Nicholsen (New York: Columbia University Press, 1992), 2:112.

13. Samuel Taylor Coleridge, *Biographia Literaria*, ed. James Engell and Walter Jackson Bate (Princeton: Princeton University Press, 1983), 2:26.

14. Paul Valéry, *Aesthetics*, trans. Ralph Manheim (New York: Pantheon, 1964), 111.

15. Valéry, *Art of Poetry*, 63–64.

16. Valéry, *Aesthetics*, 48.

17. Ibid., 103–4.

18. Geoffrey Hill, *The Enemy's Country* (Stanford: Stanford University Press, 1991), 5.

19. Ibid., 66.

20. Fernando Pessoa, "The Art of Representation," in *Always Astonished*, trans. Edwin Honig (San Francisco: City Lights, 1988), 52.

21. Hill, *Enemy's Country*, 97.

22. *The Literary Criticism of Dante Alighieri*, ed. and trans. Robert S. Haller (Lincoln: University of Nebraska Press, 1973), 101.

23. Walt Whitman, *Song of Myself*, sec. 51, in *Leaves of Grass*, ed. Sculley Bradley and Harold W. Blodgett (New York: Norton, 1973), 88.

24. Hill, *Enemy's Country*, 5.

25. August Kleinzahler, *Green Sees Things in Waves* (New York: Farrar, Straus, Giroux, 1998), 3–4.

26. Gerhard Falkner, *Über den Unwert des Gedichts* (Berlin: Aufbau, 1993), 72. "Je mehr ein Gedicht erzählt, umso weniger hat es zu sagen."

27. Philip Larkin, *Collected Poems*, ed. Anthony Thwaite (New York: Farrar, Straus, Giroux, 1989), 165.

28. Christopher Ricks, *The Force of Poetry* (Oxford: Clarendon, 1984), 274.

29. Charles Bernstein, *Content's Dream* (Los Angeles: Sun and Moon, 1986), 44.

30. Valéry, *Art of Poetry*, 185.

31. Wallace Stevens, *Opus Posthumous*, ed. Samuel French Morse (New York: Knopf, 1957), 205.

32. Friedrich Schlegel, "Lyceum Fragments" 7, in *Lucinde and the Fragments*, trans. Peter Firchow (Minneapolis: University of Minnesota Press, 1971), 144.

33. Bernstein, *Content's Dream*, 49.

34. Susan Stewart, *The Fate of the Senses* (Chicago: University of Chicago Press, 2002), 32.

35. Langston Hughes, *Collected Poems*, ed. Arnold Rampersad (New York: Knopf, 1994), 87.

36. Stewart, *Fate of the Senses*, 223.

37. William Wordsworth, preface to *Lyrical Ballads*, in *Critical Theory since Plato*, ed. Hazard Adams and Leroy Searle, 3rd ed. (Boston: Thomson Wadsworth, 2005), 483.

38. Evelyn Nien-ming Ch'ien, *Weird English* (Cambridge, MA: Harvard University Press, 2004), 13.

39. Adorno, *Notes*, 1.38.

40. Perloff, *Radical Artifice*, 53.

41. Wright, *Cooling Time*, 68.

42. My discussion of style and affiliation derives generally from Donald Davie, *Purity of Diction in English Verse* (London: Routledge, 1952).

43. Pound, *Literary Essays*, 283.

44. Ibid., 362.

45. Robert Hass, *Sun under Wood* (Hopewell, NJ: Ecco, 1996), 44.

46. Ibid., 39–41.

47. Coleridge, *Biographia*, 2.58.

48. Pound, *Literary Essays*, 21–22.

49. Valéry, *Art of Poetry*, 54.

50. Edmund Burke, *A Philosophical Enquiry into the Origin of our Ideas of the Sublime and Beautiful*, ed. David Womersley (London: Penguin, 1998), 188.

51. Stanley Cavell, *The Claim of Reason* (Oxford: Oxford University Press, 1979), 178.

52. Wordsworth, preface, 484.

53. Paul Valéry, "Last Visit to Mallarmé," trans. Anthony Bower, in *Selected Writings* (New York: New Directions, 1950), 220.

54. Ezra Pound, *Gaudier-Brzeska* (1916; New York: New Directions, 1970), 115.

55. Bakhtin, *Speech Genres*, 71.

56. C. D. Wright, *Steal Away* (Port Townsend, WA: Copper Canyon, 2003), 208.

57. Pound, *Selected Prose*, 37.

58. Richard Rorty, *Contingency, Irony, and Solidarity* (Cambridge: Cambridge University Press, 1989), 7.

59. Ibid., 20.

CHAPTER 4

1. Some poets acknowledge the awkward overlap of poetry and philosophy. Lyn Hejinian, for instance, writes, "It would be . . . grandiose of me to claim status as a philosopher. And yet, in the end, it is as philosophy—as the making and seeing of connections . . .—that poetry participates in knowing what we can and can't know about the world and how to live in it. Poetry's ability to contribute to the work of doing philosophy is intrinsic to its medium, language. Every phrase, every sentence, is an investigation of an idea." *The Language of Inquiry* (Berkeley: University of California Press, 2000), 384.

2. Angus Fletcher, *Colors of the Mind* (Cambridge, Mass.: Harvard University Press, 1991), 3.

3. Raymond Geuss, "Poetry and Knowledge," *Arion*, ser. 3, 11.1 (Spring-Summer 2003), 1–31.

4. Paul Valéry, *The Art of Poetry*, trans. Denise Folliot (New York: Random House, 1958), 182; hereafter abbreviated as *AP*.

5. See, e.g., Rodolphe Gasché, *The Honor of Thinking* (Stanford: Stanford University Press, 2007), 279, 295.

6. Robert Duncan, *A Selected Prose*, ed. Robert J. Bertholf (New York: New Directions, 1995), 27.

7. William Bronk, *Life Supports* (San Francisco: North Point, 1981), 216.

8. Bob Perelman, "Parataxis and Narrative: The New Sentence in

Theory and Practice," *The Marginalization of Poetry* (Princeton: Princeton University Press, 1996), 60.

9. Ezra Pound, *The Literary Essays*, ed. T. S. Eliot (New York: New Directions, 1954), 4.

10. John Dewey, *How We Think* (Lexington, MA: D. C. Heath, 1933), 4; hereafter abbreviated as *HWT*.

11. Ernest Dimnet, *The Art of Thinking* (New York: Simon and Schuster, 1928), 170; hereafter abbreviated as *AT*.

12. T. S. Eliot, *Selected Essays* (New York: Harcourt, Brace and World, 1960), 246.

13. Arnold Stein, *John Donne's Lyrics* (Minneapolis: University of Minnesota Press, 1962), 12, 15.

14. On distraction and metaphysical poetry, see Angus Fletcher, "The Distractions of Wit in the English Renaissance," in *Colors of the Mind*, 52–67.

15. *The Inferno of Dante*, trans. Robert Pinsky (New York: Farrar, Straus and Giroux, 1994), 5.

16. Robert Duncan, *Fictive Certainties* (New York: New Directions, 1985), 65.

17. *The Collected Works of Ralph Waldo Emerson*, ed. Robert E. Spiller et al. (Cambridge, MA: Harvard University Press, 1971–2003), 2:195.

18. Ibid., 2:63.

19. Basil Bunting, *Briggflatts* (London: Fulcrum, 1966), 41.

20. John Koethe, *Falling Water* (New York: HarperCollins, 1997), 21; subsequent references to this poem are indicated parenthetically by section and line number. My understanding of this poem is indebted first to a paper by Susan Stewart given at Princeton in 2003, and later to extended conversations with Mark Strand about Koethe's writing.

21. John Koethe, *Poetry at One Remove* (Ann Arbor: University of Michigan Press, 2000), 82.

22. F. Scott Fitzgerald, *The Great Gatsby* (1925; New York: Charles Scribner's Sons, 1953), 182.

23. Koethe no doubt intends to allude to a famous essay on the difficulty of conceiving of a subjective experience (what it is like to be a bat) as an objective phenomenon; see Thomas Nagel, "What It Is Like to Be a Bat," *Philosophical Review* 83.4 (October 1974), 435–50.

24. This self-canceling process occurs sometimes at the grammatical level, when a pronoun might refer to one or another antecedent, or at the level of figure, as when he contrasts "the stringent / Vacuum and

the sound of a lawnmower" (2.6–7). The vacuum referred to here is an abstract absence, or emptiness, but a "vacuum" is also a colloquial term for a domestic appliance not altogether unlike a lawnmower; at this level of pun, there is no contrast between "the given" and "an idea of heaven" (2.1, 3).

25. Ludwig Wittgenstein, *Philosophical Investigations*, trans. G. E. M. Anscombe (Oxford: Blackwell, 1958), 128. I am indebted to an unpublished analysis of Koethe's philosophical argument by Justin Evans, "The Philosophical Process in John Koethe's *The Secret Amplitude*."

26. Koethe is the author of *The Continuity of Wittgenstein's Thought* (Ithaca: Cornell University Press, 1996).

27. Koethe, *Poetry at One Remove*, 3.

28. Helen Vendler, *Poets Thinking* (Cambridge, MA: Harvard University Press, 2004), 27.

29. Jorie Graham, *The Errancy* (New York: Ecco, 1997), 20–22.

30. Ezra Pound, *Selected Prose*, ed. William Cookson (New York: New Directions, 1973), 374.

31. See Donald Davie, "Ideas in *The Cantos*," in *Ezra Pound* (1975; Chicago: University of Chicago Press, 1982).

32. Ernest Fenollosa, *The Chinese Written Character as a Medium for Poetry*, ed. Ezra Pound (San Francisco: City Lights, 1964), 28.

33. Linda Welshimer Wagner, ed., *Interviews with William Carlos Williams* (New York: New Directions, 1976), 53.

34. Ezra Pound, *Guide to Kulchur* (New York: New Directions, 1938), 51.

35. Fenollosa, *Chinese Written Character*, 28.

36. Ezra Pound, *Literary Essays*, 52.

37. Gasché, *Honor of Thinking*, 266, 349.

38. Fenollosa, *Chinese Written Character*, 7.

39. Ibid., 12.

40. Rae Armantrout, *Veil* (Middletown, CT: Wesleyan University Press, 2001), 123–24.

41. Cleanth Brooks, "The Heresy of Paraphrase," in *The Well Wrought Urn* (New York: Harcourt, Brace and World, 1947), 197.

42. Ibid., 195.

43. Michael Palmer, *The Lion Bridge* (New York: New Directions, 1998), 214.

44. Roger Caillois, *The Necessity of Mind*, trans. Michael Syrotinski (Venice, CA: Lapis Press, 1990), 91.

45. Ibid., 64, 94.

46. *Shelley's Poetry and Prose*, ed. Donald H. Reiman and Sharon B. Powers (New York: Norton, 1977), 229.

47. Fletcher, *Colors of the Mind*, 113.

48. *Collected Works of Ralph Waldo Emerson*, ed. Spiller et al., 3:6.

49. John Dryden, "Essay on Dramatic Poesy," in *The Literary Criticism of John Dryden*, ed. Arthur Kirsch (Lincoln: University of Nebraska Press, 1966), 80.

50. Gasché, *Honor of Thinking*, 262.

51. Wallace Stevens, *Opus Posthumous*, ed. Samuel French Morse (New York: Knopf, 1957), 228.

52. Geuss, "Poetry and Knowledge," 2; see also Glenn Most, "Poetry, Knowledge, and Dr. Geuss," *Arion*, ser. 3, 11.2 (Fall 2003), 197–201.

53. Gasché, *Honor of Thinking*, 302.

CHAPTER 5

1. Friedrich Nietzsche, *The Birth of Tragedy*, trans. Walter Kaufmann (New York: Random House, 1967), 59.

2. T. S. Eliot, "The Music of Poetry," in *On Poets and Poetry* (New York: Farrar, Straus, 1957), 32; Nietzsche, *Birth of Tragedy*, 49.

3. Marina Tsvetaeva, *Art in the Light of Conscience*, trans. Angela Livingstone (Cambridge, MA: Harvard University Press, 1992), 51.

4. See Leo Spitzer, *Classical and Christian Ideas of World Harmony*, ed. Anna Granville Hatcher (Baltimore: Johns Hopkins University Press, 1963), esp. chap. 1.

5. John Hollander, *The Untuning of the Sky* (Princeton: Princeton University Press, 1961).

6. George Steiner, *Real Presences* (Chicago: University of Chicago Press, 1989); in this and the preceding paragraph I am drawing generally on chapter 1 of this volume, but see esp. 18–19.

7. Plato, *The Republic*, ed. G. R. F. Ferrari, trans. Tom Griffith (Cambridge: Cambridge University Press, 2000), 401e.

8. Ibid., 401d.

9. Other models, subtler ones, are surely imaginable, but these two have mattered to me, and they enable me to clarify my argument.

10. Philip Furia, *Skylark: The Life and Times of Johnny Mercer* (New York: St. Martin's, 2003), 258.

11. Johnny Mercer, quoted in Max Wilk, *They're Playing Our Song* (Mount Kisco, NY: Moyer Bell, 1991), 135.

12. Gene Lees, *Singers and the Song II* (New York: Oxford University Press, 1998), 45.

13. Furia, *Skylark*, 274.

14. Mercer, quoted in Wilk, *They're Playing Our Song*, 133.

15. Furia, *Skylark*, 121.

16. Johnny Mercer, *Our Huckleberry Friend*, ed. Bob Bach and Ginger Mercer (Secaucus, NJ: Lyle Stuart, 1982), 102.

17. Furia, *Skylark*, 14.

18. Ibid., 130–31.

19. Yvor Winters, *In Defense of Reason* (Denver: Swallow, 1947), 81.

20. Ibid., 140. To hear my musical illustrations, see http://humanities.uchicago.edu/blogs/vonhallberg.

21. Ibid.

22. Florence Farr, note, in W. B. Yeats, *Essays and Introductions* (New York: Collier, 1968), 22.

23. Furia, *Skylark*, 173.

24. Ibid., 263.

25. "There's a Moon Out Tonight" (words and music by Al Striano, Joe Luccisano, and Al Gentile) was a big hit for the Capris in 1955.

26. *The Collected Works of Ralph Waldo Emerson*, ed. Robert E. Spiller et al. (Cambridge, MA: Harvard University Press, 1971–2003), 1:169.

27. Anthony J. Gribin and Matthew M. Schiff, *Doo-wop* (Iola, WI: Krause, 1992), 13.

28. Susan Stewart, *Poetry and the Fate of the Senses* (Chicago: University of Chicago Press, 2002), 110; see chaps. 2 and 3 passim.

29. Paul Valéry, *The Art of Poetry*, trans. Denise Folliot (New York: Random House, 1961), 63; hereafter abbreviated *AP*.

30. See William K. Wimsatt, "One Relation of Rhyme to Reason," in *The Verbal Icon* (Lexington: University of Kentucky Press, 1958); Donald Wesling, *The Chances of Rhyme* (Berkeley: University of California Press, 1980); Hugh Kenner, "Pope's Reasonable Rhymes," *ELH* 41.1 (Spring 1974), 74–88.

31. David Ferry, *Dwelling Places* (Chicago: University of Chicago Press, 1993), 6–7.

32. Anthony Hecht, *Melodies Unheard* (Baltimore: Johns Hopkins University Press, 2003), 66–67, 82.

33. Ibid., 77.

34. W. B. Yeats, "The Symbolism of Poetry" (1900), in *Essays and Introductions*, 159.

35. Vladimir Jankélévitch, *Music and the Ineffable*, trans. Carolyn Abbaté (Princeton: Princeton University Press, 2003), 122, 124–25.

36. Robert Pinsky, *Democracy, Culture, and the Voice of Poetry* (Princeton: Princeton University Press, 2002), 78.

37. Marjorie Perloff and Robert von Hallberg, "A Dialogue on Evaluation in Poetry," in *Professions*, ed. Donald E. Hall (Urbana: University of Illinois Press, 2001), 102.

38. T. S. Eliot, "The Music of Poetry," in *On Poets and Poetry*, 25.

39. Robert Pinsky, *The Figured Wheel* (New York: Farrar, Straus, and Giroux, 1996), 7.

40. Debra Fried, "Repetition, Refrain, and Epitaph," *ELH* 53.3 (Fall 1986), 615–32.

41. The first refrain is from Thomas Campion, poem 10 of *A Book of Ayres*. The second is from Fulke Greville, *Caelica* 69. The third is from *Caelica* 16. The fourth is from George Peele, "Hot Sun, Cool Fire." The fifth is from Swinburne, "A Forsaken Garden." The last is from *Caelica* 7.

42. Basil Bunting, *Complete Poems*, ed. Richard Caddel (New York: New Directions, 2000), 59.

43. Yeats, *Essays and Introductions*, 163.

44. Eliot, "The Music of Poetry," in *On Poets and Poetry*, 20.

45. Leibniz, quoted in Lydia Goehr, *The Quest for Voice* (Berkeley: University of California Press, 1998), 25.

46. Fernando Pessoa, *Always Astonished*, ed. and trans. Edwin Honig (San Francisco: City Lights, 1988), 29.

47. Thylias Moss, *Last Chance for the Tarzan Holler* (New York: Persea, 1998), 38.

48. John T. Dziegelwicz, SJ, "The Conditions of Music" (Ph.D. thesis, University of Chicago, 1980), 251; see also W. B. Yeats, "Speaking to the Psaltery," in *Essays and Introductions*, 19.

49. Richard Wagner, "A Music-School for Munich," quoted in Goehr, *Quest for Voice*, 118.

50. Nathaniel Mackey, *Bedouin Hornbook* (1986; Los Angeles: Sun and Moon, 1997), 21.

51. Carl Dahlhaus, *The Idea of Absolute Music*, trans. Roger Lustig (Chicago: University of Chicago Press, 1989), vii.

52. Ibid., 79.

53. Roland Barthes, *The Responsibility of Forms*, trans. Richard Howard (Berkeley: University of California Press, 1991), 250.

54. Lydia Goehr traces the view that music tries to express what cannot be expressed in music to Schopenhauer (Goehr, *Quest for Voice*, 19–20).

55. Ibid., 159.

56. Igor Stravinsky, *The Poetics of Music*, trans. Arthur Knodel and Ingolf Dahl (Cambridge, MA: Harvard University Press, 1942), 127; quoted by Goehr, *Quest for Voice*, 142.

CHAPTER 6

1. Sharon Cameron, *Literary Impersonality* (Chicago: University of Chicago Press, 2007), 165.

2. Wordsworth, preface to *Lyrical Ballads*, in *Critical Theory since Plato*, ed. Hazard Adams and Leroy Searle, 3rd. ed. (Boston: Thomson Wadsworth), 488.

3. David Damrosch, *What Is World Literature?* (Princeton: Princeton University Press, 2004), 12.

4. Martin Heidegger, *Poetry, Language, Thought*, trans. Albert Hofstadter (New York: Harper and Row, 1971), 77.

5. Aristotle, *Poetics*, chap. 9; in *Introduction to Aristotle*, ed. Richard McKeon (New York: Modern Library, 1947), 635–37.

6. Jacopo Mazzoni, "On the Defense of the *Comedy* of Dante" [1587], trans. R. L. Montgomery, in *Critical Theory since Plato*, ed. Hazard Adams, rev. ed. (Fort Worth, TX: Harcourt Brace Jovanovich, 1971), 171.

7. Stephen Owen, "Stepping Forward and Back: Issues and Possibilities for 'World' Poetry," *Modern Philology* 100.4 (May 2003), 546–47.

8. Thomas Gray, *Essays and Criticisms*, ed. C. S. Northrup (Boston: D.C. Heath, 1911), 93; cited by Jean H. Hagstrum, *Samuel Johnson's Literary Criticism* (Chicago: University of Chicago Press, 1952), 88. (Mimetic literary genres, such as novels and dramas, are less problematically appraised by the historicity criterion.)

9. *Elegy and Iambus*, ed. and trans. J. M. Edmonds (Cambridge, MA: Harvard University Press, 1944), 1:88–91; Laura Slatkin called to my attention this poem of Mimnermus and the possibility that Aristotle's taste was so inclined.

10. Ralph Waldo Emerson, "The Poet," in *The Collected Works of Ralph Waldo Emerson*, ed. Robert E. Spiller et al. (Cambridge, MA: Harvard University Press, 1971–2003), 3:6.

11. Cameron, *Literary Impersonality*, 89. In this excellent study, Cameron criticizes Emerson for a shallow sense of personhood. He does not acknowledge "the legitimacy of material self-interest" (101). Impersonality entails a sacrifice of self-interest: Emerson suppresses the pathos of this contest that many find validating; no pathos of the agon, no

credibility, in her analysis (102). The same objection may be made to musical impersonality. Poems do not struggle their way to a sonic profile. They often seem, because of the craft of poets, effortlessly musical: this is the lightness of musical language. Critics like Cameron or Kenneth Burke who require a dramatic account of impersonality will not be satisfied by my sense of impersonality.

12. Samuel Johnson, *Poetry and Prose*, ed. Mona Wilson (Cambridge, MA: Harvard University Press, 1967), 161.

13. Ibid., 491.

14. Edward W. Said, *The Question of Palestine* (New York: Random House, 1979), 76–77.

15. Samuel Johnson, *Rasselas and Other Tales*, ed. Gwin J. Kolb (New Haven: Yale University Press, 1990), 43.

16. Mark Payne, "On Being Vatic: Pindar, Pragmatism and Historicism," *American Journal of Philology* 127.2 (October 2006), 159–84.

17. Stuart Hall, for instance, characterizes the term "universal" as inevitably hoodwinking: "Old and New Identities, Old and New Ethnicities," *Culture, Globalization and the World System*, ed. Anthony D. King (Minneapolis: University of Minnesota Press, 1997), 68.

18. Helen Vendler, *Poets Thinking* (Cambridge, MA: Harvard University Press, 2004), 10–36.

19. Immanuel Kant, *Critique of Judgment*, trans. Werner S. Pluhar (Indianapolis: Hackett, 1987), 183–84 [§ 49].

20. Joseph Addison, *The Spectator* 418 [1712]; in *Critical Theory since Plato*, ed. Adams, 286–87.

21. Ibid., 287.

22. Giambattista Vico, *The New Science*; in *Critical Theory since Plato*, ed. Adams, 295.

23. Sir Philip Sidney, *Defence of Poesy*, ed. Dorothy M. Macardle (New York: St. Martin's, 1968), 33.

24. Stanley Cavell, *Philosophy the Day after Tomorrow* (Cambridge, MA: Harvard University Press, 2005), 66.

25. Johann Wolfgang von Goethe, "Maximen," in *Werke*, ed. Helmut Holtzhauer and Hans Böhm (Berlin: Aufbau, 1968), 7.519; my translation.

26. Wordsworth, cited in *Norton Anthology of English Literature*, ed. M. H. Abrams et al., third ed. (New York: Norton, 1974), 2:175.

27. Wallace Stevens, *The Necessary Angel* (New York: Knopf, 1951), 144–45.

28. Judith Butler and others have recently argued that the left needs

the concept of universality as much as the right ever did, though the point has not yet been taken. She sums up contemporary academic views when she observes, "The universalization of the particular seeks to elevate a specific content to a global condition, making an empire of its local meaning" ("Restaging the Universal: The Role of Universality in the Constitution of Political Logics," in *Contingency, Hegemony, Universality*, ed. Judith Butler, Ernesto Laclau, and Slavoj Žižek [London: Verso, 2000], 31). There are two different problems with this particularist skepticism about disinterestedness. First, it undermines exploratory writing in favor of frankly engaged and instrumental poetry. Second, it inhibits political collaboration. Ernesto Laclau observes that "there is no politics of pure particularity. Even the most particularistic of demands will be made in terms of something transcending it. As, however, the moment of universality will be differently constructed in various discourses, we will have either a struggle between different conceptions of universality, or an extension of the equivalential logics to those very conceptions, so that a wider one is constructed . . ." (Laclau, "Constructing Universality," ibid., 305). And Žižek has advocated retention of the concept of universality as "paradoxical" (ibid., 10).

29. Roland Barthes, *Mythologies*, trans. Annette Lavers (New York: Hill and Wang, 1972), 339, 341.

30. Paul Valéry, *The Art of Poetry*, trans. Denise Folliot (New York: Knopf, 1958), 76.

31. Ezra Pound, *Selected Prose*, ed. William Cookson (New York: New Directions, 1973), 32–33.

32. Ibid. Pound is invoking the particular whose significance is general, a topos of poetic theory. William Wimsatt observed,

> Whether or not one believes in universals, one may see the persistence in literary criticism of a theory that poetry presents the concrete and the universal, or the individual and the universal, or an object which in a mysterious and special way is both highly general and highly particular. . . . In one terminology or another this idea of concrete universal is found in most metaphysical aesthetic of the eighteenth and nineteenth centuries. (*The Verbal Icon* [Lexington: University of Kentucky Press, 1954], 72.)

33. Friedrich Schiller, *On the Aesthetic Education of Man*, ed. and trans. Elizabeth M. Wilkinson and L. A. Willoughby (Oxford: Clarendon, 1967), 155.

34. Theodor Adorno, *Notes to Literature*, ed. Rolf Tiedemann, trans. Shierry Weber Nicholsen (New York: Columbia University Press, 1991), 1:38.

35. John Ashbery, "The Skaters," in *Rivers and Mountains* (New York: Holt, Rinehart and Winston, 1966), 39.

36. Friedrich Wilhelm von Schelling, "On the Relation of the Plastic Arts to Nature," in *Critical Theory since Plato*, ed. Adams, rev. ed., 461.

37. Stephen Owen, "What Is World Poetry?" *New Republic* 203.21 (November 19, 1990), 28–32.

38. George Steiner, *After Babel* (London: Oxford University Press, 1975), 176.

39. *Shelley's Poetry and Prose*, ed. Donald H. Reiman and Sharon B. Powers (New York: Norton, 1977), 485.

40. Stephen Mitchell introduced his version of the Psalms, cited above in chapter 2, with this caveat: "My primary allegiance in these psalms was not to the Hebrew text but to my own sense of the genuine. . . . When I disregarded the letter entirely, it was so that I could follow the spirit, wherever it wanted to take me, into a language that felt genuine and alive" (*A Book of Psalms* [New York: HarperCollins, 1993], xv).

41. Leo N. Tolstoy, *What Is Art?*, trans. Aymer Maude (Indianapolis: Bobbs-Merrill, 1960), 149.

42. Walter Benjamin, *Selected Writings*, eds., Marcus Bullock and Michael Jennings (Cambridge, MA; Harvard University Press, 1996), 1:257.

43. Ezra Pound, *The Literary Essays*, ed. T. S. Eliot (New York: New Directions, 1951), 34–35.

44. Robert Hass, *Twentieth Century Pleasures* (New York: Ecco, 1984), 176.

45. Edward Hirsch, "Miłosz and World Poetry," *Partisan Review*, 66.1 (1999), 26.

46. Bogdan Czaykowski, "The Fly and the Flywheel," *Canadian Slavonic Papers* (March 1979); cited by Bożena Karwowska, "The Critical Reception of Czesław Miłosz and Josif Brodsky in English-speaking Countries" (PhD diss., University of British Columbia, 1995), 31.

47. Robert Pinsky, "Czesław Miłosz," *Partisan Review* 66.1 (1999), 146.

48. Richard Rorty, *Achieving Our Country* (Cambridge, MA: Harvard University Press, 1998), 133.

49. Terrence des Pres, "Czesław Miłosz: The Poetry of Aftermath," *Nation* 227 (December 30, 1978), 741–42.

50. Thomas Parkinson, *Hart Crane and Yvor Winters* (Berkeley: University of California Press, 1978), xvi.

51. Czesław Miłosz, *The Collected Poems,* 1931–1987 (Hopewell, NJ: Ecco, 1988), 167.

52. Hans-Georg Gadamer, *The Relevance of the Beautiful*, ed. Robert Bernasconi (Cambridge: Cambridge University Press, 1986), 120.

53. Czesław Miłosz, *The Separate Notebooks*, trans. Robert Hass, Robert Pinsky, Czesław Miłosz, and Renata Gorczynski (New York: Ecco, 1984), 3–5.

54. Adam Zagajewski has observed that in Polish the preposition is simply "crossing," rather than "bypassing" (lecture, University of Chicago, April 28, 2006). The sense of "bypassing" is different and specific. I presume that Miłosz approved this sense in the English translation of his poem.

55. Donald Davie, *Czesław Miłosz and the Insufficiency of Lyric* (Knoxville: University of Tennessee Press, 1986), 19.

56. Ibid., 28.

57. Seamus Heaney, *The Government of the Tongue* (New York: Farrar, Straus and Giroux, 1989), 115.

58. Ibid., 39.

59. Ibid., 37.

60. Robert Kelly, "A Love Affair with Silence," *New York Times Book Review*, November 9, 1986, 21.

61. Ibid.

62. Paul Celan, "Death Fugue," *Commentary* 19.3 (1955), 243.

63. Anon., "Silence and Death," *TLS*, October 15, 1971.

64. Anon., "Poems, Noems," *TLS*, December 7, 1967, 1190.

65. *New York Review of Books* 36.21 (January 18, 1990).

66. George Steiner, "A Terrible Exactness," *TLS*, June 11, 1976, 710.

67. Anon., "Silence and Death," 1265.

68. George Steiner, "North of the Future," *New Yorker,* August 28, 1989, 95.

69. Rika Lesser, "Paradoxically German," *New York Times Book Review*, April 26, 1981, n.p.

70. Paul Celan, *Selected Poems and Prose*, trans. John Felstiner (New York: Norton, 2001), 156–57.

71. John Felstiner dates the poem to January 3, 1961; *Paul Celan: Poet, Survivor, Jew* (New Haven: Yale University Press, 1995), 314, n. 72.

72. Paul Celan, *Poems*, trans. Michael Hamburger (New York: Persea, 1988), 110–11.

73. Paul Celan, "Der Meridian," *Gesammelte Werke*, ed. Beda Allemann and Stefan Reichert (Frankfurt/Main: Suhrkamp, 1986), 3:201.

74. Paul Celan, letter to Hans Bender, in *Collected Prose*, trans. Rosemarie Waldrop (Riverdale-on-Hudson, NY: Sheep Meadow, 1986), 26.

75. Celan, "The Meridian," in *Collected Prose*, 48.

76. Celan, *Gesammelte Werke*, 1:156; my translation.

77. Berel Lang implies such consensus when he refers to the demands made by the Shoah as "unequivocal." *Holocaust Representation* (Baltimore: Johns Hopkins University Press, 2000), 33.

78. Ibid., 17.

79. Susan Gubar, *Poetry after Auschwitz* (Bloomington: Indiana University Press, 2003), 94.

80. Ibid., 245.

81. J. M. Coetzee, "In the Midst of Losses," *New York Review of Books*, 48.11 (July 5, 2001), n.p.

82. Steiner, "North of the Future," 94.

83. James K. Lyon shows that after the war Celan chose quite deliberately to *improve* his German; he read Heidegger with particular attention to conventional German terms (not to Heidegger's neologisms) that were then unfamiliar to the foremost German poet of the postwar era. *Paul Celan and Martin Heidegger* (Baltimore: Johns Hopkins University Press, 2006), 24–27.

84. Steiner, *After Babel*, 247.

85. Ezra Pound, *Gaudier-Brzeska* (New York: New Directions, 1 970), 24.

86. Friedrich Schleiermacher, "On the Different Methods of Translating," in *Theories of Translation*, ed. Rainer Schulte and John Biguenet (Chicago: University of Chicago Press, 1992), 53–54.

87. Heidegger, *Poetry, Language, Thought*, 23 (emphasis in original).

88. Walt Whitman, "Song of Myself," sect. 17, in *Leaves of Grass*, ed. Sculley Bradley and Harold W. Blodgett (New York: Norton, 1973), 45.

89. Pascale Casanova, *The World Republic of Letters*, trans. M. B. DeBevoise (Cambridge, MA: Harvard University Press, 2004), 154.

90. Ibid., 142.

91. Ibid., 17.

92. Ibid., 119.

93. Frank O'Hara, "The Day Lady Died," in *The Collected Poems*, ed. Donald Allen (1971; Berkeley: University of California Press, 1995), 325.

94. Edmund Burke, *A Philosophical Enquiry into the Sublime and the Beautiful*, ed. David Womersley (London: Penguin, 1998), 75. Harold Bloom makes the point in regard to the literary-critical assessment of Milton: "On all issues of religion, politics, society, and economics, the Tory [Samuel] Johnson and the Radical Dissenter [William] Hazlitt are totally opposed, but they praise Milton for the same qualities, Hazlitt as memorably as Johnson." Bloom, *The Western Canon* (New York: Riverhead, 1994), 184.

95. Immanuel Kant, "Introduction," *Critique of Judgement*, trans. J. H. Bernard (New York: Hafner, 1951), 15; quoted by Rodolphe Gasché, *The Idea of Form* (Stanford: Stanford University Press, 2003), 14; my understanding of Kant is much indebted to Gasché's excellent study.

96. Gasché, *Idea of Form*, 8.

97. Kant, *Critique*, trans. Werner S. Pluhar, 87 [§ 20].

98. Bloom, *Western Canon*, 59.

99. *Collected Works of Ralph Waldo Emerson*, ed. Spiller et al., 1:57–58.

CONCLUSION

1. Victor Zuckerkandl, *Sound and Symbol*, trans. Willard R. Trask (Princeton: Princeton University Press, 1956), 15–16.

2. Cited by Simon Jarvis, "Musical Thinking: Hegel and the Phenomenology of Prosody," in *The Idea of the Literary*, ed. Nicholas Harrison (Edinburgh: Edinburgh University Press, 2005), 58 (first published as *Paragraph* 28.2, special issue).

3. Jean-Luc Nancy, *Listening*, trans. Charlotte Mandell (New York: Fordham University Press, 2007), 27.

4. Ibid., 65.

5. Jarvis, "Musical Thinking," 60.

6. It is difficult to develop the view that musical meaning is nonverbal. Even the philosopher Peter Kivy, who maintains the position that music is cognitive, testifies to the painful uncertainty of the nonverbal sense of meaning: "Musical thought is *thought*, musical understanding *understanding*. And whether or not one believes that thinking is linguistic through and through, one can hardly stray very far from language without feeling that one has perhaps strayed from thought

as well." Kivy, *Music Alone* (Ithaca: Cornell University Press, 1990), 121. Frank Sibley notes that the same problem affects all statements of meaning or of thought: "Thinkers choose words to express what they are thinking or have thought. . . . Just as we do not think in anything, we do not experience or listen in anything, either words, pictures, music, or musical terms. We do not grasp, realize, or perceive the character of music—or of faces, paintings, or scenery—in words or in anything else." Sibley, "Making Music Our Own," in *Approach to Aesthetics*, ed. John Benson, Betty Redfern, and Jeremy Roxbee Cox (Oxford: Clarendon, 2001), 149. Why a whole literature has developed concerning the discursive gap separating statements of meaning from the experience of music is unclear.

7. Arthur C. Danto, *The Abuse of Beauty* (Chicago: Open Court, 2003), 160.

8. Ibid., 118.

9. Hart Crane, *The Complete Poems and Selected Letters and Prose*, ed. Brom Weber (Garden City, NY: Doubleday, 1966), 46.

10. See John Hollander, *The Untuning of the Sky* (Princeton, NJ: Princeton University Press, 1961), chap. 2, esp. p. 28.

11. Laura (Riding) Jackson, *The Failure of Poetry, the Promise of Language*, ed. John Nolan (Ann Arbor: University of Michigan Press, 2007), 84.

12. Bradford Cook, ed. and trans., *Mallarmé: Selected Prose Poems, Essays, and Letters* (Baltimore: Johns Hopkins University Press, 1956), 55.

13. Wallace Stevens, *Opus Posthumous*, ed. Samuel French Morse (New York: Knopf, 1957), 226–27.

14. Friedrich Schiller, *Essays*, ed. Walter Hinderer and Daniel O. Dahlstrom (New York: Continuum, 1993), 65.

15. Edmund Burke, *A Philosophical Enquiry into the Sublime and the Beautiful*, ed. David Womersley (London: Penguin, 1998), 86.

16. Schiller, *Essays*, 29.

17. Robert Pinsky, *The Figured Wheel* (New York: Farrar, Straus and Giroux, 1996), 41–42.

18. Jackson, *Failure of Poetry*, 32.

19. Ibid., 153–54.

20. Ibid., 23.

21. Ibid. 106.

Index